Learning from
Scant Beginnings

Learning from Scant Beginnings

English Professor Expertise

John V. Knapp

DELAWARE

Newark: University of Delaware Press

Associated University Presses
2010 Eastpark Boulevard
Cranbury, NJ 08512

The paper used in this publication meets the requirements of the American National Standard for Permanence of Paper for Printed Library Materials Z39.48-1984.

Library of Congress Cataloging-in-Publication Data

Knapp, John V., 1940–
    Learning from scant beginnings : English professor expertise / John V. Knapp.
        p.   cm.
    Includes bibliographical references and index.
    ISBN 978-0-87413-026-3 (alk. paper)
    1. Milton, John, 1608–1674—Study and teaching.   2. Literature—Study and teaching (Higher)—Case studies.   I. Title.
    PR3588.K49   2008
    821'.4—dc22   2007047685

PRINTED IN THE UNITED STATES OF AMERICA

Contents

Acknowledgments

FIRST THANKS GO TO TWO MASTER TEACHERS, WITHOUT WHOSE HELP, inspiration, and just plain hard work, this manuscript would never have seen the light of day. The first was my dissertation Director in the Department of Educational Psychology at the University of Wisconsin-Madison, Prof. Leona Schauble. She represents my understanding of Plato's ideal: the large-souled teacher, willing to instruct, to inspire, to cajole, to listen, and, when necessary, to push and prod in her own eagerness and pleasure in helping me read, revise, rethink, and in general improve this writing. My gratitude for her labors helped keep me revising this work for publication long after the formal dissertation was completed.

I also want to thank the members of my dissertation committee: Profs. B. Bradford Brown, who taught one of the very first UW courses for both of us—back in the Pleistocene; Charles Kalish also from Educational Psychology; Margaret Egan-Robertson from Curriculum and Instruction, and Martin Nystrand, from the UW English Department, who got me thinking Adialogic@ well before it became *de rigeur.*

The second master teacher is my colleague at Northern Illinois University, Prof. William C. Johnson, *Prof. J.* in the pages ahead, who taught me by explicit example what a great teacher is and does. I have been doubly blessed in researching his teaching and then writing up this pedagogically-oriented manuscript, receiving help from two teaching luminaries, Leona and Bill.

I also want to acknowledge the hard work of my editor at NIU, Ms Gail Rover, whose keen eye and wise editorial judgment made this a much better work than it ever could have otherwise. Her work was complemented by the excellent copy-editing for the University of Delaware Press, Ms. Mary Cicora, and the work of Christine A. Retz, Julien Yoseloff, and the other editors at Associated University Presses. Of course, any problems with this book are mine alone.

Further thanks go to my colleagues and students at Northern Illinois University, whose faith in me and my work far exceeded their understanding of why I continued a second terminal degree late in my career. These include my Teacher Certification colleagues, Susan Callahan, Larry Johannessen, Judy Pokorny, Laura Bird, Christine Henderson, and the many excellent supervisors who have worked for NIU. Additional thanks go to my current chair, Philip Eubanks, and to our Dean, Dr. Christopher McCord, as well as to our former (and late) Dean, Frederick Kitterle, whose support for educating teachers in a liberal arts college was an inspiration to us all.

I must also mention several of my NIU and English Department colleagues and students who have, over the years that this manuscript was being written, given me ideas and stimulated my mind in ways too innumerable to count: these people include my Reavis Hall neighbors William Baker, Edward Callary, and Gulsat Eygen; further thanks go to our former Chair, Deborah Holdstein, and James Mellard, Herb and Irene Rubin, and members of my editorial board at *Style:* Phil Eubanks, David Gorman, John Schaeffer, and Managing editor, Linda Watson, as well as student editor, Nicholas J. Valenti.. I also want to thank several current or former students and dissertators, and now friends: Brian Edwards, Sangwook Kim, David Mullikin, Gillian Lachanski, Beth Wilson-McFarland, and of course, the co-editor for *Reading the Family Dance,* Kenneth Womack, all of whom have pushed me to come up with some good (or at least plausible) answers about what constitutes good teaching and good literature.

I need also mention our friends in Wisconsin and elsewhere: Peter Manley and Sandra Black, Ken and Gay Davidson-Zielske, Barbara and Phil Meilinger, and Hank and MaryLou Slotnick. Most of all, I want to thank my late colleague, Gustaaf van Cromphout, whose friendship over some thirty-three years was cut short all too soon by his untimely death in 2005. "A was a man, take him for all in all/ I shall not look upon his like again." Along with my department, his widow, Luz, and his children, Beatrice and Jana, and their families, I grieve for an unaccountable loss.

Finally, I want to thank my whole family without whom life would have little meaning for me. To begin, I want to thank my sisters: Shirley Carroll, husband Mike Carroll, and adult children Sean Carroll, Michelle Lug, and their families; Along with her son, Jeremy Discenza, and her granddaughter, Emma Bea, I grieve for the recent loss of my younger sister, Janet Discenza. With my wife, I mourn the loss of my late in-laws Ed and Ida Schwarz.

My hopes for the future rest with my children: Margaret A. Knapp; Lara M. Cantuti and her husband Eric Cantuti, and my newest grandson, Stephan John-Georgeo Cantuti; Joanna Saltzberg and her husband Rob Saltzberg, and my recent grandson, Jacob AJack@ Amadeo Saltzberg; Jennifer Joy Schmeiser and her husband Brian Schmeiser, and my granddaughters, Abi Joy Schmeiser and Emily Joy Schmeiser. Thinking back on the joys and stresses of my children's childhood and adolescence, my life would have been so much poorer without the happy memories of reading *The Hobbit* to them at bedtime, teaching them all how to drive, medicating their illnesses with ice cream, rejoicing in their good grades but commiserating with those that were not so good, and watching their theatrical and musical productions on stage, their cheerleading at basketball, football, and hockey games, their swim meets and their volleyball matches, and helping them move innumerable times as they went through undergraduate and graduate schools. They taught me more than I can possibly recall.

The measures of love and devotion I owe to my late parents, Victor and Ann H. Knapp, for teaching me what love for one's family meant, as well as for their generosity of love and spirit, was bestowed upon me to pass along. Hence, those debts can only be repaid by depositing all that is worthwhile in me into my children's and grandchildren's accounts, hoping that they prosper from my attempted gifts, forgive my many mistakes, remember my admiration of them, and feel how overwhelmingly much I love them.

Finally, I want to thank my wife, Joan for her patience during the three decades of high intellectual questing, for her love, in spite of the rocky roads we sometimes traveled—and weathered—and for her companionship over the years as my beloved traveling companion through mental and geographic adventures at home and abroad. I look forward to many more voyages.

So, I dedicate this book to my late friend, Gustaaf van Cromphout; to my children, Margaret, Lara, Joanna, Jennifer, and their families, and to my wife, Joan!

Learning from
Scant Beginnings

Introduction

Learning is a product of social interactions; teaching is informed benevolent intervention that enables students to go beyond where they would go on their own. Adult mediation is at the core of good teaching—a more competent adult who both participates and observes so that he or she can know when assistance is requested or needed.

—Wilhelm and Edmiston, *Imagining to Learn*

And for the usual method of teaching arts, I deem it to be an old error of universities, not yet well recovered from the scholastic grossness of barbarous ages, that instead of beginning with arts most easy, (and those be such as are most obvious to the sense), they present their young unmatriculated novices, at first coming, with the most intellective abstracts of logic and metaphysics . . . to be tossed and turmoiled with their unballasted wits in fathomless and unquiet deeps of controversy.

—Milton, "Of Education"

ENGLISH PROFESSOR EXPERTISE: A DESCRIPTION

IN IMAGINATIVE LITERATURE CLASSES AT THE COLLEGE LEVEL, WHAT do we know about the person who has responsibility for deciding and then implementing whether to teach students by "informed benevolent intervention" or by presenting "the most intellective abstracts of logic and metaphysics"? What must a university or college professor of literature know, and how must he or she impart that knowledge to those who know less? Who are these people and how do they think? To help answer these questions, this study examines the nature and characteristics of English professor expertise by closely analyzing several issues common to all those teaching imaginative literature. My focus is resolutely on the Professor. Although some recent and excellent empirical work has summarized those qualities of professorial behaviors as the "way outstanding teachers treat the people

13

(i.e., students) who took their classes," little of it traces in micro-detail over the course of a whole semester exactly *how* excellent teaching is done, the *path* to the excellence—particularly in the disciplines instructing imaginative literature.[1]

Hence, in the decades-old conflict over appropriate teaching methods in North American literary pedagogy, those emphasizing the reader have left the professor as a mere "guide on the side," a cliché which has come to dominate pedagogical thinking. While few in the university would argue for a return to the so-called bad-old-days of a one-sided transmission of ideas to passive and supposedly receptive students of the humanities, what has been lost is much conversation of significant interest about the quality of the professor. In this environment, what does such a "guide on the side" do but get out of the way of Rousseau-like Emiles (and Emilys) who supposedly learn best with minimal direction?

My interest is also on literature teaching since, as I will argue in the next chapter, the effective pedagogy of composition on both a theoretical and practical level, is possibly a decade or more ahead of comparable sophistication in literature education.[2] In order to examine literature pedagogy in both general terms and in some specificity, I conducted a semester-long study of an expert professor teaching the selected works of a major canonical author, John Milton, to advanced university-level undergraduates. It is ironic that while teaching college-level literature is perhaps *the* central public activity of most university English professors, there has been surprisingly little research into the specifics of expert professorial *practice* until very recently.[3]

This lack of systematic investigation is surprising because literature-as-storytelling has been a human cultural phenomenon for thousands of years, and teaching vernacular literature has been associated with Anglo-American universities for well over one hundred years.[4] And despite or perhaps because of this history, what we all currently observe is the inextricable dance between student expectations fulfilled or frustrated, and professors' employment of their scholarly expertise in the service of the twin goals at most universities: student learning *and* professorial disciplinary investigation.

At the secondary level, this conflict is generally muted because secondary teachers can be devoted to just one thing: good teaching. We are all familiar with the stories of how an adolescent gets hooked into the joys of the literary life by a caring but demanding secondary teacher. Here, for example, is an excerpt from Mike Rose's *Lives on the Boundary,* a book often read by those studying to become secondary schools teachers. Rose argues:

> Students will float to the mark you set . . . But mostly teachers had no idea of how to engage the imagination of us kids who were scuttling along at the bottom of the pond. . . . [They] would have needed some inventiveness, for none of us was groomed for the classroom . . . You see a handful of students far excel you in courses that sound exotic and that are only in the curriculum of the elite: French, physics, trigonometry. And all this is happening while you're trying to shape an identity; your body is changing, and your emotions running wild.[5]

But for every set of lost adolescents in a secondary school, there can be one literary guru, one "good teacher" who lights their literary fire. For Rose, this person was Mr. MacFarland:

> Jack MacFarland had a master's degree from Columbia and decided, at 26, to find a little school and teach his heart out. [Within] no time, he had us so startled with work that we didn't much worry about [his personal life]. We wrote three or four essays a month. We read a book every two or three weeks, starting with *The Iliad* and ending up with Hemingway. He gave us a quiz on the reading every other day. He brought a prep school curriculum to Mercy High.[6]
> [I] worked very hard, for MacFarland had hooked me. He tapped my old interest in reading and creating stories. [He] occasionally invited us to his apartment and those visits became the high point of our **apprenticeship.** We'd clamp on our training wheels and drive to his salon.[7]
> For a time, it was new and exciting; it allowed me to act as though I were living beyond the limiting boundaries of South Vermont [Street, in Los Angeles].[8]

So what happens at the university? Are there Mr. MacFarlands at Stanford, or the University of Delaware, or the University of Chicago, or Northern Illinois University? And since common sense suggests that there must be at least a few—albeit in rather different environments—what differences do we see between the engagement of a formerly near-illiterate fifteen-year-old by a teacher who is primarily a *teacher,* in contrast to a professor who would *like* to engage his or her students personally but who is also a scholar and writer? Who can devote Mr. Chips-like time to individual students and still "keep up with his/her field(s)," *and* publish, *and* serve on a multitude of committees, *and* maintain some semblance of a private life? Where *is* that masked super-man (or woman), and how quickly can we meet to discuss his or her secret of success?

It is almost too easy these days to fault certain insensitive secondary teachers for ignoring immature students' emotional needs. Wendy Luttrell notes: "What is most memorable about schooling is not what is learned, but how we learn. By viewing school in terms of embattled relationships, the women [in her study] held teachers accountable for what school organization and mission ignores or dismisses: the knowledge and ethics of care."[9]

Should we say the same about university professors who work mostly with young adults? Rita Kramer has discussed the follies of too much attention to "care" as contrasted to what she considers the proper focus on the students' emerging minds, but does not (perhaps cannot) prescribe the proper balance—in this case for those English education students training to be secondary teachers.[10] It becomes clear that any description of "English professor expertise" must point to some vital center, some appropriate areas of balance between teaching a subject (imaginative literature) and teaching people (students of English literature) at the university, in spite of those who believe the current "entrenched model" makes the professor, "first and foremost . . . a scholar—not a teacher."[11] No doubt that many such entrenched types exist, but departmental annual reviews are now as focused upon one's teaching as one's scholarship, or, in the opinions of many, if not, should be.[12]

If one pares away the glitter from descriptions of imaginative literature teaching in English found in most institutions of higher learning, one sees some approaches remain unchanged in over a century.[13] Lecture is still *the* operant mode of information delivery in most universities.[14] In addition, James Marshall and Janet Smith found that university-level pedagogical techniques include: 1) Large-group discussions of specific texts, guided by distributed questions; 2) some small-group work; 3) the argumentative essay, i.e., close reading of a specific text with a thesis and quotations as evidence; and 4) some student "research," as professors still require their students to look up essays or book reviews in professional journals.[15]

While such pedagogical techniques are common, professors employing them are usually motivated by and so focus upon one of the following three major areas: the text in its historical and/or cultural setting, the author, and, most recently, the reader. Although other researchers have cut up the literary pie rather differently,[16] synergistic interactions among the three areas by the critical professor have not always taken place. Rather, partisans argue that their preferred choice should be primary and that those advocating another focus are missing some crucial element, or the forest for the trees.

As we look back to just before the middle of the twentieth century and well into the 1960s, literature was most often taught at the university with primary allegiance to the text—the text as an autotelic aesthetic object with no need for much attention to the author and even less to the reader.[17] The standard delivery system was the precept or lecture method, supported theoretically by what has become known as the "(old) New Criticism."[18] *Sic transit gloria*, both for personal fame and critical fashion. Smagorinsky and Whiting, in *How English Teachers Get Taught*, indicate that this "perspective [was] rejected by virtually every text frequently assigned on secondary methods course syllabi as . . . antiquated and working against any attempt to foster personal growth of students."[19] College teaching is seen as differing little because "it fills our need to forge connections with our students."[20]

One might wonder, why such a harsh judgment on an approach that has dominated college teaching for several decades? In its most notorious and stereotypical form, the professor modeled close readings of the text through a carefully crafted lecture where the right (or infinitely better) answer to literary problems was always preferred to the novice's halting attempts to reproduce what she had been taught. Students learned to read sophisticated texts by being told (some call it indoctrinated into) a text's *real* meaning(s), observing how one arrived at such conclusions, and then, through the literary essay (or an essay examination), emulating the professor, who would judge the closeness of fit between professorial precept and student performance. Since the flow of information was generally one way, top-down, from he or she who knows a lot more to those who know a lot less, the likelihood of professorial engagement—in any consistent form—with one's students was more a fortuitous artifact of accidental contacts. These occurred, when they did, more at a student's insistence or from the professor's personal fascination than for any institutionalized purpose.

By the mid-1970s, the profession of English teaching was assailed from several directions by a) a shrinking job market; b) a surplus of scholar-teachers who had to divide literary studies into smaller and more arcane pieces in order to have anything to say that was "original"; and c) a restive college student population who had helped set in motion three major social upheavals in the United States: the civil rights movement, the feminist transformation of assumptions regarding gender roles, and campus demonstrations against the Vietnam War. Few among them considered the ideal education as consisting of listening to older professors spouting *their* opinions about literature, or life (or much else, for that matter), without also receiving some feedback from their formerly captive audience, the students. Hence, for these (among several other) reasons, a work of scholarship from the late 1930s was resurrected and soon became the new bible for teaching an imaginative text: Louise Rosenblatt's *Literature as Exploration.*[21]

An alternative teaching method, sometimes known as the *expressive mode*, attempted to include the student in direct dialogue with both professor and text.[22] This approach "corrected" earlier authoritarian methods, adjusting the teaching of fiction, poetry, and drama by placing a much greater emphasis directly on the student as reader and contributor to the in-class narrative.[23] Supported theoretically by what has come to be called the *Reader-Response* (RR) school of criticism, this alternative method identified the locus of experiencing imaginative texts primarily in the minds of the receptor, or in some instances, within the collective mind of a community of receptors.[24] As students discussed their own individual receptions of a given text and then attempted to coordinate these multiple receptions into a more orderly and unified overview, learning would take place, often regardless of the professor's own direct input. Consequently, the role of the teacher/professor came to be stated in relation to a half-truth, a cliché insisting that the best teachers were "guides on the side, rather than sages on the (lecture) stage." Thus RR often turned the so-called old-fashioned New

Critical authoritative lecturer into one who took on a largely observational role, watching his or her students take over center stage.

A variation of RR literature teaching—a student-centered pedagogy—has been called the *Developmental Approach*.[25] This slant on literacy instruction devotes considerable energy to giving students meta-cognitive insights on learning itself, "particularly when that knowledge is scaffolded through teacher-led instruction."[26] Although the teacher is thus brought back into the immediate attention (and sometimes the hearts and minds) of the students, such "strategies are too often isolated from content," privileging "the literal over the interpretive, . . . reading over writing [while it is, at the same time] . . . apolitical and non-aesthetic."[27] In both RR variations, what is still often lost are those qualities so important in the "bad old days" of the New Criticism: authorial intent, the text as an aesthetic artifact, and (most important), the teacher/professor as literary expert. As Squealer injected fear into independent-thinking *Animal Farm* residents by asking if they wanted Mr. Jones to return, so do many English educators demand to know if, by focusing on the professors, we want a return to the (hoary old) New Criticism? Who in his or her right mind would want that?

However, techniques that had seemed corrective in the 1970s had tendencies to dissolve into conversations that were often more about students' individual psyches and less about the texts under discussion. The brighter students (and even their most *au courant* professors) grew tired of hearing young Jimmy's memories about his traumatic childhood when what they had come for, ostensibly, was a discussion of Stephen Dedalus's childhood in Joyce's *Portrait of the Artist as a Young Man*. As a consequence, a group of scholars headed by narratologists such as James Phelan and Peter Rabinowitz began to pay more attention to the third leg of the triangle, the long-neglected author.[28] Foucault's oft-proclaimed "death of the author" was greatly exaggerated, as Mark Twain might have said.[29] Rabinowitz and Smith point out that as much as the two of them may argue about various types of reading strategies, they agree that "literary reading is socially rather than personally constructed."[30] Smith says further that,

> Despite my growing confidence in students' abilities, I still believe
> that teachers can help them develop interpretive strategies more

quickly than they would develop them on their own. [This is because Rabinowitz's idea of] the authorial audience challenges the pedagogy of personal relevance by establishing the importance of seeing things through the lens of another's making. [It] justifies selecting texts that call for students to keep their distance and to question constantly whether personal experiences, beliefs, and standards of interpretation that they are applying are the ones that they are called on to employ.[31]

This is all very sound advice. Here, however, the teacher encourages the student to act skeptically, coolly aloof from the personalized emotions that tended to dominate the advocacy of professors in the RR camp.

How this intellectualized behavior happens in a classroom with college-age students, struggling with their own balancing acts of emotions and intellect, would be a difficult job even for seasoned teachers to unravel. Indeed, the approaches mentioned above all tend clearly to indicate a goal, but are much less precise when describing the *daily process* of *how* the professor moves students from scant knowledge and less motivation to becoming near-expert readers of complex and sophisticated literary texts. Hence, I will argue that while each "model" has many sound elements to its procedures, none is, by itself, sufficient to describe all that an "expert professor" does in a well-taught literature class and is, therefore, inadequate to account for all the characteristics associated with English professor expertise.

Thus, following Bain who "discovered that [he and his research team] could not develop a general definition that would fit all disciplines," I will begin by conceding that even within a given discipline such as the study of literature, there are problems defining and practicing a teaching model that will fit all classes and genres.[32] Recurring tensions exist between a general model with too many exceptions to answer all or even most of the questions a specific approach might ask on the one hand, and a too specific set of teaching strategies that are unable to provide much beyond the single classroom, or the personality of a particular instructor.

STUDENT SKILLS

Before pursuing further discussion of the professor, one may well ask: what then are the skills, emotional attitudes, and types of learning behaviors required of students to read imaginative literature effectively? Any experienced teacher of literature would argue that most engaged students should be able to:

1. Develop an **intuitive feeling for words,** images, and short phrases, thus learning to identify the cognitive, emotional, and acoustic tensions that many words in an artistic context have with one another; it is understanding, as Cleanth Brooks suggests, that for the poet's language, "connotations play as great a part as the denotations."[33] This attention to the particulars of language and to the order and mixture of single words, short phrases, and images in an imaginative context is among the sine qua non of more sophisticated "aesthetic reading."[34] Students must develop the capacity not merely to see the contemporary meanings of words, but also to remain "sensitive to their histories, etymologies, and rhythms" within a context as well.[35]

2. Move easily up and down what I call the "snakes and ladders of abstraction." The student must see the **important relationships in a text;** between its specific words, images, and sentences and the high level abstractions of theme, genre, and characterization, and then beyond, to intertextual connections, generated in part by those specifics.[36] Students' movements up and down these levels become the ordinary stuff of literary reading, as teachers help them "to recognize the formulaic generic building blocks that canonical authors use to construct their texts."[37]

3. In order to develop this sense for words and relationships within the text, students must identify what Beiriter and Scardemalia call "**pattern recognition** of high significance."[38] These patterns include entities *between* the elemental building blocks of word and image and the highest levels of abstraction mentioned above: theme, genre, character, and overall artistic structure. Such intermediate elements are very often part of the "progression of the text's unfolding structure," as described by James Phelan.[39] They may include ongoing character development (along with complications setting the various characters problems to solve), the part-by-part relationships of intermediate chapters, stanzas, or acts, and their immediate relationships and symmetry (or asymmetry).

4. Develop the **motivation to read** and absorb lengthy works of prose and poetry whose immediate payoff, in relation to emotional closure and completeness, may be hours or even reading-

days away. Often, this motivation is generated, at least at first, by the teacher and by those activities the teacher has structured that students find enjoyable and useful. Part of this motivation is aided by the professor who helps students distinguish between what Rabinowitz and Smith characterize as "first time reading" contrasted to "reading from memory."[40] In effect, students recognize the first time through that reading "inevitably involves expectations that aren't met, predictions that don't work out, details that are missed, [and] patterns that aren't completed," and "that that is ok" for now.[41]

5. Add constantly to their **knowledge base** in order to improve comprehension, and thus anticipations and expectations of different types of texts. This knowledge base is informed by an awareness of genre differences, authors' biographical and bibliographical data, and by wide-ranging general knowledge that includes the historical and cultural information necessary to comprehend the work of literature being read.[42] Paul Kameen argues, referring to understanding Plato, that it is possible "for a reader to find a position to stand in, and to work from in a sophisticated readerly way, without years of training or the subordination of her readerly project to professional mediators."[43] The question is, of course, how "sophisticated" is this readerly way relative to what it could be with a teacher's help? Kameen acknowledges this "paradox" and finally suggests that he "casts his essays as provisional," a cautious position with which I am sympathetic.

6. Recognize the various **narrative voices** in texts and (following from no. 5, above) understand how knowledge of **authorial intentions** will improve the ability to read and comprehend texts. For some researchers, students' awareness of authorial intentions has become less important than the student's own cognitive and emotional operations ("The classic is the work—not the author"),[44] although all would probably agree that students must learn to focus attention on the narrator's voice.[45]

THEORY OF LEARNING

If these are the requirements for students to learn to read literature with knowledge and pleasure, the next step is to propose a theory of learning within which to ground the teacher's plans for student literary development. The most useful and appropriate learning theory to account for the observations in my study is the *Situated Learning* model developed by Jean Lave, Lave and Wenger, and others.[46] Lave suggests that students learn best via what she calls "legitimate peripheral participation" in many of the actual activities of the expert practitioners in that field: "Everyday activity is, in this view, a more powerful source of socialization than intentional pedagogy . . . knowledge-in-practice, constituted in the settings of practice, is the locus of the most powerful knowledgeability of people in the lived-in world."[47] In one pioneering essay on situated cognition, Brown, Collins, and Duguid suggest: "The activity in which knowledge is developed and deployed . . . is not separable from nor ancillary to learning and cognition. Nor is it neutral. Rather, it is an integral part of what is learned. Situations might be said to co-produce knowledge through activity."[48]

The authors make explicit their belief that to learn is to situate oneself within the very fabric of the *world* to be learned. Learning is done by the teacher communicating to the learner through what they call *indexicals:* "Indexical terms are those that 'index' or more plainly point to a part of the situation in which communication is being conducted. They are not merely context sensitive; they are completely context dependent. Words like **I** or **now,** for instance, can only be interpreted in the context of their use. Surprisingly, all words can be seen as at least partly indexical."[49] These ideas have particular interest for literary people, because for them,

> All knowledge is . . . like language. Its constituent parts index the world and so are inextricably a product of the activity and situations in which they are produced. A concept, for example, will continually evolve with each new occasion of use, because new situations, negotiations, and activities inevitably recast it in a new, more densely textured form. So, a concept, like the meaning of a word, is always under construction. This would also appear true of apparently well-defined, abstract technical concepts. Even these are not wholly definable and defy categorical description; part of their meaning in always inherited from the context of use.[50]

English professors might formally lecture on the changes in meaning and usage of such technical words as "tragedy" or "Petrarchan sonnet" or *Bildungsroman,* and would inform their students, both theoretically and practically, about what changes occur in these terms when, say, the reader of "tragedy" moves from Aristotle's definitions as applied to Sophocles' *Oedipus Rex*[51] to Raymond Williams's definitions as applied to Brecht's *Mother Courage*.[52] But merely to lecture students on the differences between the two definitions of tragedy, what Thomas Foster calls "the grammar of literature, a set of conventions and patterns, codes and rules, that we learn to employ in dealing with a piece of writing,"[53] is only part of the teacher's task.

In addition, the professor must devise *activities* that preserve the essence of expert practices and that will allow students to explore their differing emotions as they read the two texts. Rabinowitz and Smith suggest that it is "far easier for students to resist [the values of] authors when they see that authors resist each other."[54] Such activities help students clarify *through their own experience* how literary definitions are subject to change, transformation, and renewal. By virtue of the culture that uses them and those within that culture who experiment with textual variations and innovations, literary definitions concerning genre, proper modes of verbal beauty, and so on, are subject to change through usage. This, then, is an example of the sort of expert knowledge that guidance can and should provide. Thus, Brown et al. suggest that: "It may be more useful to consider conceptual knowledge as, in some ways, similar to a set of tools. . . . People who use tools actively, rather than just acquire them, build an increasingly rich understanding of the world in which they use tools and of the tools themselves. . . . Learning how to use a tool involves far more than can be accounted for in any explicit set of rules."[55] Indeed, they go on to argue that conceptual tools are the products of both "the cumulative wisdom of the culture in which they are used" as well as the "insights and experiences of individuals," and so their meanings are not invariant but are actively negotiated within the community. Hence, appropriate use is both a function of the culture and of the activities in which such ideas have been developed. Because "activity, concept, and culture are interdependent, [what they call] cognitive apprenticeship methods" are employed to "enculturate students into authentic practices through activity and social interaction in a way similar to that evident—and evidently successful—in craft apprenticeship."[56]

I will explore in some detail current conversations in the departments of college literature, both literary criticism theory and recent cognitive studies of literature teaching. While these areas offer both strengths and weaknesses for our consideration, juxtaposing the insights from the two traditions could yield important information regarding the study of teaching literature.

Ultimately, my intent is to present a profile of English professor expertise, a profile of a teacher-scholar who pays close attention to students *and* authors *and* texts *and* the learning processes required to develop competent interactions among all of them. Such expertise exhibits contours that may be understood by the average person who wants to know what his or her offspring is getting from taking courses in literature departments at the university. In the presence of expertise, students are more often engaged and responsive; *learning* is taking place. And the professor *teaches.* My purpose here is to offer a detailed map which could be profitably traced by novice and perhaps some experienced teachers-of-literature-to-be as they struggle to become more expert professors of imaginative literature.

1

Current Conversations in the Teaching of College-Level Literature

Literary scholars consider themselves to be expert in writing about literature or teaching literature but not necessarily in writing about the teaching of literature. The latter field is likely to be thin, in both senses—less productive of scholarship than the fields of rhetoric and language and less conceptually developed.

—John Guillory, "The Very Idea of Pedagogy"

Socrates himself begins . . . when he says, on behalf of Hippocrates, who wants to "study professionally" with the eminent Protagoras: "He would be glad to be told what effect it will have on him" . . . What effect will it have? How will he be changed? By his teacher? Specifically. What strikes me about this question is how obvious and basic a one it seems to be for a teacher to be asking. And how rarely it is asked. What effect will it have? Important particularly in the part of our work that prepares others to become professionals at what we do. For such a question places the pedagogical transaction at the center of the problematic.

—Paul Kameen, *Writing/Teaching*

It is the question that is wrong because it assumes that we are responsible for the effects of our teaching whereas, in fact, we are responsible only for its appropriate performance. That is, we are responsible for the selection of texts, the preparation of a syllabus, the sequence of assignments and exams, the framing and grading of a term paper, and so on . . . There are just too many intervening variables, too many uncontrolled factors that mediate the relationship between what goes on in a classroom or even in a succession of classrooms and the shape of what is finally a life.

—Stanley Fish, "Aim Low"

So set 'em up Joe; I've got a little story you oughtta know.
—"One More For the Road," sung by Frank Sinatra

26

1

In a recent *PMLA* note, Ruth-Ellen Boetcher-Joeres, the editor of *Signs,* speaks about both the difficulties and exhilaration of doing interdisciplinary work. She argues that both "feminism and interdisciplinarity alike [for example] stress collaboration," but that such joint ventures are often limited because the "met-alanguage of disciplinarity asserts itself, controlling and limiting what interests us."[1] Much the same could be said about our own internal division between ourselves as teachers of literature and as literary scholars and critics.[2] Those who insist (not without some merit) that the two should be synergistic often substitute what *should be* for what all too often *is,* in a world of merely semipermeable boundaries.[3] We all want to be good teachers *and* good scholars, but we have found relatively few models for learning how to do both well.[4]

Fortunately the times they are a-changing, and many look anew at the joys of classroom transactions.[5] Teaching as a *belle lettres* research topic is refreshingly on the move in this first decade of the new millennium, and a literary generation previously focused on theory seems to be rediscovering the pedagogical wheel. This sort of rediscovery may be a good thing, when it leads us back to the reasons why we teach the humanities at all.[6] Although at least some recovery of the obvious might seem necessary to those who have only recently come to literary pedagogical conscious-ness, much has happened in the educational world during the last twenty-five to thirty years that has gone far beyond the *lecture-paper-final examination* model that once dominated literature classrooms. After "Flower Power" temporarily shook up the often staid practices of the previous generation, many had extolled the virtues of the newer, pedagogically more interpersonal reader-re-sponse alternatives to the earlier paradigmata, but now these too have undergone rethinking.[7] Indeed, almost a decade ago thinkers in one scholarly essay had even developed a rather loose sort of plotline: "The profession has moved from raising questions about texts, to raising questions about readers, to raising questions about the conditions of possibility for any reading, to raising ques-tions about how we teach students to read."[8]

In what follows, I intend to sketch some of the pertinent re-search done in the college teaching of imaginative literature in two somewhat different domains: in the familiar area of literary study, but also in education research. This mildly tendentious survey will not be exhaustive—so much continues to be published recently, both repetitious and innovative, that keeping up has become a near-impossible task—but the educational focus may include a few sources not always familiar to members of a literature department. My aim is to discuss various larger theories of teaching imaginative literature and their strengths and limitations, rather than recipes of "How I taught Shakespeare to sophomores" or "Two ways of teaching deconstruction to undergraduates."[9] These choices have been influenced by more generalized studies of "expertise"[10] and by the still-growing body of work that discusses the teaching of imaginative literature through the lens of pedagogical expertise.[11] I will suggest that these expertise studies are both useful for and philosophically compatible with good humanistic teaching practices. Further, I would seek to allay concerns that the "mastery/apprenticeship model" necessarily leads, for example, to seeing classroom visits as enforced "surveillance mechanisms." This would be an unfortunate misunderstanding and radical diminution of an entire research direction.[12]

Several points should be noted from the start. First, much good work on teaching literature has been done by educationists whose intellectual reputation among literary people has been, at times, suspect, or worse.[13] Usually, what gets mentioned are the clichés of such endeavors,[14] spoken by many of those whose own literary work, ironically enough, is pilloried every winter holiday season by the mainstream press during MLA Conventions. Thus, rather than debating over whose pot is calling which kettle smoke-damaged, I request the reader's open mind as he or she reads some unfamiliar work about very familiar practices. For several writers in education, the subdiscipline of learning to teach imaginative literature at the college level is considered a branch of expertise studies, and in such work, those individuals study analogous educational situations useful to understanding the evolution of the literature teacher from novice educator to expert professor.[15]

A second point is how the lack of commerce between (or among) literary people and educationists about teaching literature goes both ways, to the relative intellectual impoverishment of both; some English education researchers could find quite useful this new emphasis by literature scholars.[16] Third, the recent literary interest in cognitive psychology will help college teachers of literature find all sorts of analogues in teaching literature as well as critically reading it.[17] Indeed, cognitivists began studying the human processing of imaginative literature over three decades ago[18]—long before mainstream literary critics and scholars noticed or cared. And although important, cognitive theories comprise only one paradigm in the renewed study of literature teaching.

Those interested in the teaching of imaginative literature might consider the uses of a more socially oriented educational model known as *situated learning,* and to study those thinkers who consider learning a *relationship between novice and master-crafter;*[19] unfortunately, literary scholarship employing the situated learning model is—at the moment—still in its infancy. A fourth preliminary point to make, then, is that literary teacher-scholars have a long way to go to catch up with colleagues in composition studies—who began to explore the educational components of their discipline a generation ago.[20] Fifth, some of the early efforts in this direction by scholars[21] emphasize one or more of the thematic triad of race, class, and gender as fundamental to teaching per se, as well as to classroom behavior. However, in almost all else, these writers employ traditional teaching techniques.[22] One can assume that outreach from one domain of scholarship to another, even if to a cognate field, will almost certainly require substantial reconceptualization.[23] The phrase "pedagogical content knowledge," borrowed from education studies, expresses a concept that literary people interested in teaching may wish to acquire, as Miriam Sherin suggests: "Pedagogical content knowledge . . . is knowledge specifically for teaching the domain [of imaginative literature], including understanding how to present the facts and concepts to facilitate learning [as well as] knowledge of the typical understandings and misunderstandings of students."[24] Unfortunately, it is only recently that college teachers of literature have paid enough attention to the issues and insights of those doing research on secondary literature classes; there are multiple possibilities of reciprocity in exchanges of pedagogical technique, teaching literary texts to a generation too often devoted to "Reality TV," video games, and the Internet. Those writing for the many NCTE publications aimed at secondary teachers, such as the *English Journal* and *Voices from the Middle,* as well as those whose audience is largely college teachers—*College Literature, Pedagogy,* and even *Style*—are all wrestling with many of the same problems and are worthy of further attention.[25] In application, what we see in too many public school literature classrooms, as Larry Johannessen has recently said, is a "homogenized textybook approach that contains watered-down elements of New Criticism, mostly memorizing literary terms, with a sprinkling of borrowed and watered down Reader-Response, Reading Theory, Historical, multi-cultural, gender, etc.," mix-and-match teaching.*

Secondary literature teaching is a much more difficult task in the sense that it is harder to teach a literary work to those who do not already "have some grasp of literary critical discourse and the conventions of expository argument."[26] While high school teachers wrestle with issues of immature adolescent development not found in most college students, many of their problems remain *our* problems when we face the same students a few years later.[27] As I have suggested elsewhere, "the traditional separation of literary study plus theory from its practical application in both secondary school and university teaching is itself a theoretical model whose reconsideration is long overdue."[28] Although the Modern Language Association devoted a study to *Preparing a Nation's Teachers* (1999), and later inserted a supplement on secondary teacher training to the summer 2000 *Newsletter,* things have been relatively quiet since. I hope this interest catches fire and that fruitful conversations abound; as Boetcher-Joeres has contended, collaboration is the key. For innumerable reasons, college teachers of literature have as much to learn from colleagues at the secondary level about teaching literature as these colleagues have to learn from us.

2

My guide and I came on that hidden Road
To make our way back into the bright world.
                                   —Dante, *Inferno* Canto XXXIV

Current conversations about teaching college-level literature reflect problems that have gone unresolved since literature be-

---

*Personal communication, June 11, 2003. I am greatly indebted to Larry Johannessen of Northern Illinois University, and to Elizabeth Khan, an English teacher at Conant High School in Hoffman Estates, Illinois, for help with this essay.

came a major university subject in the late nineteenth century.[29] Student-dominated conversations, at times merely inane, can evidence engagement and therefore be worthwhile. Lecturing is difficult, and while many professors lecture all the time,[30] all but a few can be boring and are therefore largely ignored by "under-stimulated" undergraduates. Unfortunately, when some English professors are asked to rectify their somnolent sagacity, several respond with the ugly old refrain that "I teach literary matters, not educational ones." Hence, among the good, the bad, and the ugly, the college teaching of literature has been dominated by a relatively few competing global visions, none of which alone has proven satisfactory to many experienced instructors.[31] Paul Kameen says it best: typically, the "teacher will have achieved ex-pertise beforehand, usually through hard private labors, and will then display that expertise, usually in the form of a lecture, an extended disquisition, or questions with prefigured answers."[32] Students then "display," says Kameen, "through various testing devices or written work, the degree to which they have come to know the proffered material," or what is typically known as *learning.* It will be worth examining these binaries in greater dis-ciplinary detail, since both teachers and students can be said to achieve and to display, even though expert teaching professors have mastered pedagogical content knowledge in a way as yet unknown to most students.

What university English professors learn and teach is almost as varied as the number of English departments. While there are no doubt still a few remaining devotees to the Cleanth Brooks model of New Criticism, and even a few followers of Northrop Frye–style Myth Criticism, what most departments exhibit these days is an almost bewildering array of schools and theo-ries—what could be called "institutional criticism"—including traditional historical scholars, a very few philologists, several leftover structuralists from the 1960s, deconstructionists, new historians, first-, second-, and even third-wave feminists, multi-culturalists whose origins stem from almost every major cul-tural grouping in North America, so-called queer theorists, some die-hard Marxists and more than a few socialist progressives, or proponents of critical literacies who focus on race, class, and gender issues under the guidance of Paulo Freire. Many of those invested in connecting the "crisis of literacy" to the "legitima-tion crisis of culture," such as Christopher Schroeder, recite some familiar themes: "These classrooms tend to grant legiti-macy either to institutional cultures, or to the cultures of stu-dents' lives, and they often ignore the ways that the praxes of critical literacy invoke a collaborative legitimacy that emerges from the dialogic interactions of these cultures."[33]

English departments also include narratologists of all sorts, and finally a number of Jungian, neo-Freudian, and Lacanian psychoanalytic critics, several of whom have influenced reader-response thinking. During the last decade the profession has also seen a number of new theoretical models, among which are the cognitivists who may be either (or both) linguistically or psycho-logically oriented,[34] the evolutionary biopoetic thinkers,[35] and of course, family systems criticism.[36]

Surprisingly, very little research has been done on the rela-tionships between the institutional theory being espoused and any particular teaching techniques. I make this claim, in spite of William Cain's rather romanticized argument that "critics and teachers who read theory are active, adventurous users of it, mixing theories that by rights should not be joined together; try-ing out, like bricoleurs, a version of one theory only to abandon it or add it to a second or third, changing and readjusting its terms."[37] There may well be many *bricoleurs* of theory but as his own coeditor Dianne F. Sadoff suggests, the strategies of "close reading," "the brilliant lecture," "small group workshops," "in-class writing," and "performatory student activities" are all still typically *practiced* and still quite familiar to any experienced teacher of imaginative literature enamored of "theory."[38] In their collection on teaching theory to undergraduates, Sadoff and Cain look to variations of such typicality, as do a few of the essays in a recent issue of *Style* (37.1, *Pedagogy*). Several exam-ples in this latter volume tie their cognitive linguistic models directly to a specific teaching practice, and while interesting in their own right, most of these practices are not grounded in any particular learning theory and those that attempt to do so dis-play merely the beginnings of such thinking.[39] Within most the-ory-driven classrooms, the familiar techniques of lecture, small-group and whole-group discussions, and the assigning of posi-tion papers take a prominent place in the repertory of teaching practices; for this reason my focus will remain on these tech-niques as typical classroom practice (versus techniques proposed by theoretical models).

Many college teachers still follow the dominant model of literary criticism from the 1940s and 1950s known as New Criticism. The New Criticism's ideologies include immanent textual meanings, intense focus on verbal tensions and the resulting textual values of irony, ambiguity, and wit. Students are instructed in a manner to search for "correct" answers to literary problems, but it is the professor who knows the *right* answer, and more importantly, enforces it with a final grade.[40] For decades this was *the* model of learning and teaching in literary study.[41]

One of the important elements within the New Criticism is a concern for the text's unity as a self-contained artifact imitating the natural order of the universe. Forty years ago, in his then-monumental summary of Western literary criticism, Walter Jackson Bate compared the Romantics' views of the natural world to the views of more contemporary criticism. He reminds us that, for the Romantics, nature was viewed as a "dynamic process or activity in which the parts [were] brought together into an organic whole."[42] Great works of art were considered to embody, either explicitly or implicitly, those same qualities of organic wholeness in which "all the elements of a work—imagery, characters, incidents, plot, etc.—directly embody or mirror or encapsulate the central theme."[43] Hence, for generations, despite formalists' strictures concerning the "heresy of paraphrase," English professors have asked their students to identify the theme(s) in *The Scarlet Letter* or *The Waste Land*, thinking that when students had found a text's "central tendency" and could recite some sort of paraphrase of it, teachers had done their job. Of course, most students were utterly mystified by teachers who tossed out one-line abstractions; to nineteen-year-olds, those skills seemed to be opaque pieces of verbal legerdemain.[44] Some of the mysteries surrounding the literature teacher oriented toward New Criticism as "keeper of the holy text" arose united with the modernist contempt for anything not part of the elite canon. In the last three decades, a reaction against so-called elitism has moved much of the profession in the opposite direction. Robert Scholes says emphatically that the New Critics, "by positioning the critic or teacher as mainly an explicator, the objects of explication—poems, little arrangements of words—were forced into an impossibly high status. Poems had to become icons to be worthy of the explicator's art.

If, on the other hand, we can allow poems to be less exalted yet still worthy of our attention, then it should be possible to speak of a craft of reading poetry that can be mastered by ordinary readers."[45]

These semimystical "priests of the eternal imagination," to use Stephen Dedalus's phrase in *Portrait of the Artist as a Young Man,* insisted that the formalist study of literature asserted cognitive authority and emotional dominion as well.[46] Hence, what novice readers (students) had to accomplish in finding the "central tendency" was discovery of the key to unlock the text's mysteries, the "objective correlative," and the concomitant "escape from personality" that took the place of unmediated emotion. Thematists escaped personality by employing the objective correlative, which could be an object, a character, or even an event—but whatever it was, it reflected the intense emotion that literature often evokes in such a way as to call up an appropriate emotion for the reader whenever the object was displayed.[47] The trick for the novice reader then was to imitate the professor by pretending at times to "stabilize" emotional reactions by a concomitant display of erudition, "explaining" why one should feel that particular way. For many, displaying a reader's raw emotion without the mediating presence of the objective correlative was considered sentimental, and sentimentality was as taboo to the literati in those days as pornography was to the church.[48] Hence, as Kameen argues, any student's ideas of "display" were almost always most profitable inside this accepted disciplinary context.

Another variation of the "escape from personality" were those critic-teachers who expected students to be a bit more argumentative. Some thematists were not so much homogenizers as dialecticians who were able to identify a text's "basic conflict between two ideas and then to argue that the action of the work dramatizes and finally resolves the conflict."[49] Of course, even in its salad days, New Criticism and its proponents of thematic unity had its own doubters. As Richard Levin chided, thematizers often run "roughshod over differentiations which exist in the 'literal structure' of the literary works." The "unity found by these critics (and readers) is of the most general—and easy—sort."[50] The jump from the gritty particulars of a text to a sweeping generalization of "what it all means" can be called the "thematic leap," a particular sin of New Criticism in general and of many English teachers and professors ever since.[51] The New Critics attempted to evaluate every text on its properties of "irony, ambiguity, and wit" (rather than sentimentality) as well as its intrinsic unity, while convincing readers that the proper search for a rewarding literary experience lies in exposing these inherent qualities in each text under question, what Kathleen McCormick has called the "objectivist definition of reading."[52]

There are still other limitations in looking so intently on a work's coherence, one of which is the diminution of character's individuality. James Phelan addresses this issue by describing thematic dimensions as *character attributes*, "taken individually or collectively, and viewed as vehicles to express ideas or as representative of a larger class than the individual character. [The] distinction between the mimetic and thematic components of character is a distinction between characters as individuals and characters as representative entities [by which we imply] that the identities of these people can be summed up by a set of ideas or values associated with those descriptions."[53]

Phelan suggests that any teacher's primary focus on generalized theme at the expense of mimetic details impoverishes his or her students' overall reading experiences. Thus, although almost everyone teaching literature has continued to follow many of its axioms (close readings are an example), the New Criticism subsequently became the "target or scapegoat of competing forms of criticism,"[54] and any teacher looking for students to ratify its dominating concerns for the unity of the text has been viewed more or less pejoratively.

As with every theoretical model, teaching practices were intimately tied in with New Critical assumptions about how one learned to become a New Critic. This mostly involved listening to the expert critic—the more prestigious the better—and then doing what he (and sometimes she) did. The teacher talked; the student listened, then imitated—sometimes by actually writing or rewriting part of a text; sometimes by recitation, other times by writing an "original" essay—and after the performance, received an evaluation of the imitation.[55] That was the primary mode of information transferal in the service of mental stimulation in the New Critical classroom. Note, for example, in Elaine Showalter's *Teaching Literature,* she is "relieved" as she cites Martin Bickman's discovery that "lecturing is an active form of thinking *for the teacher,* but a passive form for the listener."[56]

Her relief indicates recognition that passive listening is not easily conducive to active learning.

After confirming a fact known by most high school and all middle school teachers, Showalter confesses that "lecturing in a large auditorium at Princeton I have never been able to implement buzz groups [sic] and student group work; the *students* resist it too much."[57] Perhaps it is the elite mentality of Princeton twenty-year-olds, knowledgeable far beyond their years, or perhaps the size of the auditorium, or perhaps it is the condescension implied in her term, "buzz groups," but Showalter's admitted pedagogical inability here—a kind of dismissal of small-group learning because of *student* resistance—is not unusual for many academics. Gerald Graff is also dubious about the "quality" of conversation in small groups, agreeing that while the strategy "does tend to get students more engaged, it does little to raise the quality of discussion and at worst results in the blind leading the blind."[58] Neither prefaces with (although I am sure both would agree) the obvious need to "train" novice discussants in the skills of small-group debates, since the process of such skill acquisition is as important for teachers in classroom management as learning to write and to read is for students. As with so many issues in the literature classroom, we have here a chicken-and-egg problem: how and when do we do this "training" so that small-group conversations are not only motivated but productive?

Showalter's "buzz group" comment is shortly followed by her admiring citation of a Harvard business professor who has the *real* answer to good classroom conversations. This professor opines that "Mastery of questioning . . . does not begin and end with framing incisive queries about the day's material. It requires asking the right question of the right student."[59] Consistent with New Critical thinking, the expert has the "right" question and he knows—apparently by some form of Harvard Yard telepathy—which student would most benefit by responding. To be fair, Showalter then offers a few alternative pedagogical tips—dyadic exchanges, writing briefly before or during a discussion—but she concludes her observations by referencing another Princeton colleague, who goes to the *other* end of the Harvard mainstream: high *in*formality. This professor tries to "set a tone of informality, and help students 'get over their initial reaction of resistance to postmodernism or denial of its relevance.'"[60] Here we add a variation, good cop–bad cop, formal lecture or informal propagandizing; the model remains largely the same: teacher-with-the-answers delivers the truth to his or her acolytes and thus largely avoids the messy need of exchanging with students whose contingency does not always ensure an appreciation of truthful relevance.

My own form of prejudice suggests that any student who fails to appreciate 1980s-style PoMo can't be all bad! Lecturing may create the most efficient package of information deliverable by the person who had all the fun wrapping it up, but it requires a level of receptivity on the part of the listener somewhat better than that of the traveler accosted by the Ancient Mariner. "Hold off! Unhand me, greybeard loon!" has certainly been expressed silently (if not as eloquently) by generations of lecture-hall recipients of the "right question." For many college students, the questions of motivation and consistent processing of even the most profound lecture are always a problem. If we consider the various input-sources for our students, listening to directions from one's *amor* about the best places to be touched elicits one level of attention; the best lecturers cannot be said to achieve anywhere near such dizzying heights of rapt concentration.

Showalter suggests that teaching some types of literature, especially complex and language-distilled literary works such as poetry, require real pedagogic diversity and so are "traditionally the most hands-on in the literary repertoire."[61] Nonetheless, she thinks that several genres of poetry and some poets from times and places long distant appear so arcane to most students that their teachers look to weekly transfusions of information to help students' comprehension process along.[62] *How* to do that satisfactorily for all concerned, *how* to create bridges between expert and novice—other than by assigning massive doses of unmotivated "outside reading" or by giving lengthy and potentially soporific lectures—remains one of the unresolved, persistent problems in college literature teaching. The professor's literary expertise is, therefore, a necessary but not sufficient condition of quality teaching at the college (or any) level.[63]

On the other hand, what is so often missing in discussions of the sins of "merely lecturing" is the sense that a good teacher, like a good therapist, is also part of the learning system and must be included in the necessarily systemic interaction between leader and followers. By virtue of his or her credentials and insti-

tutional authority, this leader is, ideally, both insistent and nur-
turing; both representative of the potential level of the students'
growing expertise and an outsider who occasionally must en-
force group norms and institutional values.[64] In this role, the
leader "achieves and displays" wisely until students psychologically remove him or her from the job by developing their skills
and enhancing their literary interiority, even if the dismissal is
partial and temporary. Unfortunately, some lecturers may see
their work as informational-transmission only, or some variation of bringing "the truth" to the unwashed, when one could
easily point to elements of indoctrination in either such beliefs.[65] In these days of instant access to computerized knowl-
edge-bases that would overwhelm persons living two lifetimes,
perhaps mere transmission is better done by machine; *learning*
is, however, still essentially a social act—even when one begins
it alone in one's study—and socialization cannot be done adequately by either machine or words from the lectern.[66] On the
other hand, too much socialization leads to what Schroeder, in
speaking of James Berlin's "literacies from above" teaching
methods, calls "an explicit essentialism that reflects [Berlin's]
neo-Marxist agenda."[67] Hence, the dance between attention to
the subject and attention to the audience of that subject continues. The audience of people paying rapt attention at all times is
a fantasy; on the other hand, the ideal lecturer may be as difficult
to find as the ideal spouse.

3

[We] ought to reject the criticism-promoting idea that it is the
reader who invents the story . . . If the works of art that actual
authors have created are the prime target of an interpretive
hypothesis, then we should let all of the available evidence
about the causal history of the artistic structure have the
same initial status.

—Paisley Livingston

Many professors in the late 1960s and early 1970s turned to
other meta-theoretical models, ones that placed the center of the
reading experience not in a text whose truths were apprehended
largely through the intersession of a literary Holy See, but, via a
reformation of thinking, directly within the reader and his or her

community. This approach became known as "Reader-Response Criticism" (RR).[68] But as Terence Wright has recently stated, Reader-Response theory (in what Wolfgang Iser has called *The Act of Reading*) is really a congeries of theories, and whether it is considered "an art, or a science, to be treated as subjective and personal matter or regarded as a rigorous, objective discipline, RR has long been a matter of debate."[69] Norman Holland sees three basic variations.[70] The first he associates with Iser and mostly German-speaking readers; Holland suggests that the critic in Iser's model identifies "the creation of an imagined reader as a projection of the critic's own point of view." "Not cricket," he says, because this direction is "just a formalist approach wearing reader-response clothes." The second are the experimentalists, but Holland objects "to this kind of work because [he feels] the questionnaires and, in general, the experimental machinery shape and change the responses." Finally, there are those, like Holland, "who collect reader-responses in an informal way and interpret psychologically what is going on in the readers' minds" (usually psychoanalytically—cf. *5 Readers*). Holland, and others like him ask "readers to free associate in a kind of psychological experiment [and these experimenters and theoreticians] have challenged more conventional literary claims and assumptions about what readers actually do."[71]

Whatever the specific details and merits of the critical debate in theory, the practical effect of RR in the classroom has often been a striking increase in student conversation and classroom argument. This engagement has come at a cost in some instances, say Peter Rabinowitz and Michael Smith, because one often sees the absence of reasoned disputation when primary attention is paid to memorial reconstruction and individual affect. They suggest that "a strong emphasis on the pedagogy of personal experience runs the risk of homogenizing what students read and mitigates against experiencing the uncomfortable growth that can occur when they have to face a character whose life is much different from their own."[72]

Rabinowitz and Smith are echoing the "founder" of RR, Louise Rosenblatt. It might be useful to pause and consider her original work as a prelude to a more generalized discussion of how many students learn literary thinking. Indeed, it is somewhat ironic that Rosenblatt's *Literature as Exploration* (1938/76) and her later *The Reader, The Text, The Poem* (1978) have become twin foundational texts for this whole approach. In both works, Rosenblatt is straightforward in rejecting not only New Critical "objectivity," but the equally undesirable polar opposite: locating the literary experience in near-complete subjectivity.[73] As she says in *The Reader, The Text, The Poem*, the "transactional theory expounded here repudiates recent efforts to make the reader all-important."[74] In *Literature as Exploration*, she is quite explicit: "Though a free, uninhibited emotional reaction to a work of art or literature is an absolutely *necessary* condition of sound literary judgment, it is not, to use the logician's term, a *sufficient* condition. Without a real impact between the book and the mind of the reader, there can be no process of judgment at all, but the honest recognition of one's own reaction is not in itself sufficient to insure sound critical opinion."[75]

Despite her caveats, certain reader-response theoreticians continue to practice (and thus subscribe to) the several conceptual half-truths against which Rosenblatt explicitly warned her readers.[76] Some professors may unwittingly sacrifice students' critical engagement with the work being read by only asking them to look more closely to their own internal processes. Although most of us now reject the theories behind those old "new critical" methods associated with determinate meanings, teacher-dominated and vertically oriented (top-down) classroom "discussions," and relative student passivity,[77] a significant number are also skeptical of how those who report actual classroom practices have paid mostly lip-service to Rosenblatt's transactional theories. In emphasizing students' focus on the self, or reader-response, some professors noticed that students could thereby pay little attention to interacting with (what have become a scare-words) *authorial intent* or *broad literary knowledge*. As Stanley Fish has argued in another context, "The basic gesture, then, is to disavow interpretation in favor of simply presenting the text; but it is actually a gesture in which one set of interpretive principles is replaced by another that happens to claim for itself the virtue of not being an interpretation at all."[78]

Recent scholarship has reexamined the very foundations of Rosenblatt's work itself and noted how several major concepts in *Literature as Exploration* (*LE*) have evolved over several decades and five editions.[79] Their major findings suggest that, over the years, the "deletion of passages [from *LE* reduced] the agency of author and teacher in the literary transaction."[80] Furthermore, other major and minor changes in that landmark text had the effect on the authors of rendering "literary experiences fully private and not accountable to anyone and anything else save what cannot be supported by the text itself."[81] Speculating about why such changes were made, Dressman and Webster conclude that newer editions shifted "away from a broader concern for the environmental conditions that permeate reading events" because *LE*'s view of aesthetics and of reader-text relations presented was never more than superficially aligned with Dewey's philosophical stance.[82] While a more detailed examination of this fascinating article is beyond the scope of this work, it is interesting to speculate how many teacher-readers of Rosenblatt have responded to the subtle shifts in *LE*'s basic message: to place the emphasis of reading literature on the expression of the self's internal mechanisms rather than, for example, on the arguments that take place among those staking claims within the text's social transactions. By shifting the focus away from the author and text to the individual reader, teachers usually find a much more talkative class—but talk alone is not an indication of quality learning.[83]

Many contemporary teachers appear quite pleased that their students have become far more active and engaged than in the old days.[84] One RR-oriented professor wanted to actively encourage teaching texts with "reader-friendly language," expecting that, as students share responses, they will be "encouraged to listen, not of the most plausible or seemingly 'correct' interpretation, but for the diversity represented in their peers' responses."[85] *Correctness* becomes the newest casualty of literature teaching, to be avoided whenever possible and replaced by the new holy grail of *diversity of opinion*—no matter the plausibility. If those teaching in the old days spent too much time only on "the internal characteristics of individual works," the more recent emphasis upon the reader's private associations at the expense of significant attention to authorial intent and gritty textual details seems equally unfortunate.[86] It is all the more so because one of the "founders" of RR, Hans Robert Jauss, makes it clear that the students' (readers') movements from identification (or what he calls the "associative" levels of interaction: identification, admiration, and sympathy) to a more critical and ethical interpretation of both the individual character as well as the greater aesthetic meanings of the completed work and beyond—must take place for a more complete understanding of a work.

Nonetheless, Reader-Response Criticism is one of the very few newer models as popular with university professors as with many more high school and community college teachers of English.[87] In literary pedagogical theory, RR is perhaps *the* primary critical model now canonized in what Deborah Britzman[88] calls the "explicit curriculum."[89] Although certain scholars (Earthman) have seen Reader-Response as a middle ground between the objective dogmatism of the (old) new critics and the radical subjectivism of the language-oriented postmodernists (Gary Saul Morson's "semiotic totalitarianism"), other critics maintain that, in application, use of the RR model by college teachers approaches the problematic extreme of total reader-subjectivity (cf. Holt-Reynolds). In response, Michael Smith argues that where the "New Critics would ask 'What does this mean?' Reader-response critics . . . would substitute 'What does this mean to me?'" Smith suggests his coauthor's (Peter Rabinowitz) alternative: "What would this mean for the audience the author was writing for and how do I feel about it?"[90] The ideal classroom practice would, then, combine the best qualities of both the New Criticism and RR in ways that take advantage of Rabinowitz's dictum.

In this discussion generally, I have insisted on the differences between theoretical formulations and the practice of those countless and nameless teachers and professors who transform theory into practical steps for classroom use. No truly useful account of teaching literature can ignore the differences between the formulations of the *Magisters Implicata*—like Jauss or Holland[91]—and the dog-soldiers' experience of teaching literature in the field.[92] Hence, professors delighted by the intense and detailed in-class conversations of RR-oriented discussions must also not lose sight of Jauss's or Holland's warnings that students' awareness of their subjectivity should be merely the starting point of the literary experience, not the goal. Students must move on to encounter the *other*, the author's part of what is usually considered at least a dialogue.[93] Shifting the focus slightly, Rabinowitz echoes Paisley Livingston and the narratologist Gérard Genette when he (Rabinowitz) discusses "the other" via his construct called the "authorial audience," that potential audience the author has in mind when he or she creates the verbal

work of art: "Disdain for the authorial audience makes it difficult, even impossible, for readers, especially young and inexperienced readers, to be educated, molded, or discomfited by the
texts that they read—for as soon as they assume the role of both
writer and reader, they meet no one but themselves."[94] Many
novice (collegiate) readers appear unaware of the literary skills
they do not yet possess, as well as the difficulty and persistence
required to develop them. Diane Holt-Reynolds reports the
views of one student in her study on learning *how* to teach literature, which becomes a "point of departure" for examining the
transformation from merely exhibiting the characteristics of an
expert reader to teaching someone else how to develop expertise
in reading literature. Holt-Reynolds's individual did not see the
connection "between genuine expertise in a subject area like literature and a conscious appreciation of the underpinnings of
that expertise."[95] Instead, this student:

> powerfully rejected a conception of the teacher as a directive force
> [and] in its place put value on a teacher who would honor any and
> all valid interpretations. . . . How readers might be taught more than
> they already know about making personal interpretations was sim-
> ply not apparent [and the person] seemed unable to envision [reading
> literature] as a problem that might require instructional response
> [even though] she herself was able to bring critical theory, personal
> experiences, knowledge of authors' devices . . . to her own work as a
> reader and interpreter of literature.[96]

Judith A. Langer, in her highly influential study for secondary
literature teachers, claims that this state of affairs, the overem-
phasis on student subjectivity, is "far from true," yet her argument appears to leave room for further discussion. Langer
rightly thinks that good and "reflective thinking is embedded
in the social forces within the classroom. Everyone expects to
make sense and communicate."[97] No one these days would disagree—in principle.

But her colleague, Arthur Applebee, correctly asks: "If students are to learn by doing, how do [universities] avoid allowing
them to wallow in their own ignorance? If they are [to learn]
through discovery, how can schools avoid a long recapitulation
of previous discoveries, most of which are no longer interesting
or relevant?"[98] Another RR-influenced writer, while placing the

locus of interest on the reader, suggests that literary "relationships can only exist as information alongside other remembered
and imagined experiences of the reader," but acknowledges that
in "order to create critical awareness . . . some explicit interpretive process is required."[99] And Kathleen McCormick contri-
butes that while "Reader-response critics were able to say what
a text was *not*—an objective container of meaning—they were
never able to articulate what it *was*, other than as a projection of
the reader."[100] Even in arguing what a text was *not* in a literature
classroom, many RR advocates exaggerated the pedagogical activities they were ostensibly supplanting: totalitarian literature
teachers insisting on the "objective analysis of a work of literature" and reducing a text to "one true meaning."[101]

Still another RR method of apprehending literary texts is practiced by proponents of "community-based knowledge claims,"
who place the locus of the reading experience within the subjectivity of an individual who functions as a member of an interpretive community.[102.] As one team of researchers has put it, the
"essence" of reading is "reconstructing a text on the basis of a
reader's cultural resources."[103] What practical and specific steps
would a university professor of literature take to employ, say, a
Langer-type "envisionment model" in the classroom? What of
the typical class of underprepared college freshmen who are un-
skilled at university-level discourse?[104] James D. Marshall, Peter
Smagorinsky, and Michael Smith think the issues are circular:
"Students are given little practice in independent discussion,
and so, when they are asked to participate in small or large
group, they have limited command of the conventions and
achieve limited success."[105]

And what about the teacher? Where does he or she fit in? In
many RR discussions, importance is attached to the teacher's
"time on stage" without any concomitant analysis of the complex functions of that teacher's "onstage" activities.[106] In an earlier work, Langer has detailed two contrasting discussions of
literature: one conducted with students employing the principles of "envisionment," a general term for referring "to the understanding a student (or a teacher) has about a text, whether it
is being read, written, discussed, or tested";[107] the other "with
the teacher's questions used as the focus of instruction."[108] In
the first case, 54 percent of the time students attempted "to gain
enough information to form an understanding of the characters

and events," contrasted to 32 percent for the latter case. In the student response group, student language accounted for 58 percent of all words spoken, in contrast to 28 percent for the teacher-led group.

However, these figures tell us little about what was actually accomplished by the teacher's talk—or by the students'.[109] The literature classroom is a place where the teacher's knowledge of the culture, history, and context surrounding the production and reception of the texts in question is very important as a means of continuing the motivated student's participation in class conversation. It is the teacher's task to help students learn *how* the *practice* of sophisticated readers is realized. In doing so, one might expect that such a function places the teacher "onstage" for longer periods of time initially, with a graduated reduction in focus as her students master those expert practices. This view of the teacher as master of the material and student as an apprentice is quite different from the older model of professor as lecturer-with-all-the-answers. The ultimate goal here is less the explication of a difficult text and more a "guided practice," where the apprentice makes use of both his or her own personal responses *and* the acquired knowledge base of the masterful expert in order to learn a *process* that will, over time, help make the novice more expert-like.[110]

Although there were (and are) many theorists and practitioners who believe in and practice this assumption in their classrooms, one should note that this ideal is hardly new. Indeed, many influential critics from the bad old "objectivist school" sound very much like Langer herself. Almost forty years ago, a famous critic said: "Criticism cannot attain to anything like scientific objectivity; it should seek to avoid personal bias. . . . A critic cannot escape his own temperamental and intellectual limitations, and should not deny his own convictions and standards, but he should be open-mindedly receptive to works of art and to critical ideas of others. This might seem a truism if there were not critics who appear otherwise disposed."[111] Thus, while there have always been narrow-minded and domineering critics and teachers, in practice some respected teachers and critics frequently followed procedures not much different from the self-correction which may be found in Langer's discussions. RR theorists are correct in their view that any person's engagement with a literary text is initially dependent on subjective experiential factors, although this activity merely begins a process that then requires a sense of engagement with the other, in this instance an author who may have highly specific reasons for communicating.[112] Following from that assumption, to become an "expert" (or expert-like) reader of literary texts requires considerable knowledge of many texts, genres, authors, and cultures.[113]

4

> A critical debate which frequently occurs in education is the extent to which pedagogical practices are neutral in terms of their theoretical underpinnings: the extent to which teaching is a matter of possessing skills and tools. Post-modern pedagogy is a search for practices which enact a democratic use of knowledge, texts, and cultural practices.
>
> —Tim Woods

It could be useful here to sketch briefly how the profession of literature teaching developed its attitudes toward both text and reader during these years of the "theory explosion," roughly the seventies, eighties, and early nineties. Some argue that the emphasis on the reader's subjectivity as it is often practiced may be seen either as rising with early structuralism or as a "logical progression" from it[114] and, somewhat later, from deconstructionism.[115] Nick Peim argues that the "logic of the deconstructive position would therefore locate any determinant meaning granted to texts within the context of their readings, within the established reading practices that grant them meaning, value, significance—and practice of deconstruction would also, therefore, need to address these institutionalized reading practices and their contexts."[116] As is by now all too familiar, such thinking led to the assumptions known by the collective term "Postmodernism," or more irreverently, PoMo.

For many postmodern theorists, "authorial intent" and "stronger versus weaker" interpretations as procedural guidelines have been largely eliminated from critical discourse in favor of the French critics' beliefs in such concepts as the "free play of signifiers" and "infinite plural readings." As Roland Barthes has said, the purpose of rereading is to uncover "not the *real* text, but a plural text: the same and the new."[117] In the opinion of many, the pendulum had swung by the late 1980s from a spurious "objectivity" to an equally spurious but by then ubiquitous subjectivity.[118] The net result was a new generation of PoMo-influenced students, several of whom went so far as to suggest that, in interpretation, almost "anything goes"—since, in a democratic classroom, anyone's opinion is as good as any other as long as one has textual "evidence" to back up generalizations.

Lest these assumptions be disregarded as merely those of immature novice readers, one example appeared in a widely read collection of essays edited by Henry Giroux and Peter McLaren, titled *Between Borders.* Ava Collins asks: "How can we address the issue of how students assign value to texts, of how they construct their own evaluative paradigms in relation to the evaluative paradigms they encounter in the classroom, and what that relation is, when we have not explicitly addressed the issue of how value is assigned to any text by anyone, including teachers and critics, except in reference to the accepted wisdom of the canon?"[119] After juxtaposing arguments supporting this view by Barbara Herrnstein Smith and those opposed by "tenured conservative" Roger Kimball, Collins makes a by-now rather typical either/or PoMo move and sets up the straw person of opposition, not to Dostoyevsky or Shakespeare, but to "quality television": "Thus begins the argument for the purging of student experience from the classroom, the reinstatement of *absolute authority* of the professor in the domain, and the revision—or reversion—to the curriculum to encompass the Western classics that embody the Values of Civilization."[120] In the decade following what became known as the "canon wars," one of its leading theoreticians, Gerald Graff, has tried to call a truce among the warring parties by offering a commonsense synthesis of both positions:

> An unfortunate split runs through arts education, reflecting the romantic culture war between creators and critics, between the teaching of art "itself" and the teaching of arts criticism. . . . Good reading does have to be rooted in a student's primary experience of a text or work. But if that experience is to mature and be stretched beyond the place where it already is, it needs a critical vocabulary in which to express itself. It is therefore misleading to oppose the first-hand experience of reading to second-hand critical analyses *about* our reading. How we talk about a book shapes how we read the books themselves.[121]

Left unsettled is *how* one teaches a novice to learn to read both types of texts. One's view of how such knowledge is acquired depends upon one's explicit or implicit literary learning *theory.*

From what I have read in recent thinking by literature teachers, the only "learning theory" I have been able to deduce from this body of work is the relatively vague sense that getting students talking will somehow "cause" them to learn how to read a complex work of art. The teacher's job in all of this appears to consist largely of keeping out of the way—acting as the "guide on the side" and letting students talk, while occasionally pointing out this or that factual bit of information or acting as discussion moderator if the conversation bogs down. In one sense, then, the variations of Reader-Response criticism as well as the remnants of the New Criticism, as they now appear to be *practiced* in many university and high school classrooms, tend to amplify some basic problems in the teaching of literature in the classroom.[122] Such pedagogical practices have had the secondary (if unintended) effect of diminishing research in literature teacher expertise, because displaying such knowledge is so often associated with the old pedagogy of stand-up lecture, examination for the right answer, and invariant textual meanings. As Applebee et al. have recently suggested, curricula "focusing on 'right' answers [emphasize] specialized content (knowing), ignoring the discourse conventions that govern participation (doing)."[123]

If we look anew at the role of the expert teacher of literature, we may ask how such an individual could avoid the extremes, those twin polarities of near-solipsistic subjectivism and the abstracted thematization associated with the "objectivist criticism" of the bad old days. Here is where employing the modified situated learning model[124] to study professorial expertise could be useful. Although both space and purpose deter me from an elaborated discussion of the situated learning model within these pages, its use in observing a full-semester course on John Milton is recorded in the pages ahead[125] and a second example may be found in an essay detailing the literature game *"Animal Farm* Hegemony." The latter exemplifies a type of individual literary learning within a social matrix where winning or losing an argument is of less importance than establishing the boundaries of dissent and developing a felt response to totalitarian practices.[126] Both writings represent applications from the groundbreaking work of Jean Lave, Lave and Etienne Wenger, and Barbara Rogoff (*Cultural*) in what the latter calls an *apprenticeship of thinking.*

These days, no sober well-read professor unblushingly believes that (a) he or she has the only "right" answer to all the vexing problems found in complex literary texts, or (b) students can do an even adequate job of understanding major works of art merely by consulting their own pulses—with no reference to the responses of other critics or to pertinent historical and cultural information. Hence, for the college teacher of literature who wishes to induct students into the guild of practicing criticism, reexamining the pedagogical expertise of critics and scholars becomes one way of avoiding the *Scylla* of New Criticism and the *Charybdis* of Reader Response. Stanley Fish says of teaching a student about *Lycidas* that "I was showing [him], offering myself as an example, much as a tennis coach does when he says to a pupil, 'Do it like this.'"[127] The teacher's objective would be to socialize his or her students into learning how to develop the same kinds of skills used by professional teachers and critics, not so students will become junior critics, but so they will become better, more independent, and more sophisticated readers of imaginative literature. These activities are precisely those of the professor who employs a modified situated learning model to teach the basic patterns of literary reading.

Studying the expertise of a teacher in a university-level literature classroom involves investigating how that instructor manages the balancing act between helping students engage emotionally and expand mentally versus leading them down the "one true path" that only the professor seems to define.[128] Neither polarity is sufficient for a heuristically satisfying classroom literary experience, nor is either complete without some elements of the other enfolded within. I have argued that contemporary literary theory thus far offers almost no detailed explicit instruction in how to achieve this balancing act. I now turn to education and cognitive research as useful additions to our understanding of teaching literature.

5
EDUCATIONAL RESEARCH IN THE TEACHING OF UNIVERSITY-LEVEL LITERATURE

Expertise in the cultural forms of literature is so tied to our experience with language and communication and to our general education that the duration of training required may differ from our study of expertise in other domains.

—Joan Peskin

> Acting is not the type of skill . . . in which ability is acquired
> by intense reading of relevant literature. According to most
> theater practitioners, the heart of acting skill is the ability to
> commit oneself fully to the character's situation under the
> highly artificial conditions imposed by professional perform-
> ance.
>
> —Noice and Noice

Cognitive studies of learning and teacher knowledge in imaginative literature classes have lagged behind comparable studies
in other disciplines such as math, composition, and even history.[129] Although a rich body of research has helped transform
teaching in other areas, research of the same quality only recently appears to be emerging in literary studies.[130] Here we will
examine selected patterns of cognitive research in the domains
of literature and literature teaching and briefly review investigations in other domains, such as history, when such research
holds promise for analyzing the teaching and learning of imaginative literature.[131] Although there are numerous practices that
literature professors employ, I will focus on classroom conversations, both small-group and whole-group, because they tend to
dominate what college instructors say they want or are trying
to use in their teaching. While admittedly sketchy, this survey
should suggest to writers like John Guillory that the "thin"
scholarship on teaching literature is actually somewhat thicker
than one might first realize.

Most cognitivists will begin by trying to define the issues
called for by the tasks. Some types of academic problems are
"well-structured tasks," jobs that can be "broken down into a
fixed sequence of sub-tasks or steps that consistently lead to the
same result."[132] Clearly, this description does not apply to the
task of teaching imaginative literature to contemporary high
school adolescents and college-age adults, for whom the job of
mastering a literary classic can often lead anywhere *but* to the
same result.[133] Nonetheless, Applebee believes that traditional
approaches to literature teaching have "relied on classroom
practices that focus almost exclusively on memory, allowing
goals of active reasoning and participation to fall by the way-
side."[134] Memory development may be useful for solving repetitive or similar problems (one remembers a solution invented
years ago and then applies it to the current job); memory also
supports the pattern-recognition that is fundamental to exper-

tise.[135] But memory is only one component among many in solving ill-defined tasks where there *is* no history of previous solutions to recall. Literature comprehension is tested by textual explication; we give quizzes where we ask our students: "Here is a two-line passage from X; who said it, in what context, and for what reason(s)?" The teacher, having reread X many times, is fully aware of the ramifications of this passage in X in a way that the first time reader could not be. Hence, the teacher's question conflates memory, reading skills, and (most importantly) *re*reading skills in ways that require much more than memory from students first approaching a dense work of literature, and therefore much more from the professor teaching it. Yet this quiz-question type is commonplace, forcing learners in an ill-defined domain to answer as if the response were part of a well-defined problem set.

In well-taught literature classroom, reading comprehension and literary analysis often involve ill- or minimally structured tasks. These cannot be "broken down into a fixed sequence of sub-tasks or steps that consistently and unfailingly lead to a desired end result [and because they] are not characterized by fixed sequences of sub-tasks," one cannot "develop algorithms that students can use to complete these tasks."[136] The cognitive study of the ill-structured tasks involved in critically reading and understanding literature has a disciplinary history that is barely a generation old.

In the 1970s and into the 1980s, cognitive research in the teaching and learning of literature often focused on "story grammars," and tended to conduct investigations on very simple texts or fragments of texts.[137] Early researchers thought that by reducing the scope and complexity of imaginatively written texts, they would more easily discover the mental operations involved, for example, in students' comprehension. Thus, "story grammar" research attempted to provide a means of identifying the structure of mental representations formulated while reading a story. Researchers were limited, however, by two operating procedures: the first posited an ideal reader, not real ones; the second employed the principle of *cognitive reduction*. Both made these research designs problematic for literary study because complex texts have emergent properties that are not captured by reductive analysis. The evolutionary biologist Ernst Mayr points out that both living and nonliving systems "almost always have the property that the characteristics of the whole cannot (not even in theory) be deduced from the most complete knowledge of the components, taken separately or in other partial combination."[138] The emergence of novel properties in whole systems "has often been evoked to explain such difficult biological realities as mind, consciousness, and even life itself."[139]

"Perhaps the two most interesting characteristics of [emergent properties] are that: (1) they, in turn, can be become parts of still higher-level systems; and (2) wholes can affect properties of components at lower levels" (so-called downward causation). For this reason, Mayr argues, *reduction* produces incomplete explanations, "since new and previously unpredictable characters emerge at higher levels of complexity in hierarchal systems."[140] When applied to texts, these principles imply that fragments of text take on different meanings when embedded in larger texts. Thus, if models of comprehension are based only on fragments, researchers' conclusions may be misguided.[141]

The two assumptions intertwine in the study of literature, since neither an abstract reader nor a reduced text account for the *relative movement* of the students' and the teachers' conceptualizations *between the two poles of reduction and emergence* during literature classroom interactions. Readers often start by simplifying a complex textual passage, building up a *textbase*[142] that encapsulates the basic meaning of a passage. From that textbase and the reader's own understanding of the situation described within the text, the reader then reintegrates his or her newly arrived understandings into the whole work, so that larger meanings emerge.

In literary education, Peter Rabinowitz has developed an analogous way of looking at this process, primarily by examining the endings of texts. He contrasts *configuration* and *coherence* in his discussion below:

> *Configuration* is the interpretive activity by which, *during the act of reading,* a reader assembles the emerging details of a text into larger patterns [or *emergence*]. It's the application . . . of specific strategies [from the recognition] that in art there is a controlling force over the shape of events and that one can reasonably assume that the future will *in some recognizable* way be prefigured in the present. . . . *Coherence,* in contrast, is the process by which a reader makes *retroac-*

tive sense of an *already completed* [novel, play, or poem, and which arises] from a general axiom [that] any serious . . . work of literature is in fact unified, and both apparent patterns and apparent breaks and inconsistencies can be assumed to bear significant meaning. Using this principle, we are able to generalize broad themes from local meanings and to convert apparent incongruities into metaphors and ironies.[143]

When Rabinowitz discusses this process in relation to a reader completing texts and making sense of their endings, one could argue that this is a continuous process throughout the reading of most imaginative texts, a view I doubt he would oppose. The capacity to move, sensitively and smoothly, up and down these levels of abstraction distinguishes the expert from the novice reader. Teaching the tactics of this process is one of the central challenges to any university teacher of literature. Elsewhere, I have called this cognitive movement—from reduction to emergence and return—the "snakes and ladders of abstraction," after the children's game entitled (in the United States) *Chutes and Ladders*.[144]

The complicated and highly nuanced relationship between reader and text has often required reductions in complexity to facilitate laboratory study, limiting the usefulness and applicability of some research. Defining the question in certain ways delimits the types of answers one can get. In the case of story-grammar research, the emphasis was on using artificial text structures as models for mental representations. Once it was known *how* stories were represented mentally, teachers could then develop strategies for helping student comprehension using that knowledge.[145] Of course, it is now widely acknowledged that stories artificially contrived to tap supposedly invariant reader-meanings do not support playing with ambiguity, meta-

---

*A quick example from E. L. Epstein: "Poets have been aware of the possibilities of reinforcing meaning with sound ever since Homer (and probably before). It has always seemed an added grace of style (onomatopoeia) when the sound seems an echo to the sense" (*Language and Style*, 1998, 25). How does one then read a poem with onomatopoeia in mind? The reader or student first *reduces* her mental focus to the phonemic level in order to *hear* the sounds made by the collection of letters on the page; next, the reader then moves up the level of abstraction by connecting any particular collection of sounds to the words from whence they are derived; finally, the reader *emerges* from the sound and word level to that of the larger meanings, both at sentence and at macro-level in the next, and hence the "snakes and ladders of abstraction."

phor,[146] or imagistic nuance,[147] activities that mark adult readers' comprehension of artistically created literary texts.[148] The two-decade popularity of story-grammar research points to the difficulties of research paradigmata, and have diminished its theory's practice in a heterogeneous classroom.

In focusing on the reader rather than the text, Barak Rosenshine, Carla Meister, and Saul Chapman review effective teaching based on findings about how students read and comprehend imaginative literature. They ask: How do students learn to read literature in a literature class led by a teacher? Rosenshine and his colleagues suggest that teaching students how to generate their own questions is a useful heuristic. Using that strategy is not a "direct procedure or an algorithm to be followed precisely but rather a guide that serves to support learners as they develop internal procedures that enable them to perform higher-level operations."[149] This proposal differs from the standard IRE (Interrogation-Response-Evaluation) mode of questioning, relatively unchanged in most schools for generations: (1) teacher asks a question to which he or she already knows the answer; (2) student responds with what the student thinks the teacher wants; (3) the teacher evaluates the response, and if the teacher approves, moves on to the next question or the next student. If incorrect, the teacher either works on the first student respondent until the correct answer is forthcoming or attends to another member of the class for the "right" answer.[150] By contrast, Rosenshine wants to train students to ask the kinds of questions in a social setting (a classroom) they might ideally ask themselves while reading alone.

Getting the relatively immature reader to begin self-questioning involves self-monitoring, because students trained in generating questions also acquire "heightened self-awareness of their comprehension adequacy."[151] Rosenshine and his colleagues performed a meta-study of a number of experimental approaches designed to train students to learn self-questioning. The meta-analysis included studies that used "reading scaffolding"— where the teacher helped the students by modeling or demonstrating a particular skill and then gradually withdrawing his or her support as the student became more proficient.[152] Then Rosenshine and colleagues focused on studies that employed procedural prompts, specific suggestions, or procedures that facilitated self-questioning and cognitive development. They organized the results around five different types of prompts, and assessed the effectiveness of each on standardized test scores: (a) signal words (who, what, where, etc.); (b) generic question stems and generic questions (How are . . . and . . . alike?); (c) the main idea of a passage; (d) question types; and (e) story-grammar categories. Looking for "a particular kind of relationship between a question and its answer and the cognitive processes required to move from the former to the latter," Rosenshine found "no effects for this category . . . where standardized tests were used."[153]

Rosenshine and colleagues conclude by indicating that the most successful prompts were the signal words and generic questions of question stems. However, different "prompts yielded different results," suggesting that future studies "in other areas of cognitive strategy research, such as writing and summarization, be organized around the different procedural prompts used in those studies."[154] These intervention strategies alone, while interesting and potentially useful, are usually taught as isolated skills and as such, tend to lose their connection to whole practices. Moreover, instruction in skill-building alone often pays little or no attention to motivation or to the overall goal of learning.[155] Hence, such strategies are meaningful for experts using them spontaneously, but not for novices who must be trained in both strategies *and* their meanings within the larger practices of expert reading and analysis.[156]

Cynthia Greenleaf and her colleagues have argued that "isolated skill-based instruction may perpetuate low literacy achievement rather than accelerate literacy growth."[157] In her research "with students from richly different backgrounds," they have become convinced of the "necessity of not only *telling* students what to do and provide engaging and authentic opportunities for them to do it, but also painstakingly and explicitly *showing them how*, building bridges from their cultural knowledge and language experiences to the language and literacy practices valued and measured in school and society."[158] Among other experiences, she suggests that professors teach in explicit fashion such instructional strategies as RT (Reciprocal Teaching), including requiring students to practice "questioning, summarizing, clarifying, and predicting." In addition, she focuses on a "key literary practice": strategic control of the reading process; meta-cognition, or knowledge of the self as a reader" as well as "meta-discourse, or knowledge of texts and textual practices."[159]

Her apprenticeship model of teaching literary reading found that one of its more "powerful results" was "the development of students' abilities to critically evaluate and appraise texts and textual practices themselves."[160]

Such abilities must be learned over time and are considered to have "emergent" qualities. In research that is highly useful to literature teachers by analogy, Tony Noice and Helga Noice speak of theater studies that contrasted actors' memorizing texts by rote to employing "gist" strategies. They report that "participants using a 'gist' strategy not only far out-performed participants using a rote strategy, but that this strategy advantage was particularly true of students [who] recalled five times as much material (scored as nearly verbatim) as those who had tried to memorize the same material in rote fashion," as the actors focus on the ratios between specific passages and the overall critical picture such passages instantiate.[161] Given this finding, we note Rabinowitz and Smith's contrasts between reading and rereading.[162] As teachers of narrative and poetic literature, we may wish to rethink the commonplace quiz questions that give students who have read a text once a quotation (perhaps two lines from a five-hundred-page novel) and then ask them to elaborate on the speaker, its context, and its meaning. While experts see large complexities in a single line or exchange, Noice and Noice report that novice readers (students) do not, for example, ask as many questions about the text and exhibit "few goal-directed elaborations."[163]

In sum, the authors present what they claim is now a consensus among cognitive researchers of text: teachers will need to ask students "to go back and reprocess portions of the text" in order to "increase the effort participants [have] to expend on the task and, as a consequence, [facilitate] memory for that portion of the text." Thus, a "learning strategy based on elaborating the material [leads] to significant verbatim retention" since professional actors can generate up to two and a half times "as many explanatory elaborations as students." Teachers would then need to have literature students attend both "to the individual words and [to] understanding why the character used those particular words."[164] The unspoken assumption here is that all of this work on student elaborations of the text would occur *before* the teacher gives the quiz.

Other researchers have been as concerned about conducting a

class of *active* student readers and conversationalists, but do so in the context of investigating the differences between expert readers and novices in poetry. Joan Peskin found that in her study of poetry readers, the "notion of expert and novice is relative rather than static,"[165] making teaching poetry grounded on assumptions of a cognitive continuum between what experts do with a text and what novices do (or do not do).

> Although more experienced readers of poetry differed from less experienced readers in terms of their deep structure of knowledge in a manner similar to the study of expertise in other domains, [and although novices did] have well-developed expectations for understanding the category of poetry as discourse in general, . . . experts employed productive interpretive strategies (such as structure, rhythm, wordplay, and rhyme scheme as cues, scanning to contextualize, looking for meaning at the locus of binary oppositions, and making use of visual representations to highlight structural elements) [whereas] novices used these strategies minimally.[166]

The implication is that to investigate what experts do with poetic texts as contrasted to novices, one should examine a real college classroom where works are selected that may *not* be (1) short, (2) simple, and (3) mimetically "real" or discussed as if they were (only) mimetically real. In the context of complex literary analyzes, the teacher's role should include placing "particular emphasis on designing interactions so that students become more aware of the strategic nature of learning, particularly the connection between strategy use and learning."[167]

Michael Smith says much the same thing as he discusses students' learning of literary genre: "[Genre] is best understood not as a group of texts that share textual features but rather as a collection of texts that call on similar sets of rules, that invite similar interpretive strategies. [Understanding genre thus is not to suggest] that novices be made to copy experts but, on the contrary, that teachers help students understand what it is that experts do (which is quite different)."[168]

Elise Earthman has also discussed the differences between the way that college freshman and graduate students read poetry. She selected the "particular works [read] because they are simple enough for freshman to understand at the literal level yet complex enough to allow graduate students to demonstrate their interpretive abilities."[169] The design Earthman uses is the familiar novice/expert study. The findings emphasize the literary process of "filling the gaps," following the work of Iser, who argues that "non-explicit texts (such as literary works) contain gaps or blanks, places where the text is under- or even un-determined and where the reader must fill in missing information in order to make sense of the work."[170] In contrast to the graduate students, who immediately felt that certain gaps in the form of symbols were important, college freshman "did not spontaneously fill the gap in such a way that they found symbolic significance in a recognizably striking image."[171] How does one "train" freshman to *see* symbols? Might not a teacher need to model *seeing* and maybe even explicitly point out symbols before expecting novices to strike out on their own?[172]

Ola Hallden describes the paradox of learning: "If learning [is] a linear process that entails, piecemeal, . . . adding separate bits of information to one another," then there is "no meaning if there is no . . . cognitive structure into which these bits of meaning can be assimilated." In order to "solve the paradox, we must assume that the structure is in flux."[173] Analogously in literary study, James Phelan has also addressed this issue of a moving cognitive structure (what he calls a "Progression") that readers experience as they encounter an imaginative text they have never read before. Phelan thinks of Progression as a major theoretical construct: "Progression . . . refers to a narrative as a dynamic event, one that must move, in both its telling and its reception, through time. In examining Progression, then, we are concerned [both as teachers and readers] with how authors generate, sustain, develop, and resolve readers' interests in narrative."[174]

There is, then, at least one theory that offers a solution to Hallden's paradox, but has still not explicated the teacher's role(s) in instantiating that theory in the classroom. For example, what exactly are the dynamics of this structural flux? Would literary experts be able to act as experts in an unfamiliar fictional area instead of "reading against memory"?[175] M. Ann Britt et al. would say yes. Britt's students who had knowledge of "a text's narrative structure learned more information in the text than did students . . . who had difficulty with the text's structure."[176]

But if freshman students knew neither text nor a general narrative structure, nor very much about the world, then what? How can learning begin when basic literary knowledge is low and students have few domain-specific heuristics and schemata to help? What steps could the teacher take then? Perhaps the most obvious one is to ask (or even demand) that *students* ask questions about the texts they are reading—real questions. Noice and Noice indicate that "having to state why a particular fact was true forced participants [in their study] to supply elaborations that reduced arbitrariness between concepts in a sentence, and this type of elaborative interrogation seemed to promote learning."[177]

The second step might be to reconsider just how much students do and do not know. In an interesting analogy to literary issues, the historian Samuel Wineberg argues that his students do indeed bring to historical texts "a set of resources."[178] By analogy to Teun van Dijk and Walter Kintch's ideas of "textbase" and "situation models" (on which see below), Wineberg says that

> [The] reader of history creates various cognitive representations of the text [and] while [they are] sufficiently distinct from one another to merit separate categories, [they] work together in fostering historical understanding by communicating with each other and interacting in highly-complex ways. The representation of the text [i.e., words on the page] and the representation of the event [i.e., the plot] are joined by a third, the representation of the subtext . . . which embraces readers' efforts to reconstruct authorial intentions and purposes, and to determine the guiding assumptions, biases, and convictions that frame historical texts.[179]

So, even novice readers (of historical as well as of literary) texts bring to the table resources that a good literature teacher can use. The question remains: *how?* I will try to answer that in the chapters ahead.

Gaea Leinhardt suggests that teaching expertise can be "characterized by speed of action, forward-directed solutions, accuracy, enriched representations, and elaborations of knowledge rich in depth and organizational quality. We know that expert teachers run a better class, but the useful, teachable mechanisms of *how* that is done have been elusive."[180] This leads to two questions: What does a literature student need to know to start breaking out of Hallden's paradox? And how can the literature teacher help in the breakout?

One type of potential solution, the HEI (hypothesis-experiment-instruction) method, is borrowed from a Japanese model of student interaction in small-group work, created by the teacher's structuring a three- or four-way student debate.[181] Students are given a short lyric poem to discuss and are to select (or are assigned) one each of four separate but overlapping "hypotheses" provided by the professor. Each hypothesis is potentially "correct" thematically, but each is also somewhat limited from the perspective of the other three theories. After the teacher "primes" the students with helpful information about decoding this poem (or poetry generally), touching on such matters as genre, metrics, or historical background, students are to debate from the perspective of their own hypothesis and vote at the end of a time period as to which argument carried the day. They may switch sides, modify their own or another's hypothesis, or even conclude that two or more are each "correct."

What is different about the HEI method from ordinary small-group work is that each student begins with a "correct" answer, but is required to convince (or try to convince) his or her colleagues that one approach is better, more productive, or more broad-based than the others. Hence, students are to behave as if they were novice critics at an MLA conference session where three or four panelists each attempt to persuade the others and the audience whose paper deserves further consideration. In sum, these novice poetry readers play the same "game" as the experts, but inside the context of their professor providing the scaffolding for their action.

While teacher-structured small-group work offers one possibility in solving the learning paradox, we are still left with the issues of large-scale informational flows from expert to novice. Peskin's study indicates that, "in period poetry [such as Milton's] at the very least, knowledge is an important component of poetic communication."[182] Generally, university-level English teachers' expertise and classroom conversation skills have been described, analogous to other university disciplines, in global or general terms,[183] but not with the specificity found in many investigations at the middle and high school levels[184] nor in such domains as math,[185] history,[186] and in several of the sciences. For now, one might look, by analogy, to some discussions of differences between expert and novice literature readers.

Indeed, well before making recommendations to improve instruction it may be useful to examine the cognitive literature on expertise in *reading* poetry to see how useful these insights can be in *teaching* literature. Peskin recently described the differences between expert and novice *readers* (not teachers) of poetry. Her rejoinder to the RR types who claim that reading poetry is "personal and natural" is that such a definition would "blur any distinction between an experienced or inexperienced reader" and further, that "if a text could be interpreted in infinite ways, there would be a 'debilitating relativism' [so that we] would not be able to talk about 'the set of critical differences' . . . between individuals who display more or less ability."[187] In another study, Colin Martindale and Audrey Dailey also take many RR critics to task for much the same reason, explicitly arguing that the focus on individual differences misses the commonalities many readers share. Hence their wariness of merely studying individually "actual readers . . . because their readings [could often be] too idiosyncratic."[188]

Peskin thinks *expert* and *novice* "are relative terms in that the novice may indeed be fairly experienced in reading poetic texts but is less experienced than the expert."[189] As did Wineberg, Peskin says, following from Van Dijk and Kintsch, that experts construct two mental models, the mental representation of the propositional content, and the *situation model*, the cognitive representation of that area of domain knowledge that is relevant for the text.[190] The situation model provides the knowledge for constructing a model of the textbase. Informed readers have domain-related patterns of organized information they use to help create a framework for *easy processing* and *recall of details*, and also *to anticipate* what the text will say. Expert poetry readers read, for example, a lot of *other* poetry and know what language moves other poets have made. The teaching paradox continues, of course, in the problem of how to teach a novice to read poetry without his or her already having read a lot of poetry.

Peskin also draws on Jonathan Culler's structuralist model of poetic communication. Culler argues that reading poetry is *not* a natural activity but is "charged with artifice," that is, "animated by a special set of expectations or conventions that the reader has assimilated and that are also part of the implicit knowledge of the author."[191] Hence "the study of one poem facilitates the reading of the next and readers must have considerable experience in these conventions." For Culler, the primary expectations are (1) the "rule of significance"—the poem expressing a significant attitude to some problem concerning man or his relation to the universe (that is, the poet wants to say something significant); (2) the familiar post-Jamesian "convention of thematic unity"—all the parts of the poem are related to create a unified coherent whole; i.e., "all the puzzle pieces should fit";[192] and (3) the "conventions of metaphorical coherence"—since the *basis of poetic expression is the metaphor.*"[193] Next, Peskin addresses an article by Bereiter and Bird to see if strategies in prose comprehension also apply to readers of poetry—such strategies as "pausing" and "formulating higher order summaries,"[194] "backtracking when meaning breaks down," and so on.[195] Peskin's list, modified for poetry, includes: (a) structure as cue (grammatical units, stanzas, resonance between structure and content); (b) binary appositions (often as thematic devices); (c) wordplay and language as cue (puns, repetition and variations, etc.); (d) rhyme and rhythm as cue;[196] (e) scanning for patterns (up and down the page); (f) pencil representations (external aids, drawings, notes, etc.); and (g) titles (used more by novices; too obvious for experts).

Finally, Peskin speculates whether or if novices having a greater difficulty constructing meaning in poetry "will diminish their appreciation of the poem" by struggling with an interpretation.[197] Following her analysis, Peskin concludes that "experts [have a] rich deposit of schemata that enabled them fairly early to *allude to other literary texts.*"[198] Experts read widely and, in recalling a variety of other poems, used the *cues* from such works to help them understand the poem better. In addition, experts were able to contextualize quickly—"to place the poem in a general context *constrained by certain conventions pertinent to the genre* of a poem."[199] Hence, knowing the forms of the sonnet allows an expert to find where the "turn" is: after the eighth or the twelfth line. Again the teaching paradox is getting the novice to learn about sonnet conventions before he or she has had enough experience with other poetic forms to distinguish between them and sonnets. Thomas Foster's *How to Read Literature like a Professor* seems to be aimed in the right direction for just such a problem, since he elaborates, in colloquial language, several generic or structuring patterns—for example, quests, descent into the inferno—as potential containers for students to fit in this or that element of a difficult text they are reading.

Peskin also states that experts have an "explicit anticipation of what is to come,"[200] as Phelan suggests during his discussion of the text's Progression. Finally, she points out that experts "spent much longer on each poem than the novices."[201] Although these experts quickly made sense of the poem, their sense-making was only the starting point for them, since "poetry is not a finite problem but an open-ended task."[202] Experts mined their prior knowledge resources thoroughly "to provide a deeper, richer, exploration of the poetic significance and of how each poet has effected meaning, where the form echoes the content, and whether conventions were adhered to or subverted."

By contrast, "novices [both in reading poetry and history texts] who did make sense of the poem acted as novices do in other domains, deliberately constructing a representation of the task in a slow step-by-step manner but not exploring the poem in any depth after they felt they had some grasp of what it meant." Furthermore, "novices reading poetic texts show a further similarity to those [novices reading history texts] in the phenomenon of *presentism. Presentisms* take the form of a default psychological propensity to select a *context* from one's "contemporary social world."[203]

When meaning broke down for novices, they either "reread the confusing segment or did the opposite, . . . set the lines aside and read on in the hope that the confusion would be resolved in later lines."[207] Conversely, during moments of difficulty, the experts used their "higher level comprehension strategies [and focused upon] binary oppositions, wordplay and language shape and structure and rhythm as cues." In short (and here is the crucial teaching move), when "experts could not make clear sense of a passage, they moved from trying to construct a representation of what the poem was saying to *how* the poet was saying it."[205] "Novices, on the other hand, very frequently expressed frustration."[206] And of course, in a classroom filled with frustrated students, the likelihood of their paying careful attention to seemingly arcane information about matters they find incomprehensible is not high, and hence the dance between motivation or experience.

6
INVITATIONS TO THE DANCE OF MOTIVATION OR EXPERIENCE

More recent work, both popular and scholarly, suggests just how far we still have to go for good answers. Several investiga-

tions have produced some interesting results, but in the end may
have introduced more questions than produced definitive answers. In the popular press, it has become commonplace to
speak of student malaise and lack of interest in basic learning:

> Students say that they feel bored in class, submit assignments that
> under-exercise their talents, and do minimal homework. Last year
> the National Survey of Student Engagement found that 44 percent of
> first-year students never discuss ideas from their readings or classes
> with their professors outside of class. And Indiana University at
> Bloomington's 2005 "High School Survey of Student Engagement"
> found that as many as half of all students spend only four hours or
> less per week preparing for class. . . .The trends are not unrelated.
> The more young people gather to watch TV shows, transmit e-mail
> and text messages, and blog and chat and surf, the less they attend
> to their regular studies. What develops is an acute peer conscious-
> ness, a sense of themselves as a distinct group. . . . As drivers of con-
> sumer culture, mirrored constantly by mass entertainment, young
> adults understandably heed one another and ignore their seniors in-
> cluding professors.[207]

Mark Edmundson said much the same thing a decade ago: "I can
only say that I hear comparable stories about classroom life from
colleagues everywhere in America. When I visit other schools to
lecture, I see a similar scene unfolding. There are, of course, terrific students everywhere. And they're all the better for the way
they've had to strive against the existing conformity. At some of
the small liberal-arts colleges, the tradition of strong engagement persists. But overall, the students strike me as being sweet
and sad, hovering in a nearly suspended animation."[208] Edmundson went on to blame the consumer society (and mentality) for
this state of affairs: "University culture, like American culture
writ large, is, to put it crudely, ever more devoted to consump-
tion and entertainment, to the using and using up of goods and
images. For someone growing up in America now, there are few
available alternatives to the cool consumer world-view. My students [at the University of Virginia] didn't ask for that view,
much less create it, but they bring a consumer *weltanschauung*
to school, where it exerts a powerful, and largely unacknowl-
edged, influence."[209] Whether consumer society is to blame or
ourselves as professors of the humanities, Bauerlein thinks that:
"The disengagement of students from the liberal-arts curricu-

lum is reaching a critical point, however. And the popular strategy of trying to bridge youth culture and serious study of, say, using hip-hop to help students understand literary classics, as described in a June 19th article in the *Los Angeles Times* hasn't worked. All too often, the outcome is that important works are dumbed down to trivia, and the leap into serious study never happens. The middle ground between adolescent life and intellectual life is disappearing, leaving professors with ever more stark options."[210]

The educational scholarship about these stark options suggests that much of what has been mentioned immediately above is actually more complicated than complaints about the younger generation. Martin Nystrand et al. conducted the following study at the secondary level, but its findings have implications for all levels of education, including college classrooms. Nystrand et al. empirically examined "hundreds of observations of more than 200 8th and 9th grade English and social studies students in 25 Midwestern middle and high schools.[211] Their results show that authentic teacher's questions, uptake, and student questions function as dialogic bids with student questions showing an especially large effect":[212]* "While student questions appear to spur the onset of dialogic discourse within instructional settings, challenging teachers' questions (that is, those posing high cognitive levels) may pose a barrier to active student participation in classroom discourse (via student questions) by reinforcing the voice of the instructor as dominant and authoritative, though just how this might play out in any given case would seem to *depend on how the teacher handles student responses to such questions.*"[213] However, when students asked "questions about the content of instruction, [they] heightened the dialogic potential of classroom discourse," at least in part because "student questions follow up something someone else said." Students "especially have the power to enhance dialogicality of classroom discourse when the teacher, rather than answering the question and quickly getting back to the lesson plan, allows classroom talk to move in directions prompted by the question."[214] For Nystrand et al., the ideal class discuss is one

---

*Professors ask "authentic questions" when they do not expect prespecified answers. "Uptake" occurs when the professor takes a significant portion of the language in a student's answer and incorporates such language into the next question (cf. Nystrand and Gamoran, 199). Full disclosure: I was a member of this research group from 1986–1990.

where "a critical discourse mass . . . yields to open discussion in which teachers and students work out understandings face to face—the quintessential form of dialogic interaction."[215]

At least one study suggests that professors who "allow classroom talk" to move in directions prompted by students are not guaranteed to be satisfied. Further professorial attention to the emotional and social aspects of whole group discussion is equally important, as was discovered in a research project carried out just a year later. Seung Lee Do and Diane Schallert tried to understand the role of affect in classroom discussion, both within a class discussion and across several classes, among college seniors. They found that when "students' general affective response to the current context was positive, they paid more attention to what was occurring in class at that moment, moving immediately to deep listening and talking."[216] However, "if students were in the throes of some sort of negative affect, their tendency was to go from attending to tuning out, sliding quickly out of listening or talking into tuning out. . . . [The] most frequent antecedent to tuning out is an experience of strong negative emotion of an accumulation of smaller aggravations. [Students] stopped paying attention or participating in the discussion not because they were simply being lazy [an implication often made by the popular press] but because they were trying to protect themselves from strong negative emotions in the context."[217] Do and Schallert interpret this withdrawal as a "coping response, a way to regulate affective processes and increase student well-being in class discussion."[218] For these researchers, the social aspects of the class, the presence of a cohort of peers, could make the relative success of whole-group discussions "subject to the pressures of what peers may think or feel about whatever was said in discussion." As the study's class progressed through the semester, students "took on particular roles and routines within the cohort group, mostly because they had come to know each other so well."[219] Hence, professors "may do well to consider more closely the potential effects of social aspects in the class on students' emotional well being. This is not as simple as it may seem."[220] Such regulation is as much in the control of the individual student as anything the professor might say or do, since "students needed the ability to regulate their negative emotions, especially toward the social aspects of the class, to stay focused on listening to the content of the discussion."[221]

Or are those false dichotomies? The college teaching of literary matters still has far to go for good answers.

Conclusion

We have surveyed several connections between the major theoretical models of teaching imaginative literature and the practical outcomes of a too-slavish devotion to any one theory. Those doing research in literary teaching still will need to catch up with colleagues in composition theory, a subdiscipline that did not come into its own without following two distinct procedures: attention to the empirical investigation of what researchers actually did relative to what they thought they did, and the creation by practitioners of a concomitant revolution in their teaching methods that arose from the mix of observation and theory. Much exciting work is being done in cognitive domains outside the usual ken of literary people; we would do well to take some of this "educational work" seriously.

We know where we want to go—where do we start?

1. How can we prepare students, aesthetically, to learn complex literary reading in such a way as to move naturally up and down the "snakes and ladders of abstraction"? That is, how does the professor of literature help his or her charges to notice there might be significance in roses blooming outside Hester's jail cell, in Hawthorne's *Scarlet Letter?*
2. What are some new and interesting methods for teaching important literary information to novices of that cultural world that might make such nuggets of aesthetic lore meaningful? (This chicken-and-egg motivational problem is older than chickens or eggs and has yet to be solved by the mere power of the grade.)
3. Is there a way for teachers to arm students with the tools of "literary criticism"—such as deconstructionism, feminism, new historicism, and family systems, thus supplying them with information about the text *and* its surrounding cultural matrix *and* the specifics of criticism—without overwhelming the student or retreating to (mere) lecture?

2
Step One
Scant Beginnings

An adequate account of how complex knowledge is built up
from scant beginnings remains to be worked out.
　　　　　　　—Bereiter and Scardamalia, *Surpassing Ourselves*

We simply don't yet have . . . sophisticated, discipline-spe-
cific discourses [in literary studies] for talking about what it
is that we do for at least half of our living: teach.
　　　　　　　　　　　　　—Paul Kameen, *Writing/Teaching*

To Begin

IN BOOK II OF PLATO'S *THE REPUBLIC,* SOCRATES, GLAUCON, AND GLAU-
con's brother, Adeimantos, are having a conversation about education that could easily serve as a guide for those reading ahead.
Socrates asks, "How shall our guardians be trained and educated? . . . [We] must not leave the discussion incomplete, but
we would not make it tediously long." Glaucon's brother as-
sents and seems eager to participate: "Indeed, I expect this inquiry will be of great help for our purpose." Socrates then
charms his audience into a lengthy exchange by suggesting:
"Then certainly, my dear Adeimantos, we must not let it go,
even if it turns out to be rather long . . . Then let us imagine
their education, as if we were just telling stories to amuse a long
leisure hour."[1]

In the next few chapters I will tell a series of stories, perhaps
not of a structural complexity to challenge Plato's, but adequate
for the amusement of anyone interested in *how* a typical group
of undergraduates proceed from "scant beginnings" to a fairly
sophisticated understanding of one of the great poets and essay-
ists in the English language, John Milton.

What I Did and Why I Did It

I chose to conduct one semester-long observation and analysis of a single upper-division English class in order to describe in specific detail university-level professorial expertise in the teaching of literature. I selected the case-study approach because in reviewing the research literature on teaching, it became clear to me that what was needed was a detailed analysis of *how* a university professor juggles the complex set of tasks necessary to teach difficult, imaginative texts. This type of fine-grained description would provide the best behavior models for those interested in pursuing these teaching practices.

The Participants

THE STUDENTS

Prof. J's 8:00 a.m. class (he calls it "Red-Eye Milton") was composed originally of thirty-one students, four of whom eventually dropped the course. On the first day, I explained my research project to the entire class and asked for volunteers to participate. Twenty-five of the thirty-one students volunteered to participate, nineteen females and six males. Those who elected not to participate were informed that no materials would be collected from them and, to whatever extent possible, videotaping would not include them. Participants included one African American male, one Asian Indian female, one Hispanic female, and twenty-two ethnically white students. The four students who dropped the course were all original participants: two white males, one Hispanic female, and one white female. The ethnic diversity of the participants is somewhat less than the enrolled student body of the university as a whole which had, in 1997, approximately a 24 percent minority population. However, the class is reasonably representative of English majors, who are somewhat less diverse than the university student body as a whole.

THE TEACHER

The teacher in all of this is a colleague of mine at Northern Illinois University, English Professor William C. Johnson, Ph.D.

(hence, "Prof. J"). At this institution, Prof. J has won both the Presidential Teaching Award (given to three individuals each year by the president of the university) and, in a different year, the student-and-faculty-awarded Teacher of the Year for Excellence in Undergraduate Teaching, awarded annually to three out of twelve hundred or more teaching faculty. Prof. J's reputation in the English Department during his more than thirty years of teaching stands among the highest rated in a department known throughout the university for very high-quality teaching standards. In addition, for many years Professor Johnson has been Director of Sigma Tau Delta, the international honor society for undergraduate English majors. As such, he has regularly traveled both in the United States and abroad, speaking on issues relevant to university-level English teaching and college English majors. In short, I chose a teacher widely considered to be an expert in the teaching of literature by a large number of qualified people over a very long period of time. Prof. J, whose scholarly expertise is in English Renaissance literature, has also published many reviews, articles, and a university press book on the subjects he has taught, which include Spenser, Shakespeare, and Milton.

My purpose was to identify how an expert professor introduces his college students into the practices of expert readers of great literature, such as Milton's. In particular, I sought to describe how the professor erected a scaffold of expert literary practices for students and then gradually withdrew it, as students assumed control of those activities themselves. Because my interest is expertise in teaching, my focus is on the professor: his planning, in-class behaviors, implicit theories of student learning, and knowledge both of Milton and of the pedagogy required to teach Milton. As Prof. J said to me: "I hope I'm not sounding arrogant, but I think an important part of the process [of teaching students literature] is the teacher, acting as a catalyst."[2]

Why Milton?

The writing of John Milton is considered one of the cornerstones of English literature; courses in his works are offered every year (if not every semester) at the university where Prof. J teaches. Indeed, all English majors are required to take at least one major author's course from a list which includes Chaucer,

Shakespeare, and Milton. Hence, the Milton class is taken by approximately 25–33 percent of all English majors and, according to the director of undergraduate studies, the students in this course represented a broad spectrum of all students majoring in English (1997 statistics).

What is interesting about this particular course is the ostensibly narrow focus: one writer and one period of the seventeenth century. The amount of information required by a novice to operate even within this particularized "field" (Milton) encompasses biblical and classical literary models, late Renaissance education, history, theology, and science, as well as the usual genre modifications typical of any coherent literary period. For most undergraduates, reading Milton requires an enormous amount of "extra-textual information or background knowledge," little of which is known by American university students prior to the class.[3]

The necessity for "extra-textual information" in teaching Milton (even though his works have been, as our former colleague Frank Court notes, a "staple of English department programs" since the nineteenth century)[4] highlights the significance in the different approaches to literature teaching discussed in the previous chapter. There has been much practical pedagogical research on teaching various sophisticated literary works to college students,[5] yet few of these studies do more than describe painfully familiar teaching problems, provide one or more recipes for fixing them, and conclude with exhortations like, "Milton deserves active readers who commit themselves to the communication process."[6]

In her essay of two decades ago, Professor Melchior describes some typical issues she faced when teaching Milton to university-level undergraduates: (1) "Some students could not read the words and make meaningful sentences out of them" (that is, they exhibited deficiencies in text-modeling);* (2) "Almost all of them lacked a context for the text" (little or no background knowledge of seventeenth century British culture, politics, and literature); (3) "Those who succeeded in surmounting both of these obstacles still had difficulty; they wanted to be 'note-

---

* This could be seen by some as a perennial problem. A couple of years after this study was completed, Professor Anne E. Berthoff complained that unless one is somehow "distracted" from the obvious, "our students are unpracticed [among other limitations] in close observation" (672).

taking bystanders' to the reading process, and would therefore have missed encountering the work as aesthetic communication" (deficiencies in literary schemas).[7] Student engagement with issues within the text as well as with the author and his or her intentions is one of the challenges faced by any expert teacher of difficult classical literature.

Procedures

For this study, I observed and videotaped Prof. J for twenty-seven of the thirty scheduled classes constituting the fall semester. Class met on Tuesday and Thursday mornings from 8:00 a.m. until 9:15 a.m., when he taught junior-senior level undergraduates this English course on the writings of John Milton. These twenty-seven classes provide data for a case study of how an expert English professor teaches a group of English majors, who previously knew little or nothing about John Milton and his writings, to become independent readers of these texts.

Data Sources

FIELD NOTES

During the fall semester, as I observed and videotaped the scheduled Milton classes of Prof. J, I took extensive handwritten field notes during each class to supplement the videotaping. Immediately after each class, I reviewed my notes and corrected any omissions. Some days later I retyped all field notes, and with these in hand I reviewed each videotape in detail and amended the field notes a second time.

INTERVIEWS

I interviewed Prof. J on two separate occasions for approximately one to one-and-one-half hours, once before the beginning of the semester and once in late October. During these interviews I asked him about his philosophy of educating students, his classroom methods and procedures, and his expectations of an undergraduate class of English majors. After most classes I also spoke briefly with Prof. J, asking him about his motivation for particular classroom activities or for more information about interesting teaching maneuvers.

Some of the questions I asked Prof. J during the initial interview included:

1. How do you expect students to cope with the moral and ethical issues Milton presents to them from a distance of three hundred years?
2. How can you gauge a student's readiness to learn about the complexity of Milton, when it may be beyond the student's ability to define it for himself?
3. What do you hope to accomplish in the first two-to-three weeks of the semester?
4. [After being informed that J requires his students to spend from five to seven hours preparing for any given class period]: Is the primary focus in the seven hours of preparation on the students' intellectual structures or knowledge? . . . Are your preparation decisions largely (or mostly) influenced by what they actually know about Milton—or what you think they should know?

EXAMPLES OF CLASS WORK

Prof. J copied and provided samples of class work from all students who participated in the study, randomly selecting a broad range of submissions to include:

(a) several different weeks' worth of class notebooks written by students as homework before each class, taken via the method he refers to as "Cards o' Doom";
(b) samples of midterm examinations;
(c) samples of student term papers;
(d) three sets of sample short quizzes written at the start of some classes.

Data Analysis

All videotapes, field notes, and student-generated materials were reviewed repeatedly as the case study was generated. In addition, I examined all student-generated work, the interviews, and read or reread each of Milton's texts as it was covered in class. I used these materials to generate a day-to-day narrative of class conversations, activities, and teaching events. Since my objective was to describe the significant episodes and teaching moves made by Prof. J during each of the classes, my analysis is organized in sequence and the classes are divided into six groupings, called Steps One through Six.

These "Steps" are identified by considering two dimensions: (1) the growing complexity of the texts and the consequent learning development required of students as they move through the course; (2) the changing genre characteristics of each set of texts, from relatively short fourteen-line sonnets, through Milton's adolescent prose writings to his more complex and longer poetry and drama, and concluding with his masterpiece, the epic poem, *Paradise Lost.* At the end of each class and each Step, I summarize the important teaching considerations and student developmental learning patterns observed during the classes that constitute that period.

Step One

In this first day of class, we will take a look at the foundation Prof. J puts in place to build upon during the ensuing semester. At the beginning, the professor's essential task is motivation; helping young adults learn to love (or at least to enjoy) both the literature and the class conversations about literary works of the imagination.[8] This task requires the teacher to help build a "community of interpreters"[9] by setting up common structures (literary problems to be resolved) and goals, and by creating a classroom atmosphere where students feel comfortable enough to share their ideas and to use their newly acquired bits of knowledge in interpreting the texts.[10] Much evidence suggests that complex intellectual tasks are often made somewhat easier by conversations (Plato calls them *stories*) among those engaged in the same labors.[11] As one researcher put it, during such conversations, the "cognitive dimension [is] deeply embedded in the social framework."[12]

Alas, unlike learning skills such as computer programming, the appreciation and discussion of great literature is not, in our time and culture, a requirement for successful negotiation in making a living.[13] Hence, any professor in the humanities assumes the double burden of passing along skills and knowledge *and* of persuading students that eventually they will like what they read and may even, in those distant halcyon days after college, regularly give up a *MySpace* session or a TV show for the "pleasures of the text."[14]

WELCOME TO CLASS

For Professor J, eight o'clock on a Tuesday morning seems like a particularly great time to begin. "Welcome to 'Red-Eye Milton!'" he announces smilingly to his thirty half-awake English majors and minors. Prof. J passes out course syllabi, discusses attendance policies, and after one or two other preliminary statements he points out: "I can't make you like Milton—you will or you won't like [him] by the end of the course—but you will *learn about* the seventeenth century, and Milton, and about yourself."

Prof. J structures his class into the six sections I call "Steps," which correspond to texts to be studied, literary skills to be mastered, and historical/biographical information to be added to the students' knowledge base. Each *Step* develops and then builds upon students' specific textual knowledge and mastery of biographical details and skill practices, which aids the students in displaying what they have learned and thus interpreting their encounters with the literary and historical materials discussed. The Steps are each structured around a text or set of texts, initially organized chronologically according to the period in Milton's life when they were written. Organizational substructures include the genre(s) of each text, within which are embedded the literary skills as well as the biographical and historical knowledge that Prof. J assumes his students will need to help decode each work. Hence, for Prof. J, causing learning via a highly detailed, explicit, and fairly directive course outline is of major importance.

Prof. J begins the students' introduction to Milton by giving them a page-long set of assignments for the next class day. These lengthy written assignments are given out each class period. They include feedback from the current day's work, as well as a structuring for the next few days reading and thinking (see appendix A for both *Assignment Sheets* (hence *AS*) and for the class *Schedule*, which lists in outline form the texts assigned for reading). The completed assignments are to be kept in each individual student's *Course Project Notebook*, which is collected through a random process Prof. J calls the *Cards 'o Doom*. Each week, he gathers one small group's (four to six students) work and reads the work of each member. Thus, each student's *Notebook* is evaluated by Prof. J three to four times during the semester. Notebook grades are the traditional A–F, complemented by a paragraph (or more) of written analysis of its strengths and limitations (see appendix A for a sample evaluation).

Prof. J begins the process of building Miltonic learning from relatively modest beginnings by laying foundations on several levels: biographical information, technical matters relating to sonnet reading, and source hunting. In the handout he distributes during the first class, Prof. J asks students to:

1. Read a bare outline of the chronology of Milton's life;
2. Locate [in the Hughes (1957) edition of their Milton text] the assigned sonnets (nos. 7, 18, 19, and 23), read them, and make a list of "the criteria for identifying a poem as a sonnet" (*AS* no. 1);
3. "Identify [their] source(s) for this information," a question meant to identify how much these students remember from their "English 200: Introduction to Literary Studies," a course usually taken upon entry into the major.

Following students' multiple readings of each poem, they are to look in the *Oxford English Dictionary* (*OED*) or in the textual notes for any words not understood, and *then* and only then are they to attempt an analysis of the four sonnets. Prof. J provides six prompts, asking basic questions about speaker, audience, genre characteristics, and Milton's thematic focus—his "human concerns, or real human desires." Finally, Prof. J reaches the "important" issue, how these poems relate to the student personally, when he asks: "What, if anything, in them speaks to you in your own *humanness?*"

From the outset, Prof. J exhibits expert "English pedagogical content knowledge"[15] in a variety of ways. He asks students to learn some specific facts about Milton and about the genre of the sonnet, as both sets of "facts" are specifically related to their humanness—a key to the students' motivation in wanting to read this information in the first place. By opening the semester with these specific questions, Prof. J models for students a careful attention to the text, to language in general, and, by asking them to consult the *OED*, to the shifting meaning of specific words. Only then, he states, should the students begin to interpret the sonnets themselves.

This modeling of basic literary processes (authorial intent through biographical information, attention to word-level issues, and connections to students' own lives) is particularly important for anyone teaching a literature that is removed in time and space from students' experience. With seventeenth century literature, the reader-response teaching paradigm so popular these days with teacher-educators is not, at least initially, as fruitful as it is for student readers of contemporary fiction whose own life experiences help them with basic textual decoding. Moreover (according to some critics), in a RR environment, such experiences often *become* the matter for study. Fleishman, for example, refers to this romantic subjectivism as "the fall into self-consciousness," one that has left many English departments "without much connection to its scholarly antecedents, except as they provide examples of the 'value-laden, interested, [and] ideological.'"[16]

In reading Milton, by contrast, students must be helped with the ordinary process of decoding the text of an unfamiliar (early modern) type of English,[17] set in a past [1608–74] remote from their own experience, which exhibits values rather distant from their own assumptions. In addition, since the original King James Bible was so deeply embedded in all that Milton thought, said, and wrote, contemporary students must also become familiar with that version—a parallel text to complement the reading of almost anything by Milton. Merely reading or decoding at the word or sentence level poses the first challenge to any professor of Milton teaching advanced undergraduate English majors. In a smooth series of cognitive adjustments (via what I have called the "snakes and ladders of abstraction"),[18] Prof. J begins at this word level and moves through genre distinctions and expectations, ultimately reaching the larger issues of thematic and philosophic abstractions having to do with the self of the student.

As one of his daily routines, Prof. J introduces the practice of vocabulary-building through what he calls his *words du jour*. On

Day One, for example, he uses and explains words (and their etymologies) such as *caveat, agon,* and the Latin phrase *peccata
forte* meaning to "sin boldly," first made famous by St. Augustine centuries before Milton. In this way, J models attention to
specific vocabulary in order to get students to work on Milton's
word use, the first level of abstraction in understanding historical poetry and an activity that Gerald Graff[19] suggests helps novice readers enter into the "conventions of written [and spoken
academic] discourse."[20]

> J continues his introduction to these literary studies, addressing his
> first class:
> "An assignment might say that, in this poem, there are these
> three unusually employed words. In the library, in the *OED* for ex-
> ample, look up something about these particular words. So, there are
> different ways of "getting into the text" (in effect, multiple ways of
> finding *patterns of high significance*). Not only are you [students]
> going to learn about particular poems and particular prose works,
> but you'll be learning the craft of literature—how people put things
> [in a text] together; how we as readers take them apart, and also how
> we as readers apply them to our lives. How you grow when you read
> literature . . . [for example] . . . What do you learn about yourself
> when you read [James Joyce's] *Portrait [of the Artist as a Young
> Man]*? What does 'Original Sin' have to do with us?"
> As Judith A. Langer has said: "Students' ability to engage [in litera-
> ture-specific dialogue and] the sorts of discussions illustrated [in
> chapter 8 of her book are] useful indicators of their literacy. Such
> participation is often more revealing than a traditional measure of
> their ability to read, write, or replicate literal meanings or other's
> ideas."[21]

MORE ON OPENING DAY

First, Prof. J invited students to learn about the seventeenth
century, about Milton (the man *and* the writer), and "about
yourselves." As he describes how Milton saved *"everything:*
grammar school papers, notebooks from childhood, all of his
writings," he asks students: "How many of you have saved your
old grammar-school papers?" Thus, Prof. J begins weaving a semester-long narrative in which he explicitly connects elements

from the students' own past lives with that of Milton himself, as well as early readers of Milton and of *Paradise Lost*.

Prof. J helps students in acquiring new knowledge by making **explicit links with their prior knowledge.** He is convinced that these acquisitions are not merely cognitive; J is also looking to develop students' **emotional identification with Milton as a prelude to analyzing the text.** During an early interview, Prof. J mentioned that he wanted students "to get to know Milton as a person, and not just as a writer who lived and died three hundred years ago and is considered very dull and dry."[22]

He continues: "We'll use the literature to come back to Milton as a person; sometimes I'll try to get back to the question, 'What does this (literature) mean to *you* [the students]?' "[23] The first day begins this *reciprocal* process of students learning through both emotional identification and textual analysis. Hence, for J, when students:

1. talk about Milton as a young man,
2. they identify themselves with what he is doing.
3. Meanwhile, they are developing the technical expertise of sonnet analysis;
4. and in doing all three simultaneously, Prof. J suggests: "The bigger picture is that we're softening that hard, frightening view of Milton they (students) may have heard of."[24]

He builds on the students' knowledge of and identification with Milton, in part, through the medium of daily writing assignments wherein students follow (in a modest way) Milton's own educational experiences of regular written exercises.[25]

Second, in the context of daily writing assignments, Dr. J explicitly states that "one can come at a piece of literature from a thousand different ways." With this declaration, J signals a concept similar to Perry's[26] developmental ideas of *multiplicity* in students' intellectual and ethical interpretations, arguing that these works have been reinterpreted by countless generations of students and scholars. Thus Dr. J's expert exhortation: since there is so much to do, students *must* do daily written assignments. The "assignments are geared to help you get into the text" [since] most students "don't know what to focus on because there is so much." The assignments are "to give you a start; to give you help." All of the above is designed to attune students to "pattern recognition of high significance."[27]

Prof. J believes that his homework assignments and repetitive practice are crucial to students' learning in his classroom. He argues that he is "real serious about this—you [students] need to prepare these things ahead of time" because what "we're doing in class will be based on the work you've done out of class . . . If you haven't done the reading; if you haven't done the assignment, you won't have anything to do in the group or in the class." He jokes, "It's sort of like sin and the confessional: If you don't do one, you have nothing to talk about in the other."

Third, Prof. J often **uses metaphors** from both *Paradise Lost* and from Milton generally to illustrate his points, modeling through his attention to specific language the activity of "systematically integrating descriptions and references from multiple levels of the text(s) referenced."[28] Class conversations become another major motivator in Prof. J's teaching model. As seen in the paragraph above, he uses a metaphor from *Paradise Lost* to explain one reason why students must do homework and come prepared for discussions.

And Prof. J is in very good company. As R. S. Prawat says of one of C. S. Peirce's major ideas, *abduction:* ideas about abduction—a mental process "originating outside of language . . . as an imaginal or iconic phenomenon . . . [but relying] heavily on verbal discourse—[is] one of metaphoric projection."[29] Prawat thinks metaphoric abduction "represents an interesting blend of the social and the individual." Hence, metaphors are like a pump for the heart in the sense that such metaphors are "semantically complex signs that represent a blending of the imaginal or iconic, the indexical, and the symbolic . . . Abduction . . . is a metaphoric process [possessing] a key attribute: it consists of old and new meaning."[30]

The next step involves another part of Prof. J's weaving process as he relates Milton's Puritan ideal of ethical choice, his own continuous evaluation process, and the students' behaviors in class. Prof. J acknowledges the students' workloads in other courses, but asks them to give the assignments in this one an honest "try." He says, "Be honest—to me, to the profession; to yourself—i.e., don't *fake* assignments, 'cause you're the one who loses. We'll only have time to survey this material—it's too much otherwise." Prof. J reminds them that it is "part of [his] job to assess; I'm doing it all the time. I'm in there to help, [reminds students of office location]." He explains that the highest percentage of the final grade is the "J factor," because he is "constantly interacting with students as we work together in small groups, larger groups, and so on."[31] To his students, he says: "You'll have choices on your research or "investigative" papers; Milton was very big on choices." Prof. J is constantly **weaving the ethos of the subject matter into the ethos of class conduct.**

In order to discover the class's baseline knowledge, Prof. J directs his students to take a clean sheet of paper, draw a line down the middle, and write everything they know about the seventeenth century on the left side and everything they know about Milton on the right. Then he begins the *Question and Answer* part of the opening day:

J: "What other writers in the seventeenth century do you know?"

J contextualizes, beginning with what students know and adding (in an oral narrative) the missing history and names, such as Henry VIII, the founding of Church of England (C of E), James I, Milton becoming a Puritan, Charles I, the Civil War in England, Oliver Cromwell, Milton's life and marriages, and his eight-year overlap with Shakespeare (Milton was born in 1608; Shakespeare died in 1616), Marvell, and Pope.

J tells the class: "You don't have to write that down; I'm not going to quiz you." He explicitly signals the contrast between **intellectual exploring** and grubbing for grades in the traditional classroom. J jokes, "You [students] can say nasty things about Milton or *Paradise Lost,* too; it's legit" here in this class.

J suggests that students will, later in the course, like *Paradise Lost,* and delivers a smiling exhortation to read it: "It's a wonderful story!" He tells them the anecdote of Milton casually giving his one and only manuscript to a neighbor to read. The neighbor complained that there was no redemption in *Paradise Lost* and that Milton needed, in current jargon, to give the epic poem a "happy ending." That is how *Paradise Regained,* Milton's second great epic poem, came to be written. Reactions to this story indicate that student engagement is high; students smile, shake their heads, and in general implicitly agree that this is indeed an unusual way for a masterpiece to be extended.

Prof. J's story-like in-class narrative and its tone of implicit, shared marveling at how casual Milton was with the only copy of one of the world's great literary masterpieces sets the stage for one of his preferred styles of direct instruction, **the anecdote.** As a former colleague of ours, Neil Norrick, has suggested: "If we achieve rapport by turning our separate personal experiences into shared experience, and if jointly produced narratives and personal anecdotes allow us to accomplish this along with amusing each other and laughing together, then certainly these two sorts of talk exchanges must range high among our strategies for creating conversational involvement."[32] Student engagement develops as a direct result of Prof. J's willingness to risk the silence any teacher (or comedian) fears, that no one (or few) in the audience will think a joke or story as funny as the deliverer believes it to be.

Prof. J reminds them that the syllabus he has presented is a map, not an inflexible blueprint, and draws attention to his own mistake (on a handout), using that as a tool to teach a *word du jour:* St Augustine's *peccata forte* means to "sin boldly" if one is going to make mistake. Prof. J models that mistakes are part of the learning process, and so **turns a mistake into teaching opportunity.**

To his students, J says: "Do any of you have any questions?" but then immediately corrects himself (for you teachers-in-training, the more productive form to use is, "What questions do you have?"). Here, Prof. J models how the good teacher signals both the assumption that students are actively engaged in the conversation and the teacher's willingness to entertain the results of that involvement. Through casual joking and a lighthearted ability to laugh at himself and his own (minor) slips of the pen, Prof. J establishes a crucial balance in tone that will develop throughout the teaching and learning of this semester.

Thus ends the first class period of "Red-Eye Milton."

Summary

Dr. J's Expert Behaviors	Relation to St. Learning	Cognitive Function
"I can't make you like Milton."	Reader-Response Motivation.	Emotional infusion
Written assignments	Develop knowledge base	Scaffolding

Identify sonnet characteristics	Genre familiarization	Pattern recognition of high significance; systematic integration of multiple levels of text
Authorial intent	Speaker and audience	Procedural knowledge; links author and reader; hypothetical model of the author
Attention to word-level meanings; *Words du Jour*	"Snakes and ladders of abstraction"	Declarative knowledge; detailed description of specialized language
Movement from word to genre level	Snakes and ladders of abstraction	Procedural and declarative knowledge
Milton's life and seventeenth century information	Knowledge base	Declarative knowledge; author/reader link
Linking Milton with students' lives	Motivation and new knowledge links	Prior knowledge activation and new acquisition
Alternative interpretations	Modeling cognitive reframing	Pattern recognition of high significance
Use of metaphors and metaphoric language	Snakes and ladders of abstraction	Declarative and procedural knowledge
List knowledge of Milton and seventeenth century	Activate prior knowledge	Declarative knowledge
Intellectual exploration	Reader-response motivation	Emotional infusion.
Turn mistake into teaching moment	Modeling reframing	Procedural knowledge and activating motivational schema.

3

Step Two
Milton's Sonnets

[In] a certain sense, we cannot formulate a proper ideal for being an English teacher. We can, however weave a wreath of words around this subject and cast it into the stream of time . . . [w]eaving is a textual process, the creation of a textile or web out of mere threads . . . [That is the] image of the English teacher as an instructor of textuality, a weaver of texts who teaches such weaving to others.

—Robert Scholes, *The Rise and Fall of English*

CLASS SESSION 2

PROF. J BEGINS STEP TWO OF HIS MULTISTEP COURSE SEQUENCE WITH a lengthy roll call of some fifteen minutes, a procedure he follows again in the third class meeting. During this time he memorizes names and faces, joking with the students and exchanging small anecdotes and stories. The casual tone and leisurely pace of these roll calls masks their serious purpose: one must first develop trust and familiarity between individual students and their professor, and among the students themselves, to conduct a class of active participants.[1]

After completing the roll call, Prof. J reviews the previous day's information, not by drill-like question and answer, but more in keeping with the story-like exchanges that have just transpired. While the content of both sessions involves one unit of study, I will discuss each day in turn, pointing out the most important experiences of this second class period and then adding any new information while discussing Day Three.

In this second period, Prof. J asks questions in a rather casual way, wondering if anyone remembers "when Milton was born." When one student answers with 1608 (the correct date), Prof. J responds with the same note of marvel in his voice as he had about the student's anecdotes earlier, and with an almost extravagant praise: "An A for the day for you!"

Following this review, J begins a short conversational lecture on Milton's early life, much like anyone who wants to discuss his knowledge with friends. He mentions that students in Milton's time arose at 5:00 a.m. to attend chapel, saying their prayers in English, Latin, Greek, and finally in Hebrew. He continuously contrasts the lives of Milton's peers (nicknamed "Paul's Pigeons" because instruction took place in London's St. Paul's Cathedral) with the students' lives on campus. In this way, prior knowledge and new information are interrelated, and delivered within the same personalized and tonal framework as the non-threatening and non-pressured roll call was done. This seemingly casual direct instruction stands in vivid contrast to the often-clichéd notion that the teacher's control of information delivery must be "dry as dust" and largely lacking in intrinsic interest for bored students.* All thirty pairs of eyes are focused on this purveyor of seventeenth century educational practice, who compares current student life on campus with such seventeenth century academic attributes as very early morning mandatory chapel, its several languages of instruction, the precocity of the students, and the rigors of routine.

Within the context of this delivery of new information, Prof. J's "words du jour" make their initial appearance, connecting some of the previous lecture material about Milton's father being a "scrivener" to the word *scribe* (public writer).[2] J then begins to weave word associations among several seemingly disconnected items: (1) Melville's short story, "Bartleby, the Scrivener," whose famous phrase, "I'd prefer not to," is jokingly likened to the typical contemporary student's response to a writing assignment; (2) the sound change from *v* in scrivner to *b* in scribe is associated with regularized Indo-European sound

---

* In effect, Prof. J's blending of interactive chat *before* class and his lecture style *during* class allowed what Martin Nystrand et al. have called a "public space for unofficial student voices" (*Opening Dialogue*, 15). Prof. J's style contrasts with what Lensmire ("The Teacher as Dostoevskian Novelist," 1997), using Bakhtin's theories, calls the "polyphony" of student interactions versus the teacher's purported "impoverished and deadening monologism." While there is no doubt that many lecturers may be likened unto human Quaaludes, that sleepy procedure is not *necessarily* true of all lecturers nor of all lecturing—as witnesses that of Prof. J. Cf. Jay Parini, *The Art of Teaching* (New York: Oxford University Press, 2005), 58–69.

changes; (3) this pattern of transformation is then connected to the language differences between Milton's early modern English and the students' "Chicago-ese," often pronounced, smiles Prof. J, with a distinct local (DeKalb, Illinois) accent; (4) the other areas where the sound change could be noticed, such as in the name of the near century-old American publishing house, *Scribner's*.

Words du jour painlessly infuse vocabulary into the students' minds at the rate of between two and four new words per class period, all of which are directly related to the literary and historical matters about Milton under discussion. Prof J is in good company here, since Gerald Graff, among others, has argued that quoting specific language—from "Bartleby, The Scrivener," or from Milton—"operates as a bridge that enables students both to imitate the foreign language of academia while giving that language their own spin or even reacting against it."[3]

Step Two of "Red-Eye Milton" focuses on a relatively easy formal literary structure, Milton's fourteen-line sonnets.[4] J does this for two reasons: these poems came early in Milton's poetic development, and the skills students will ultimately need to read the epic poem, *Paradise Lost*, are practiced in embryonic form with these sonnets. For Prof. J, the skills of seeing poetic patterns and their variations are crucial, and in keeping with what Charles Anderson suggests: "Learning is a matter of seeing a pattern. It is also the desire to do well, to carry out a complex work with excellence. That indeed, is the power we want to draw forth, nurture, and perfect . . . [because it is] precisely our effort to discern an underlying pattern [that guides our inquiry into teaching and helps us] to catch on to what the university is all about."[5]

Teaching the fourteen-line sonnet is an excellent way to begin literary pattern recognition. According to one scholar of the subgenre, the "sonnet was invented about the year AD 1230 in southern Italy, [and] is probably the longest-lived of all poetic forms. Its duration and shape are determined before the poet begins to write."[6] By custom, simple (Italian) sonnets have "*proportion*, being in eight and six [lines], and *extension*, being in ten- or eleven-syllable lines, and *duration*, having fourteen of them . . . crucial to the sonnet's success and distinctive voice is the link between proportion and thought."[7] Spiller suggests that this kind of "formal or generic preempting of the author's decision is actually helpful,"[8] and cites Alastair Fowler, who opines that: "Far from inhibiting the author, genres are a positive support. They offer room, as one might say, for him [or her] to write in—a habituation of mediated definiteness, a proportioned mental space; a literary matrix by which to order his experience during composition."[9]

I cite these ideas at length, because in teaching the sonnet form one must persuade the student that just as he or she plays tennis with the net set up and within previously agreed-upon rules of procedure, so, too, does the poet play inside boundaries. Like all really great players, however, some rules may be creatively interpreted to benefit a given player's game-in-progress. Hence, it is imperative for the teacher to help the beginning student of Milton work through the complex relationship between what the poet is trying to say and the structural properties of his argument. In creating a sonnet, *what* is said cannot readily be separated from *how* it is said,[10] via what Paul Fussell calls "meter-making meaning."[11]

As an expert both on Milton's sonnets and on the difficulties associated with teaching Milton, Prof. J thus begins instruction on Milton's *writings proper* by addressing fairly high level abstractions concerning the type of poem a sonnet is—a concern that Milton himself certainly had to consider before writing. After beginning the opening day with word-level considerations, Prof. J moves in this second period to almost the opposite end of the abstraction spectrum: the genre, or, more precisely, the subgenre. This "double-barreled" procedure oscillates from the bottom to the top of the levels of abstraction, paving the way for the formation of students' new thinking patterns.

This reading skill, moving from the word or the image to theme and idea, is perhaps one of the most complex mental processes that any novice must acquire to become a successful consumer of classical literature; it is also one of the most difficult to teach. At the university level, such teaching is typically accomplished via the formal lecture method, telling the students what the critical consensus of opinion is about the meaning of sonnet X, image Y, meaning Z, and all their interrelationships. Presumably, students somehow master (perhaps by imitation) this process and are expected to transfer this skill, thereby to do the same to another text by the same or (some teachers hope) even by a different author. In reality, only a minority of English majors, even undergraduates from colleges in Oxford University, are able to read a new text critically via this process of the "snakes and ladders of abstraction."[12]

Conversely, Reader-Response theories and practice per se often do not add much to the repertoire of students' skills. Jane Agee describes a professor of teacher-training in English who "envisioned moving [his] group of pre-service students from their reading of [in this instance] *To Kill a Mockingbird* toward understanding reader-response-centered approaches to teaching literature."[13] Working in small groups and in whole group discussions, they were to discuss the works studied and come up with written summaries of the major issues they had identified. At the end of the semester, this admittedly rather new professor was happy with his students displaying "a variety of opinions and a variety of responses, and that's okay. The goal [was] just to think about and move toward a coherent stance . . . [Nonetheless,] he voiced reservations about the effectiveness of small groups and his own discomfort with giving up so much power . . . [He] did not feel what they wrote justified the time he had allowed for small-group discussions."[14] It seems clear that small group work, in and of itself, does not miraculously translate into literary epiphanies. Another example: After teaching a student-centered literature class in which students had seemingly explored everything *but* the works of literature on the syllabus, Jane Tompkins asked them "Why they thought it was that [they] had never succeeded in talking about literature; ([students] had done all sorts of things in that class but rarely had a good literary discussion). They said it was because *they didn't know how*"[15] [emphasis added]. To begin *his* semester-long development of these student skills, Prof. J initiates a series of comparative questions derived from the class *Assignment Sheet,* distributed the period before and assigned as homework. As J discusses this assignment, he also lays out the incremental poetic trajectory of the course, from the fourteen-line sonnets to the twelve-book epic. Referring to his questions, Prof. J asks, "What are the characteristics of the sonnet?" Once the students repeat the basic formulae of the early sonnet form, J moves up the scale of complexity by asking how these forms are modulated: "What are some of the structural differences between English and Italian sonnet?" Having expressed the more obvious of those differences, students are then focused on one of the particular sonnets of Milton when Prof. J asks, "What are some basic themes, ideas, and values in Sonnet VII? What are its genre characteristics as a sonnet?"

After establishing the basic "playing field" of Italian and English sonnets, Prof. J moves the students into small groups to discuss their individual findings from the homework assignment. Although students indicate (mostly nonverbally) that they could find selected mechanical elements (end rhymes, number of lines) during this day's activity, they are as yet unable to connect such items to the larger themes and arguments of the poem.

> J: Without looking back at the text, did Milton follow these patterns?
> Sts: (Shared looks; some shrugs; silence.)
> J: They do somewhat, but not entirely because he [Milton] breaks the patterns—because there are other forms he can use, too.

Well, asking and then answering one's own question—in the context of student silence—is a time-honored alternative to the teacher tearing out his or her own hair by the roots. The reader will recall, however, that we are not reporting the happy conclusion of a successful semester here, but rather investigating a class in process—a process containing warts and all. Thus we see, early on, the real difficulties inherent in teaching abstractions, problems hardly unique to J's class. While most college students are able, initially, to find specific textual fragments of meaning, they are not usually capable of emerging from the detailed trees into a clear view of the whole sonnet forest; nor, conversely, is it likely that they will then look reductively back down to a detail or two for support to bolster any high level assertions they have made at this early point in the semester.

Prof. J then returns to whole group discussion, based on the combined student findings in small groups and homework assignments. His purpose is to **introduce students to genre constraints, formalistic property variations, and creative poetic play** within these rules. The structure of how he does this is listed below, A-G.

A. Prof. J: "The rules say [for sonnets, a rhythm scheme called] 'iambic pentameter' almost always. However, there are variations, and really good poets—really good writers—break the rules. We see Milton breaking the rules; he said that 'he made *new* rules.'"

Prof. J implicitly signals to students yet another connection between the ethos of the subject matter and their own education: Students may question the rules, perhaps even break some, so long as they bring well-thought arguments to class.

B. Prof. J repeats his earlier question: "So, what's the difference between Italian and English sonnets?" and then proceeds to help students tease out the play inherent within the formulaic. When a student responds that English sonnets have a different structure from the Italian and proceeds to elaborate selected details on the differences, J asks, "What *are* three quatrains and a couplet?" The student is momentarily stumped. He has given the "right" answer, yet J wants him to move beyond drill-like answers to the *reasoning* process behind alternative sonnet structures:

> J: "Note the movement of thought—the poem takes you from one place to another, so you are studying a thought in process. Some people think in *4, 4, 4, 2* lines (Shakespearean sonnet); others in *8 and 6* (Italian sonnet). [Together] they (groupings of eight and six) represent two places of thought. So what happens in the second phase (the sestet)? The sestet grows out of first group (octave), going in a direction and then taking a *tornado*—Italian for 'turn.'" [J's next *word du jour.*]

C. J then asks, "Where did you go to get this information?" J uses quizzical student responses to suggest sources of library information on the formal properties of poetry.

Following this mini-lecture he moves to a specific sonnet and a larger abstraction: "What are some of the basic themes (you have found) in Sonnet VII?" J then suggests that "the kinds of things to ask [in his assignment] about this poem are good things to ask about any poem." Hence, J points to two student cognitive processes: (1) self-regulation; (2) pattern recognition of high significance.

D. J repeats an earlier question: "Who is the speaker?" [Answer: A young man, twenty-three-years old.] J continues: "Does it have to be a man?" He shows the class a picture (from a textbook) of Milton. "He looks young, but one cannot always tell the internal from the external." This contrast between visual appearance and inner reality triggers a question for Prof. J about the parallel issue inside his students' minds:

J: "How many of you have thought, when standing in a crowd of people, 'If only they knew what I was really thinking?'" With this thread, J is moving students up and down levels of abstraction, from general knowledge to specifics of text to his students' own experience and prior knowledge. "To whom is the speaker speaking?" This elementary literary question stumps the students momentarily. [Answer: A college friend, who has accused Milton of "dreaming away his years 'in the arms of a studious retirement.'"][16] After no one answers, J asks one student to read the poem out loud; the class discusses the relatively weak sense of direction they *and* Milton might share in their college years. J then relates this discussion to the text by quoting from Sonnet XIX, "He also serves who stands and waits." He tells them that even though a parent or teacher may be keeping her eye on you, like Milton, you must find your own way. J tries to connect students' prior knowledge to this new concept by asking them to imagine that the "Master's eye" image in Sonnet VII is like the "eye" on a dollar bill, "Where," he says, "Uncle Sam may be watching you."

With Sonnet VII, Prof. J has successfully woven a number of discussion threads around a work of literature. He includes the meaning of this sonnet in particular, genre considerations of types of sonnets in general, Milton's life and other biographical data, and the larger abstract connections between these and the students' own experiences with parents and teachers who want to know "what they're going to do with their lives."

E. J then moves on to help students with poetic pronunciation. He describes how the rhyme scheme helps one to understand specific seventeenth century English pronunciation—"du'eth" rhymes with "truth." He asks the whole class to say the word out loud; they do, and then repeat it again.

F. J instructs them on some major themes in Milton: "Milton's God is always *doing*—Milton is perhaps one of the originators of what is known as the Puritan work ethic. Even as a young man Milton knew he was destined to do great things, although his college friends wanted to know where he was heading by going home after college and 'reading his life away' there."

G. A student asks, "What did the lecture (on Milton's day) have to do with poem?" J's response: "Good question. My lecture was just background." His word *just* may be somewhat modest, since he is continuously building up in his students a storehouse of both abstract and concrete knowledge about Milton and the fabric of the world surrounding him and his writings. This student's question points to another issue, *thus far only implicit* in J's structure of the class. Not yet conscious of the whole literary tapestry needed to read successfully all of Milton's writings, this student is typical of those taking a class about a time far distant from their own. His question may be merely a variation of "will this be on the test?" What is interesting is J's sense of incremental complexity, and how he intends to get students who know nothing about the seventeenth century or Milton to internalize basic concepts and to gain familiarity with Milton's style, techniques, and favorite themes.

This second class day of "Red-Eye Milton" illustrates another basic problem in teaching college-level literature: how does one deliver complex material from another time and culture to support students' understanding without primary reliance on lengthy and highly detailed lectures? In this second class of the semester, J includes in daily class work:

1. Conversations and handouts (including some library work) on genre-level issues;
2. Personal charisma;
3. Mini-lectures that at times move to an almost atomistic level (*words du jour*);
4. Lots of *opportunistic* teaching (J uses student comments both to deliver basic information and to reinforce material already discussed).

His focus is to scaffold student movement toward meaning from the level of word to genre to larger theme, all with considerable recursion at each individual level as well as at combinations of levels. This movement, referred to as the "snakes and ladders of abstraction," now seems beyond the capacity of many (if not most) class members; their learning to do so will be one of the major issues J will address during the fourteen weeks of class. If they do, we will see them able to coordinate, for example, both the de-contextualized "rules" of the sonnet and their instantiation into one of Milton's particular sonnets. At this early point, however, our question remains: just *how* will this expert professor help them to do it?

SESSION 3: SECOND DAY OF STEP TWO

Prof. J repeats many of the opening patterns of the previous class: a leisurely taking of roll while learning names; joking, and offering personal anecdotes. He begins class with a review of *words du jour* from prior sessions (notably, *peccata forte*), as well as a review of the genre properties of the sonnet. J then directs the students to open their books to the next sonnet to be discussed. He begins with a direct move to a key thematic and genre consideration when he says: "One thing we didn't discuss last week is the tradition of love sonnets. Is this sonnet (XXIII) about love? Are any of Milton's sonnets about love?" Typical of early on, one student gives a "clipped" answer:

St: "Sonnet XXIII is not. "
J: "Right! What Milton has done is to take the sonnets and *transform them for his own reasons.* In the sonnet on the Piemontese (XVIII), for example, Milton asks for revenge on their murderers. This is not a lovesick request."
J: "Turn to Sonnet XIX, and will Mr. X read out loud." (This student knows how to read poetry well. Following the reading, J begins the questioning by reviewing several of the concepts—the poem's speaker, audience, purpose, and so on—discussed in detail the previous period.)
J: "Is there a specific calling in the poem?" (No answer, because students are not able, early in the semester, to transfer information from one poem of Milton's to the next).
J: "Anyone help out?"
St: "God wants you to be patient."
J: "What is Milton's talent (the answer to which was discussed the class before)? After a student gives a good answer, J rewards student with lavish praise: "Excellent, good answer!"
J: "How was God described [in this sonnet]?"
St: (Recalling a high-level generalization from a mini-lecture in a previous class): "God as taskmaster and Puritan."
J: "What does God like [in the poem]? Does He [God] need anything from the poet?"
St: "It's a good way of reciprocity—as a gift."

Thus far, J and the class are simultaneously reviewing yester-day's thematic material and analyzing the current sonnet. Al-though J has been asking largely "report-type" questions thus far,[17] he suddenly asks a class-stopper; a higher-order thinking question (HOT Q) to which no one has an immediate, drill-like answer.

> J: "But *why* does God (who is all powerful, all-knowing) need *you* to do . . . X [anything]?"

When no student answer is forthcoming, J says he will leave the query hanging there, a question to keep in mind as students continue to read Milton.

> **Comment:** J's questions and question-sequences this pe-riod, in contrast to the last one, are often merely recita-tion,[18] with J's narrative building up a mental model of meaning(s) of this sonnet with the occasional pursuit of a higher-order-thinking (HOT) type question. Hence, the al-ternation in the two classes: delivering information, and re-peating it to ensure students' absorption is coupled with multiple references to this information as it relates to stu-dents' lives.

In a new move toward *intertextuality*, J reads, dramatically, from the book of Matthew. J starts interpretation at the literal level, and then moves to Milton's imagistic borrowing from it. As he reads from Matthew 25, the parable of the talents (money) invested well or not, he focuses on the word *talent*. The reading moves into J's own narrative (a story rather than a lecture) to explain the context and the readership of the King James version (Milton was immersed in the Bible, as were most educated peo-ple in the seventeenth century). J then relates the meanings of his narrative, the biblical story, and the historical information, to Sonnet XIX. He begins his questions again as he reads Sonnet XIX out loud, emphasizing the very words he has just read from King James.

This is a **key element in teaching poetry:** J models the process of understanding complex poetry by **reading out loud,** allowing his students to hear the sounds from an excellent reader. As he reads both Sonnet XIX and the passage from Matthew, he pauses to ask questions, does comparative sound patterns, and poses suggestions for alternative interpretations.

> J: "Any questions?"
>
> St: "In all four sonnets Milton uses the Italian format, but seems to change the sonnet form, especially the end rhyme scheme. Yes? And if so, why?"
>
> J: [Delighted] "Yes, part of his modifications—Milton changes rhyme scheme—all good writers do that; they show you that they *can* do it; then they change it again to reflect a tradition rhyme (to show that they can do that, too). All great artists do that. Notice that in the traditional sonnet, each sentence or clause ends at the end of a line [line integrity]. Milton changes that, and runs his line into the next" (a poetic technique called *enjambment,* although J doesn't use the word here but will wait until Step Five, Class no. 16).

In effect, this student's question has triggered the next step in learning about reading formalized poems, learning thus far that has largely been given either by J directly or read by them as part of an abstract taxonomy of sonnet conventions. Now, the student has, herself, seen the variations in specific poems and has been able to conclude, at a high level of abstraction, that poets do indeed vary the rules to suit their own purposes. This is the first instance of a student actually applying the rules to a concrete example. She has articulated their imitation of genre constraints and the subsequent variations and modifications. J thinks that students must learn both processes, of tradition and then variation on tradition, as he seizes the moment to show students the verbal flexibility in great writers.

Summary

Although much of the class conversation on this third class day (and second day of the Unit) still takes the form of report-type questions, J is highly energetic and interactive, giving students "high signs," "OK" signs, and so on, for good answers or for accurately reviewing previous work. He introduces new concepts by yoking them to previous ones and to students' own experiences, thus providing them with epistemic access into the mysteries of Miltonic poetry. If one thinks of *incremental com-*

plexity, J seems to be setting the stage for more complex discussions later.

9:02am: J ends this discussion of sonnet form and moves to the next unit (with approximately thirteen minutes left in the third class period).

4

Step Three
Longer Poems

The art of poetry is the art of knowing language and people
equally well. It is an art whose focus is in two dimensions at
once: toward an inert technical arcana of syllables and
sounds and syntax and metaphor as well as toward the animated actualities of human nature and human expectation.
                    —Paul Fussell, *Poetic Meter and Poetic Form*

SESSION 3 CONTINUES

PROF. J EMBARKS ON THE NEXT STEP OF "RED-EYE MILTON" NEAR THE
end of Class Session 3. Moving from the sonnet to the longer
(thirty-plus-stanza) poem, "On the Morning of Christ's Nativity," Prof. J and the class address the complexity of reading and
comprehending narrative line in more elaborated poetry. In particular, J's class considers Milton's imaginative narrative of
what happens, both literally and symbolically, on Christmas
mornings when Christ is reborn.

"One will find in it themes, devices, and techniques he was to
use later in his more mature works, yet they first are used here
in both meaningful and moving ways."[1] J again signals students'
attention both to Milton's intellectual development and their
own. He reminds them that reading the poet successfully means
watching for repeating patterns and recurring poetic motifs. One
such theme is the Puritan compulsion to *do;* to become an active
agent rather than a passive vessel.

J suggests to his students a connection between this feeling of
doing for Milton and their own responses to the well-publicized
death of Diana, Princess of Wales. He reminds them, "You said
to me you wanted to *do* something, but didn't know what." Dur-

97

ing these last fifteen minutes of Session 3, Prof. J says to his charges: "Without looking in the book, what do you consider other people were doing [on the morning of Christ's birth]?" He immediately follows up his own question with a gloss on the word "consider," a *word du jour.* "Con *sider*—the last syllable comes from the word *sidereal* or 'star,' and it was a star guiding the three kings." J explains that Milton also thought of a gift for the Christ child—and creating *his* gift, the poem, also allowed him to *do* something.

At this point, Prof. J hands out the *Assignment Sheet* (See appendix A) for the next class and asks students to read Milton's letter to his best friend, Charles Diodati (in their text). Before doing so, however, he requests that each writes out on a sheet of paper his or her "own beliefs of religion and friendship." J tells them he's not "looking for anything," but just wants them "to think, to help them focus on the letter and then the poem." After listing their own beliefs, they are to "reread the letter and then the poem." Similar to Bartholomae and Petrosky's technique[2] of getting students to list and consider their own agendas first and then examine a professionally written text for comparable patterns, Prof. J suggests that after the students' own self-examination, they are to trace several themes in "Morning"—specifically, light/dark, time, music /sound/silence, and nature—and to specify the big issues in the poem; the ones unasked by Milton but which are implied and alluded to.

Summary

During the waning moments of the third class, J gradually introduces students to the tasks required in poems much longer than sonnets: to note comparisons and contrasts, to trace imagery patterns and techniques, and, ideally, to relate the poem to their own lives—a bridging process—and to connect one text (Diodati's letter) with another ("Morning") through a type of intertextuality.

SESSION 4: CONTINUE STEP THREE

The fourth class period begins with Prof. J reviewing concepts and identities from the previous sessions. R. F. Thompson says that the evidence from neuroscience suggests such mental reviewing of names and concepts, or what he calls "distributed practice," is "much more effective" for both semantic and motor skill learning "than seven hours in a row of massed practice."[3]

J then displays pictures of St. Paul's Cathedral and briefly lectures on the contrasts between British education in the seventeenth century and the instruction his own students are receiving near the twenty-first century. The most significant contrast, for this class, is between the American educational practice of "lock-step" advancement through the grades and the British sense of "forms" in the seventeenth century, where one stayed until one learned enough to move on. Prof. J concludes the review by telling his students, "Now we're up to date" from the previous class.

At this point (roughly fifteen minutes into the period), Prof. J refers the class to the handout entitled **Milton Links,** a set of three yellow sheets explicitly asking students to connect elements of their own lives to the issues in Milton under discussion (see appendix A-6,7). He begins by asking general questions such as, "What makes a good friend?" After some discussion, J says that these are qualities Milton found in Diodati. "One trusts one's friends with intimate details and this letter is like two guys writing inside jokes."[4] J takes great pains to **weave connections** between the students' own lives and the text under discussion.

After several minutes of class conversation J moves to the letter, the "sixth Elegy." He makes a point of Milton's playfulness: "Milton's letter (in Latin verse) is like an exercise to see how well they can do this; [how well these friends can] carry it off."

Then, J moves specifically to the text—*Eligia sexta* (Christmas 1629)—and begins what amounts to report-type questions. But unlike mere drill, these conversational patterns also contain new information and, most importantly, emotionally charged motivational statements:

J: "Who are the Muses?"
St: "Keepers of the arts."
J: "Good way of saying that—"Keeper of the arts." (He then rewards

the student's response and delivers a mini-lecture on Muses as the nine daughters of Mnemosyne. J models delight in *words du jour,* or excellent choices in language). [*Word du jour* (WDJ), *Mnemosyne.*]

J: "Isn't that neat." (J's exhortation is one of the major elements when exposing students to aesthetics). "Bacchus *is* the god of wine. [jokes]: "I'll drink to that."

J then reminds them of one of the previous week's *word du jour,* "telos" (end of time), as that word is used to contrast Christ's coming on the one hand and Milton's assumption of the end of Paganism on the other. J resumes this combination mini-lecture and report-type questioning sequence:

J: "Milton starts thinking about big themes in his poetry at this early an age . . . What has Diodati written?"
St: "A letter to a friend, in Latin verse."
J: "Nice letter to a friend, isn't it?"
St: "Was this during the semester he was home?"
J: "No; it was done a couple of years earlier."

One is immediately struck by the student's use of Milton's biographical information, employed to help make sense of this new poetic material. J reminds the class that Milton's poetry is oral and *is meant to be recited.*

J: "Many of the seeds are here ("Morning of Christ's Nativity") for *Paradise Lost.* All of this (discussions of friendship) led us to today's poem."

J keeps pointing out **organizing structures** for students to relate what they're learning to all of Milton's poetry. Prof. J now goes to the blackboard: "I asked you to write of some of the themes and issues in this poem [short list, 'Morning of Christ's Nativity']. This was the first of Milton's serious compositions, composed when he was twenty-one, near your [students'] age. What *are* the themes you wrote?" Here J is merely asking for students to trace, using their Assignment Sheet # 2, the basic "themes and techniques" in the poetry read. Thus far, the professor is neither looking for nor requiring students to give *critical* or interpretive answers.

> **Comment:** Herein lies one of the crucial issues in teaching imaginative literature: How does one encourage or even demand that students encounter the "snakes and ladders of literary abstraction," and/or respond emotionally to an element in a text when their baseline knowledge of the context of the literary piece is still minimal? During independent reading, there is no easily understood director pointing the student's eyes and understanding to the proper place on his or her mental "stage." As discussed in chapter 1, textual analysis is a complex mental process requiring both a detailed knowledge base and a set of procedural skills not easily acquired. For this reason, Prof. J spends significant time early in the course on both the detailed knowledge base *and* the literary structures upon which students will necessarily develop these procedural skills.

As J asks his initial questions about the "Morning of Christ's Nativity," his students respond:

St 1: "[It's about] Christ."
St 2: "[It's the] end of Paganism (*telos* and end of time)."
J: Reviews *telos* [WDJ] and suggests that "Then, sin stops—on Judgment Day."
St 3: "Christ is called the 'dreaded infant.'"
J: "[He is called thus because] the pagan gods are terrified of him. Like Yeats's 'Leda and the Swan'—where Zeus comes to Leda in the form of a swan, has his way with her, and she bears Helen of Troy—everything in the world is changed after the child is born."

J's narrative uses a literary analogy between Greek mythology and modern Irish poetry to make connections with Milton's poem. J is weaving a web of prior knowledge and cultural allusions in order to make these new concepts clear. In doing so, J now introduces another *word du jour*. He says that this poem is an *incarnational* poem; *carne*, from flesh, like "chili con carne."

During this sequence an interesting phenomenon occurs. J has asked questions of the class in general, without specifying a particular student. During one previous exchange in the discussion, a student named Darryl answered a factually based question with what was clearly an unrelated response. J politely asked someone else, and that student's answer made it clear that Darryl had not understood the question. J did not embarrass him, but it was clear that Darryl was not happy with his own response. As J continued his report-type questions, he circled back within three to four minutes to Darryl and asked a relatively easier form of the same question.

> J: "Darryl—what is different, in the poem, about light and darkness?"
> D: "Light is associated with God."
> J: "See, you did know [the answer to the previous question]."

So as not to highlight this exchange (and so further embarrass Darryl), J immediately builds on the same concept but in a more general fashion:

> J: "What else is different?"
> St: "Nature is different [too]."
> J: "Good job, Sara!" [J rewards student for good answer.]
> J: "What else is different, with the shepherds who get the news first.
> St: "They are told [by the angels] to 'fear not.'"
> J: "Who are shepherds [to] fear not? Jason?"

J goes to another student with a previously weak answer (Jason) and gives him another opportunity as well. Thus, in the context of covering the issues students need to know, Prof. J is also **paying attention to the emotional** expressions and ego-needs of his students.

As J asks these fairly basic questions about narrative line and cast of characters, he also weaves in students' previous remarks about the death of Princess Diana and then jumps several levels of abstraction from plot and characters to genre. Next, J asks a direct question from the homework assignment: "How is this poem different from traditional Christmas odes?" and responds enthusiastically to the student's answer about this being the pivotal point in the poem.

Having discussed two of the four themes on the handout, J returns the class to the first three lines of the poem and connects the poem's beginning and end. By contrasting the rhetoric of the poem's opening and closing, J models the analysis of poetic structure by getting students to learn to move from gritty textual details to larger abstractions, and to return.

> **Comment:** The poet Jane Hirshfield speaks of this movement from details to larger abstractions as part of a poem's rhetorical information: "The poem itself is essential rhetorical information."[5] In keeping with what was learned from the (old) New Criticism of the 1940s and 1950s, each element of the poem is expected to be meaningful: (a) placement of a word on the page; (b) sound qualities matter, punctuation and caesuras (musical-like stops) responsive to themselves and to their context; (c) reading sentence-by-sentence rather than only line-by-line; (d) rhetorical organization of the whole poem, rhetorical unit (of meaning) by rhetorical unit, rather than only stanza by stanza; (e) structure as cue. We know, for example, that the last line of a five-line limerick will rhyme with the first, for a larger reason than merely end-rhyme unity.

Here is a final example of Prof. J's movement from larger thematic issues down to the word level and then up again, on this occasion by using a questioning technique called "uptake" (he incorporates some portion of a student answer into his next question).

J: "Do you notice anything about line three (in poem)?"
St: "It's contradictory, 'Of wedded maid, and virgin mother born.' It's like an oxymoron."
J: "What is an oxymoron?"

Following the students' responses, J adds information by explaining line 3 in the early part of the poem. (*WDJ: paradox = doxy = kind of thinking*). J also introduces the rhetorical strategy of *chiasmus*, or crossing references. Here, J moves from the half-line level in the poem to the word level (*paradox*) via *words du jour*, up again to the concept level (*chiasmus:* "Of wedded maid, and Virgin Mother born"—here, predicate and subject, then subject and predicate),[6] all the while setting the stage for what is one of the key concepts in Milton, Christ's ontology as both godlike yet human.

J's assignments for next class: (1) Skim over the poem again and . . . pick up more of these images you had for homework in the previous class. (2) Here is a homework handout—the same type as Milton's college assignment, a rhetorical exercise like, "Which is better, day or night?" Prof. J asks his class to see "L'Allegro" and "Il Penseroso" as companion pieces, moving them from considering one, more complex poem than any of the sonnets, to considering two poems. Both poems are textually interrelated and both, while containing elements of Milton's early poetic practices, are evolutionarily a step above his students' academic exercises.

Session 5: Continue Step Three

As is typical of his opening class activities, Prof. J suggests that they all "pull things together before we start." What follows is a five minute drill-like review of the major concepts the class discussed the week before. Note the consistent use of "uptake" in J's responses to his students, as he incorporates a student's ideas and/or words into his next question.

> J: "Let's start with 'On the Morning of Christ's Nativity.' What's the difference between 'nativity' and 'incarnation'?"
> St: "Being made flesh?"
> J: "How does one change form?"
> St: "One changes form via a 'metamorphosis.'"
> J: "That's why we don't have a lot of baby images. Milton at twenty-one writes a Christmas Hymn. What are some things told about the baby (Jesus)?"
> St: "Radiating light."
> J: (*Repeating*): "Radiating light."
> St: "Becomes the redeemer of mankind."
> St: "Becomes the 'dreaded infant.'"
> J: "What does this 'dreaded infant' do?"
> St: "Gets rid of pagan gods."
> J: "Watch for images of music—add a hymn of praise, a gift to God."

J's incremental technique (above) includes weaving a tapestry with bits and pieces of student responses and his own additions.

J next moves students into small, informal groups and asks them to take out the blue sheet (Assignment no. 2, handout from previous class). J: "Let's help each other to see how rich this texture is; lots of references to 'time' and so on." He then asks the five groups (four to five students each) who picked various themes (time, nature, music, light/darkness, to "Share with one another what you have found, as well as notes from the other groups [reports] and add these to your own list. What did you find on that theme?" J recommends **recall strategies,** such as using notes at the bottom of a page and so on.

After ten minutes during which student groups compare homework notes from the previous weekend, J begins the small group reports. Here, the students explain to the whole class what they analyzed about the poem through a combination of homework and small-group discussion. J begins by repeating, in part, the discussion of light/dark images from the last class period, but then extends it further:

J: "Who has the light, God or Christ?"

St: "Well, they're the same."

J: "Light is a major image. Tell us a little bit more about that. What else?"

St: "So many references (all over the place). Light symbolized good; dark, bad."

J: (Repeats this student's response and says) "It's a common association Milton sets up."

J: "Does light just reflect or shine or does it do more? [Repair] What else does it do? (It's not just passive); not just *is*; it *does!*"

St: "The light of the stars refuses to stop shining (because Christ is born)."

St: "Light gives hope."

J: "Hope for what?"

St: "To Milton's audience, for one's own journey. Light becomes a star."

J: "What else? Anything else light does?"

St: "Light becomes a force."

J: (Rewards students): "Excellent, well done. It's [light] an active force, pushing darkness out. This is a great theme in literature— about light pushing out darkness." [Creates an association, yoking new concept to students' prior knowledge.] "You've all experienced this—you're sitting around a campfire as a child, telling ghost stories and you're safe as long as you're in the circle of light. In the darkness there are . . . *things*." [Uses pseudo-mysterious voice.]

St: "There are some interesting differences in descriptions of fire; see [for example] line 28." (Student has picked up J's sensitivity to variations and modulations of light imagery and says so, using word and sentence rhythms similar to J's.)

St: "On l. 28, the altar is surrounded by clear light, in contrast to l. 210 where the light did a dismal dance about 'the furnace blue.'"

J: "Good point. Interesting word, *dismal* [WDJ]. It literally means 'bad day,' or *mal dis*. [Returning to the first reference]: "The word is a play on 'hallowed fire' and comes from a reference to the Bible, The book of Isaiah, where the angels take a burning coal and touch it to the tongues of the prophets; hence, fire both destroys and purifies."

Comment: J has taught the students to pick out images and to give them both local and contextualized meaning within the whole poem. Then he **builds upon student response** (after rewarding them for a good answer) by (a) discussing root words, etymologies, and the like, and then (b) contextualizing the response further by embedding it in extratextual sources (the Bible). His style is still, so far, quite directive in the sense that *he* is controlling class discussion. This style is obviously at odds with much of RR philosophy as discussed earlier, but as René Wellek, one of the major critics associated with the (old) New Criticism, has pointed out, Reader-Response theory or *Rezeptionsaesthetik* "is unable to bridge the gulf between these two problems: the reader's reactions and the signs of historicity—parody, imitation, allusion, conventions—embodied in the works themselves."[7] Clearly, Prof. J believes that his students must internalize the "historicity" of Milton before they can confidently venture out to voice their own opinions. J's teaching philosophy is, therefore, directed toward balancing the students' growing knowledge of such historicity with their own interests and motivations; such a balancing act on his part requires their trust in Prof J's ultimate goal of their intellectual independence.

This balancing act for college professors is often not intuitively obvious. The cliché is that high school teacher's primary emotional allegiance is to his or her students, while the college professor's passion is primarily to his or her discipline and its materials. Even so sensitive a psychologist as Harvard's Robert Kegan makes the bifurcation in describing his own career path: "I found that I had a love of and a gift for teaching and working with kids. I was able to do so in ways that were more expansive than what I imagined I'd be able to do as an English professor, where I'd be making literary texts the main object of my affections."[8]

After further questions and answers from the next two groups (comparable to the discussion above), J moves to Group Four, who had possibly the most difficult task of the day, that of analyzing Milton's complex use of time, particularly in stanza fourteen, lines 133–41. J makes an interesting observation about meta-cognition and literary discovery (note below J's explicit statement about literary cognition).

At this point, **J reads out loud:**

> For if such a holy Song
> Enwrap our fancy long
> Time will run back, and fetch the age of gold,
> And speckl'd vanity
> Will sicken soon and die,
> And leprous sin will melt away from earthly mold,
> And hell itself will pass away,
> And leave her dolorous mansions to the peering day.

St 1: "Time is referred to as a tedious song. I thought (the phrase) 'age of gold' would have been judgment day—but the (next image) I didn't understand."

St 2: "Well, how about . . ." (voice trails off; student is confused).

J: [Signals *complicated stuff* in stanza 14]: "This is exactly how one does good literary searching and researching. (You think), 'I don't know what this means and I think it's important,' and then you start looking at it and questioning."

J: "Anybody know anything about the 'Golden Age'?"

Sts: [no response].

J: [Explains "Golden Age," briefly.] (To St): "Amanda, you suggested (earlier) an Adam and Eve kind of thing—an idyllic state. Here, the incarnation is so glorious that we've moved back to the golden age." (To class): "Does that make sense?"

St: "Well, there's a footnote (in text) that tells the answer."

J: (Joking) "Right! When all else fails, read the book." [In summarizing his own remarks, J adds in the **student's insights** and the note from text.]

J: "We're progressing in time to go back—back to the Garden."

J: (To small group, rewarding them): "I appreciate your group tackling that complexity."

St: (Helena) "Is this (stanza) the major turning point in the poem?"

J: "Yes, in terms of time (generally) and in terms of the poem's time, it is, too."

> **Comment:** For the first time in class, a student (Helena) has
> volunteered her insight that the poem's pattern appears to
> coalesce around this particular stanza. In effect, she *has*
> moved up the "snakes and ladders of abstraction" from
> word, line, and stanza level to whole-text level.

Prof. J then moves on to Group Five. He begins by reminding
them of a connection from a previous class: music is god = god
in music.

St 1: [Looks through poem and tries to explain l.163 in stanza 17.]
J: "What point are you making?"
St: [Reads from lines 53–61, stanza 4, contrasting noise and the word
"peaceful" in the opening line of the next stanza.]
J: "Nice contrast there (in images) between end of stanza 3 and open-
ing of stanza 4."
St 1: "It's heavy music."
J: (Jokes) "Like heavy metal? Anything else?"
St 2: "Look at stanza 8 and 9, especially line 89."
J: "It is an embellishment on the Pipes of Pan."
St: [Adds to J's explanation that the word, "kind" meant "kin" in the
seventeenth century; then reads from line 89, interpreting that
Pan appears distracted.]
J: (Also builds on stanza) "Look at the very description of the angel's
singing, 'warbling.' Pun on *divine.*"
J: [As J explains about sound at the end, the student notes that Line
239 ties music into time.] "Excellent! Time and sound are con-
nected; time and sound are meter (in poem)."
J: "Why should *time* have an ending?" [asking them to look in last
stanza] Tells them, "Good job."

This period, for the first time, the students and J **appear to collaborate** on weaving the class narrative line. J's "rewarding" of
students has helped give them to sense that they, too, can contribute and help create the tapestry that is the class discussion.
After a further discussion of issues Group Five thought worthy
of reporting, J concludes class with the following:

J: "Ok—any questions you [students] might have?"
[Summarizes]: "This poem is a wonderful combination of images, in
which we've taken a journey from light to dark, from sound to si-

lence." He then talks about images appearing in the next two poems, "Il Penseroso" and "L'Allegro."

J: "What else in relation to light and dark, larks and nightingales? What other elements?—Who's Orpheus?"

St: "He makes such good music, he's able to bring her [Eurydice] out of Hades."

Prof. J explains about Orpheus, the musician. Then he repeats Thursday's assignment: "Between today and Thursday, reread "L'Allegro" and "Il Penseroso." He then has one student choose a card *(Cards o' Doom:* one of the five small groups will have their written work reviewed).

End of Class Session 5.

Summary

Prof. J is clearly directing conversation in his classroom, a practice which seems at odds with current "conventional" RR pedagogical wisdom; that students learn about a work of poetry best when primarily exploring their own responses to it. As many a teacher of noncontemporary literature will attest, asking students for responses—when they have scant knowledge of the cultural materials required to *have* a response—is asking for the nearly impossible. So Prof. J creates a kind of **"infusion model,"** where he interjects bits of information while, at the same time, he labors to build student rapport and create an environment that feels safe and learner-friendly.

Although I believe Dona Kagan has greatly overstated her case, her focus on the professor establishing classroom rapport accords with J's practice thus far. As Kagan writes, the "heart of teaching and learning lies in the teacher's rapport with students; this supersedes the influence of pedagogical method. How academic material is presented is a relatively commonsense task; it is important only that it be organized logically and clearly."[9]

Hence, during this Third Step in his semester course, J values and works at maintaining a very good rapport with his class, arriving early and "schmoozing" with them, joking about difficult passages in the poetry, and bringing up connections he has learned from their reported experiences. What is interesting is the relative weight of teacher-directed and student-directed analysis of the poetic materials. In the episodes above it seems clear that *both* teacher and students have begun *jointly* to weave a class narrative, albeit the "Loom-Master" is still Prof. J, and a more balanced *weaving* is, at this point, still ahead.

SESSION 6: CONTINUE STEP THREE

This class represents the end of the first three weeks of the semester. By now, Prof. J knows his approximately twenty-nine students by name and quickly takes roll, then passes out sheets of paper for a brief two-minute reading quiz. During this preliminary shuffling of papers, J reminds students of name pronunciation and has them "mouth" the Italian word, *L'Allegro!* J jokes, "It's Italian; use your hands!" In short, by now—even at 8:00 a.m. and with a quiz imminent—the class's atmosphere is one of relaxed, energized fun.

J gives his students a short quiz, but claims it is "not a test . . . Even if you don't know what might it be, guess. Get into a *Miltonic* mode." At 8:05, several students walk in late. J doesn't say anything at the time, although after class he will speak privately with a couple of habitual latecomers. J then returns the selection of class notebooks he has reviewed, noting that these "varied from general to detailed. It's *very* important to pay careful attention to detail; it is important to read carefully." Drawing attention by analogy to a Chicago architect, J tells them that "God is in the details! Pay attention to details." These good-natured exhortations are usually followed up by brief, after-class conversations with individual students. This might be considered just old-fashioned "jawboning," but Prof. J has previously invested the time to know his students; these are, therefore, specific **discussions from a position of relatively close understanding** rather than "nagging from a distance."[10]

J then begins to cover the quiz. While the *Question-and-Answer* exchanges immediately below are little more than post-hoc drill, one should note that even in this most mundane of classroom activities, J manages to insert his personality and joy in the actual lines from the poems

J: "Who does L'Allegro hence?"
St: "They (both poems) *hence* each other."
J: "At what part of the day does the 'L'Allegro' person go out?"

St: "Dawn."

J: "In 'Il Penseroso,' what does Melancholy look like?"

St: "Melancholy looks like—a nun."

J: (Smiles and recites with relish ll. 31 and 32 of "Il Penseroso"): "Come pensive nun, devout and pure, Sober, steadfast, *and* demure."[11] [J deliberately stresses the final conjunction and the iambic beat, as all attend to his reading.]

J: "What does Milton like to read?"

St: "Tragedy!" (with a nod back to the reading of "demure").

J: "When were these written in Milton's life?"

St: "Age of twenty-one." [Again, the age of most of these students.]

J: "Right! These were like college exercises, contrasting day and night."

Following the fifteen minutes it takes to complete both the brief quiz and the analysis of the quiz answers, Prof. J asks the class to "count off by fours," as he develops the more formal **small-group** structures that will remain as such for the rest of the semester. Even counting off is fun, as J jokes in the process: "This'll loosen the cobwebs and get us into the kind of thing that Milton is doing."

In this first small-group exercise of fifteen minutes, J will move the students from listing elements of prior knowledge to the acquisition of new knowledge. While this initially looks like parallel seat work, it will soon become apparent that it is not.

Prof. J's instructions: "These are the ground rules of brainstorming; don't elaborate, just do it: Draw a line down the middle of your paper and write as many things as you can [about the following]: There are two parts of life—in and out of school. Describe each part of life by doing the following for about one to one-and-a-half minutes:

Left side:

1. Write about several benefits of working ("Pick any job you want, but you can't have mine."); draw a line under each of those benefits;
2. List the things associated with that kind of lifestyle;
3. Write the name of a person you associate with that lifestyle.

Right side: Assume you like being in school; write an analogy between your own life [the known] and Milton's [knowledge recently heard];

1. In one minute, list the benefits of being serious student, and put a line under each;
2. What associations with this kind of life (colors, music, art, etc.) do you have?
3. Think of a teacher or someone associated with that life, an exemplar! Who would exemplify that life?"

Concluding the students' writing activities J solicits answers to each writer's schema. "Recall that in a debate, you don't know which side you'll argue for."

J: "If I asked you to argue for the opposite [of what you believe], could you?"
St: "I couldn't!"
J: "Think of the imaginative qualities required to do so—as in Milton, for example."
J: "Let's take a vote. Who thinks Milton favored 'L'Allegro,' or favored 'Il Penseroso'? Why?" J explains: "This is the kind of process—*dialectic*—that Milton does in 'L'Allegro' and 'Il'Penseroso'; it's an assignment comparable to what you [students] just did.
J: "How many would say you liked better 'L'Allegro'?" [Raise hands.] "How many 'Il Penseroso'?"
J: "Milton gives us positive qualities either of 'L'Allegro' or 'Il Penseroso.' What private associations did you have? Colors?"
Sts: "Green, red, yellow, melon color."
J: "What does the 'Il Penseroso' narrator do late at night?" [Repairs]: "Where does he go during the night?"
St: "To the tower."
J: "And what does he do in the Tower?" (J asks rhetorically). "What else? He reads and is contemplative; cf. *Canterbury Tales*, Plato, philosophy.[*WDJ*] *Via activa* versus *via contemplativa*; what makes both of these attractive?"
St: "'Il Penseroso' compared to a nun. Like Mother Teresa in the news the other day?"
J: "What was Mother Teresa's life like?"
St: "Both active *and* contemplative."
J: "It's fun as you work through these things (to think) how *imaginative* they are."

Most students have between six and eleven associations on each side of their papers. Both opening activities appear designed to integrate the newly received information about Milton's poetry as being, thus far, outgrowths of his [Milton's] school exercises.

> **Comment:** J has asked his students to write, not a poem re-
> motely near the sophistication of Milton's, but an exercise
> similar to the type from which Milton drew his inspiration
> and honed his poetry-writing skills. This **experiential
> teaching method** suggests part of Prof. J's educational phi-
> losophy: Students can neither understand nor appreciate
> the work of even a major figure like Milton without seeing
> him, at least at first, as **being somewhat like themselves.**
> One way to do that is to give them an academic exercise
> comparable to the type that informed Milton's own poetic
> inspiration.

Keeping his students in their small groups, J then suggests that
they share their homework insights with one another. Because
many are uncomfortable with this idea, perhaps expecting the
competitive environment typical of university classes, their collaboration at first appears minimal. As they continue through
the semester, however, these same students gradually will become socialized into mutually synergistic activities. What had
previously been one-line responses to J's question are becoming
more elaborate, in part because J's gradually less-specific
promptings allow his students to develop their own calculus of
elaboration.

Group Reports: (Example of Group One):

> St 1: "In 'L'Allegro,' the images are pretty auditory but partly visual;
> in 'Il Penseroso,' there is mostly silence and contemplation."
> J: "Say more about that, would you?"
> St 2: "The first poem was about song and harmony, but the second,
> 'Il'Penseroso,' is more about peace and quiet."

Students appear to have moved, in this instance, from the specifics of poetic imagery to a higher level of abstraction concerning not only the whole poem, but its companion as well.

> St (from Group 4): "Both poems use similar verbs—the tenth line
> ends with 'ever dwell.'"

This kind of answer indicates awareness of parallel processes
within the poetry and knowledge of its grammatical progression

by the student, a real step up the "snakes and ladders of abstraction"; from specific word (verb) to formalized concept repetition, in two separate but connected poems.

J starts with a simple contrastive set and then shows how students are to work through details via recursive movements:

> J: "Without looking at your text, which poem of the two is longer?"
>
> J: "Is one unhappy with life? Look at cycle: when does 'L'Allegro' begin? When does 'L'Allegro' end the day?"
>
> St: "At sunset?"
>
> J: "What are last things that happen in 'L'Allegro'?"
>
> St: "Eat, drink, and stories [elaborates]. [Then,] beyond the sunset, one writes in early evening."
>
> St: (from Group 5): "Note the difference in the use of the *walking* metaphor. In 'L'Allegro' (l. 57), Milton describes 'walking not unseen,' whereas in 'Il Penseroso' (l. 65) the phrase is 'I walk unseen.'"

This student is able to **connect verbal images in contrasting situations,** possibly as a result of J's prompting them in the Assignment Sheet no. 3) to pay particular attention to verb choices in the first ten lines.

J announces that the following week will be devoted totally to reading and understanding "Lycidas."
End of Class 6.

SESSION 7: CONTINUE STEP THREE

Prof J opens this Tuesday morning with a brief warm-up quiz on "Lycidas," even as he returns the last quiz (on "L'Allegro" and "Il Penseroso"). As he carries out these minor housekeeping chores he tells the class, "We did Thursday what I don't like (to do); we did not read 'L'Allegro' out loud. Milton is one of the most musical of the English poets. So, this week we'll all read 'Lycidas' out loud, [since] poetry is mostly feeling."

J continues: "You have quite a bit to do on 'Lycidas' (1637), the best of the 'minor' poems." He then reviews the essential points from his own mini-lecture during the previous class.

Following the quiz and review [above], Prof. J begins one of the more interesting classes I have ever witnessed. Since one of the major tasks in Step Three is to create connections—in this case from a culture and a poet distant in both space and time to the students' own lives—the teacher must constantly search for **bridging mechanisms,** methods of helping students to see relationships between the seventeenth century and their own time and interests.[12] Prof. J employs the raw emotional shock from Princess Diana's untimely death (an experience then only three weeks past) to connect students' emotions to the genre of the eulogy and the specific example of Milton's "Lycidas."

> J: (To class) "We have today a rare opportunity to comprehend how our grief over Princess Diana may feel like Milton's grief over the death of his schoolmate. Let's move into groups." [Class divides into previous grouping arrangements.]
>
> J: (To Group 3): "What are some of the analogies to the deaths we've recently witnessed: of Princess Diana, Mother Teresa, and Sir George Solti? What are some of the differences between your reactions to the death of Diana and that of Mother Teresa (who was eighty-seven years old)?"
>
> Sts: "Shock, (a) at the way she died; (b) at her being so young; (c) It did not have to happen that way; d) the *way* she died, like a made-for-TV movie; (e) Irony—blaming one person and holding someone accountable: one's self, God, [in this case the] paparazzi, the car driver, the royal family, and Prince Charles."
>
> J: "This is all *part of the grieving process.*" [J mentions Elizabeth Kubler-Ross and her ideas of the patterns of grief; he quizzes the class about their experiences with death generally.] "Are there differences between the death of an older person and of someone one's own age? Does anyone recall the death of JFK?" [Of course, only one student in the room was even alive when the president was assassinated, and she was five years old at the time.]
>
> St: "In general, there is a weeping, [followed by a] release. You want to get on with [your] life."
>
> J: (Asks them about the church service at Westminster). "What marked the eulogy?"
>
> Sts: "Praising a great person. Diana's brother was angry at the public and at the Royals."
>
> J: "At the end of a funeral service, where does this emotion ultimately go?"
>
> Sts: "One is at peace; we will somehow try to live in another way because the dead loved one has gone to a better place [and variations of this sentiment]."
>
> J: "They spoke good words about Diana. Indeed, the word *eulogy* reminds me of another *word du jour, eu + logy,* 'good words.'"

After about fifteen minutes of this general conversation (without a mention yet of "Lycidas"), Prof. J gives the class a brief group assignment:

> J: "Make a short list (in each group) of some of the things that go along with funerals, and were part of Princess Diana's funeral."

Group sharing follows. J asks a student to go to the board to write, joking with him and giving him a hand at the end.

> Group Three's results: "There was a gathering of a lot of people, slow-moving people; lots of flowers; the casket was displayed and the procession lasted for a long time; there was a military accompaniment, somber music, and a gathering of the family weeping; they had candles, incense, pall bearers, and bells tolling—once for each year of life."
> J: [WDJ] "*Tolling* like bank 'teller,' (someone or something accountable)."
> J: [at 8:45am]: "OK, turn back together in groups. Now: [**Key question**]: Which of these [ideas, issues] connects to 'Lycidas'?"

Comment: This **bridging exercise** was a very interesting teaching move. Prof. J uses popular information (Diana's death) to elicit authentic student reactions; then he takes those *patterns of genuine grief* in their own lives and connects them, culturally and historically, to today's lesson and to the genre consideration of Milton's elegiac poem.

After fifteen minutes of small-group work, hunting connections, J brings the students back to the whole group again. They are now capable of connecting the more general commentary about Diana's funeral to the various genre elements in "Lycidas," and to do so with explicit reference to line numbers:

> J: "What is a wedding song doing in a funeral?"
> St: "Weddings celebrate life; a funeral celebrates death—they are mixed (here)."
> St: "Look at l. 123: [It was a] lean and fleshy song."
> St: "(l. 87): The strain was of high mood (mode)."
> J: (l.14): "Connect the water image, the tear, and the melody."
> St: (ll. 28–36) "(They) all deal with music."

J: "(Do you remember) anyone in stories who has gone into water and come out again? What do you know about dolphins?"

St: "They're healing creatures."

J: "What about the Bells?" (l. 135)

St: "A part of the music."

J: "Rhythmic changes; look at lines 37–38 (J recites): "Now thou art gone. [reads slow and heavy, like tolling of bells] In sum, the poet goes some place we all go in responding to death, but with a double meaning to work through their grief."

St: "Why was King Edward going to Ireland?"

J: "We don't know for sure, but he sank within sight of the shore (and died along with others)."

Class 7 ends.

Session 8: continue step three

Prof. J begins with a discussion and lecture, and starts with his congratulations to the students:

J: (To class) "Most of you did a good job relating funeral experiences with public expressions of grief." J reviews, making the **transition** from ordinary human experience (prior knowledge) to formal properties of poem.

J: "We've all experienced the death of people we know and some we really didn't know. These experiences are part of our culture. It's very natural (nature-like) to experience grief. Although I doubt he [Milton] made a list (as he did in 'L'Allego' and 'Il Penseroso'), these types of experiences are all part of the package Milton is putting together, partly because he just knows them because he is human, and partly through the traditions. Now, the traditions come into the formal elements of the poem. I asked you to look up some things about the formal parts of the poem—this is a 'pastoral' poem."

Here, J reviews connections made in the previous class, gives relationships, and **defines a key literary word.**

J: "What would be some actions expressing grief? If Marcel Marceau were to 'act out' the poem, what would his actions be? What kinds of emotions are expressed?"

Sts: (Severally speak out): "Anger;" "grief, . . ."

J: "Milton takes these emotions, sights, sounds, and images, and weaves them into a traditional form called the *pastoral*. If [the poet] chooses pastoral, (like an epic—*Paradise Lost*—or a sonnet (recall early class)), he (Milton) has to do certain things."

[J weaves the students' past common experiences, previous class work, and formal properties of the sonnet into a blend, explaining the text ("Lycidas") under discussion.]

J: "What is a *pastoral*? I asked you to look up elements of pastoral! Why wouldn't shepherds know anyone other than shepherds?"
St: "'Cause it's an *elegy*—shepherds writing about dead shepherds."
J: "Milton *invokes* the muse" [J gives etymology: *vocate.*] "One uses *invoke* as 'to speak,' or 'to call.' Milton uses it as a 'calling.'" [J is constantly working on vocabulary.]

This particular class session appears rather flat. The students are not really with him today, some twenty minutes into the class. In contrast to the intensity of the previous session, this one feels all the more subdued. However, Prof. J senses their mood and jokes about the "cat invoking its mews (muse)." When next a student responds back with a joke, J joins in, engaging whole class. J evidences an interesting **problem-solving skill**—getting an uninvolved class hooked into the discussion and class materials. Later, J uses his natural sense of humor to cajole his charges into participating in the narrative of the class, even though this morning (a little after 8:00 a.m.) it seems the very last thing they want to do.

St: "There's a flock involved."
J: (With mock concern) "Pardon?"
St: "I said it carefully!" (Student is also smiling.)
J: (Laughs, joking back as class mood picks up): "I noted that; I appreciate that."
St: "Well, the flock and shepherd are connected."
J: "Connected with what? Milton connects shepherds and flock with clergy. Hence, pastoral is about shepherds, also pastors in church—hence we [readers] are a flock."
J: "What is a bishop?" [Repair]: "What does a bishop look like?"
St: "Carries a staff that has a hook."
J: "At this point, Milton gives us a transition; Milton uses the discussion of generalities about death that we all feel, that we all have, and takes them to make specific connections, references to

Edward the King. In effect, Milton goes from generalities to literary conventions to personal things. He expresses his **personal experiences** within the framework of the elegiac conventional poem.

J: "I want to stop and actually read some of the poem. How many of you did read this out loud? We'll share experiences; **don't be afraid** of being corny. If you don't know a word, fake it. You now know the 'movement'—from the poet saying 'I'm not ready' to 'I'll have to do it, so I will.'" [J asks students to read out loud with no specific prior preparation]: "Who would like to start—Melanie?" [However, this mode of reading out loud with no preparation will change shortly; see end of class.]

Sts: [Read out loud; *seratim*. Here, J makes no mention of the technique of enjambment, hence some mangle the lines. *No intervention—no attempt to explain meanings.*]

J: "If you cannot pronounce a word, look at the meter" [But students (apparently) are not yet aware of metric analysis.]

Comment: J continues his gradual withdrawal from drill-type queries (see immediately below) as students begin asking questions and elaborating more in their answers. His initiations are also less anticipatory, designed to give students more control over the direction of the conversation.

J: "Let's go back to the beginning of the poem [and do an] *explication de texte*. What does Milton do that is unusual [here]?"

St: "Milton belittles himself." Then, the student elaborates on his answer (much of it indistinct).

After a few more questions of explication, J winds up the discussion of "Lycidas" by congratulating the class in his best John Wayne voice: "Ya done good!"

Next week the class will read Milton's only play, *Comus*.

Summary

By this point in the semester, Prof. J is able to motivate his students to start the real work of understanding an arcane poet like Milton because he has made a point of connecting their lives (most in their early twenties) with several of the specifics of Milton's. He began this process the first day, by showing up regularly before class began and chatting with those who (at an early 7:55 a.m.) were already there. He asks one student about his sick mother, another about her daughter's problems in kindergarten, and a third about the previous weekend—of some social importance to the student.

From this casual banter, it is not a long step to class discussions of Milton's rather unusual post-educational experiences—staying at his parent's home for five years *after* graduation and reading—and comparing and contrasting those experiences with the students' own current lives and problems. The students are more than willing to ask questions, make comparisons, and thus immerse themselves in seventeenth century college life. The meanings in the poems seem almost naturally to flow from such contexts, and to further ensure that students see such relationships, Prof. J gives them several of the same type of academic exercises that Milton experienced.

It is axiomatic that the teacher's personality and the day-to-day personal connection between instructor and pupil is *crucial* at the middle school level, and only slightly less so in high school. Further, one of the professional irritations between high school teachers and college professors is the formers' ideology of closeness to students' lives. So-called pragmatic high school teachers routinely acknowledge its need while theoretically oriented college professors claim that their "academic culture" is different; that their students are older and beyond the need for hand-holding.[13] What appears clear from the evidence presented in Prof J's class is that the "human connection," the triadic emotional *and* academic relationships among professor, students, and imaginative materials, are no less important, albeit different, at the college level as they are for younger students, particularly for literary materials distant from students in time and space.

As the class sessions progress, Prof J continues and refines several earlier teaching habits:

1. His *words du jour* now have taken on regular and important meanings for students who automatically look for root derivations of important poetic words.
2. The level of discourse has steadily risen (without necessarily dramatic changes) from mostly drill-type question-and-answers to more thoughtful and interactive responses,

often reflecting information students have only recently learned themselves.

3. The class motivation remains relatively high for an 8:00 a.m. class on a fairly arcane subject (even for English majors); this comes from J's public recognition of thoughtful student answers and the mutual respect with which student and professor exchange not only information but gentle humor.

4. The complexity of student thoughtfulness increases continuously as Prof. J moves from image to personal connection (Princess Diana to "Lycidas") to thematic and character issues back down to image again.

5. Finally, J's continuously weaves the students' personal life experiences and emotions with those of Milton's life and his poetry. For this class, Milton seems to have lost his original aura of remote and crystallized Puritan intellect. By the end of this fourth week, Milton is just another interesting poet needing somewhat more than a little further explaining.

5

Step Four
Drama and Nonfictional Prose

Pedagogical content knowledge also includes an understanding of what makes the learning of specific topics easy or difficult; the conceptions and preconceptions that students of different ages and backgrounds bring with them to the learning of those most frequently taught topics and lessons.

—Allan H. Shulman

CLASS SESSION 9

PROF. J NOW MOVES THE CLASS TO THE GENRES OF DRAMA—MILTON only wrote two, with *Comus* the major one—and nonfictional prose. It is this latter genre for which Milton is probably best known, aside from *Paradise Lost.* His discussions of education, freedom of speech, and political openness still ring true, and many humanists consider Milton's writings essential referents for any person who claims to be educated.

In this class, Prof J introduces Milton's drama, *Comus,* as he continues several of the practices we have noted in earlier steps. The genre of drama requires a few modifications to classroom procedure, most notably the increased involvement of students speaking parts of the text out loud.

To begin, J return quizzes from the week before and launches a fairly traditional question-and-answer session. He then opens with a brief lecture to the class about *Comus,* "a masque." In this context, J asks a student the date of the masque. When the student gives the wrong answer, J smiles: "Well, close. It actually was 1634." This exchange illustrates again that his focus is less on correct answers and more the continued positive interactions among students, professor, and the class materials.

J then defines the *masque* by saying, "I am sure you all know this," and provides cognates (via his now-familiar *words du jour*) of that word's employment in Milton's practice: it is "something underneath the surface, like a *masquerade,* or *mascara.*" Prof. J asked the students (in Assignment no. 5) to define the characteristics of the genre, and now lectures on types of genre generally: poetry, drama, fictional prose, nonfictional prose, and lastly the *masque,* which he says is a subgenre. This is J's first explicit discussion of genre characteristics, although he began Class Session 2 with a brief overview of sonnet-genre patterns.

> **Comment:** Much of what follows is teacher-directed based on homework for that day, and formulated via report-type (memory) questions and short student answers. This format recognizes that most students would have little skill or knowledge in ways to synthesize this information on their own. The combination of asking mostly report-type[1] questions interlaced with mini-lectures is Prof. J's way of introducing students to such information painlessly. One would note, however, that J's style is hardly the dry-and-dreary one-way dissertation so often characterized by those advocating the primacy of student-centered activities in the classroom. J's loom weaves threads of new information, anecdotal asides, questions about students' experiences, and frequent exhortations to see this *masque* as something that, upon reframing, could actually look rather familiar, like the family outing.

Prof. J begins the question-and-answer session by asking students to consider what their own motivations might be in attending a masque:

J: "Why would we (contemporary people) want to see masques?"
After various student speculations, J continues with some basic
    groundwork:
J: "Where is the play set?"
St: "At the patron's home."
J: "Where do the kids end up in this play [masque]?"
Sts: "They're actively involved, singing, dancing . . ."
J: "With whom do they dance?"
St 1: "Members of the audience."
St 2: "This reminds me of the [long-running Chicago] play, *Tony and*

Tina's Wedding!" (Student describes this "interactive production" in detail.)

J: "Excellent example—that really works well to describe Milton's masque."

Here, J and the student consider in some detail the connections between the two productions. The dancing at the end of *Tony and Tina's Wedding*, J suggests, would be similar to a masque run by the mythological "attendant spirit" who also happens to be the master of ceremonies.

J: "Comus's crew—what do they look like?"
St: "They're very proper and formal."
St: "Was this a (reader's theatre) or a real play?"
J: "A real play, staged and directed by someone named Henry Lawes. Milton was twenty-six, just out of school. And what was (Milton) doing (after college)? Reading! At the age of twenty-seven, what was he doing, reading, etc.?"

Comment: Here Prof. J develops a way of looking at a literary text via what, in another context, is called the "authorial audience," the "specific but hypothetical collection of individuals the author assumes will read his book; this audience resides primarily in the author's mind."[2] This is precisely the construct that is most often ignored in RR theories and practices because it requires the reader to make inferences about authorial intentions, inferences based on concrete particulars in the text and, when necessary, from extratextual evidence not immediately available to the average reader. The problem that emerges next is one most teachers face at one time or another: How to keep the crispness of students' attention when the teacher must deliver crucial information that is not immediately recognized as important by the members of the class.

J: "I want to ask you [students in class] not a rhetorical, but a real question. What if you were to put on a play in a small college in Iowa in front of people you do not know? What do you, as the author, *need* to know?"
St: "Characters."
J: "Yes, you'd need to know about the family for whom the production was being given."

J then delivers a *mini-lecture:* the Lawes family and Charles Di-
odoti's family (Milton's best friend) were close in London.

At this point in the class discussion the students do not appear
engaged and are not on-task; even tired. J's previous question-
and-answer sessions have been characterized by a high degree of
interaction and student engagement, but for whatever reason on
this morning in late September the class appears sluggish and
unresponsive. As mere observer, I could not find out—not from
the students, Prof J, or from my own reflections—why the rest
of this day went as it did. What is of interest are the **coping
mechanisms** Prof. J employs to deal with a class either unready
or unwilling to talk.[3]

> J: "Who was Henry Lawes—and what was his connection to Edger-
> ton family? [pause] It's in your notes . . ."
> Sts: [No response; frankly, dead silence!]
> J: "He was working as the children's music tutor." [J provides the
> answer, but with no tension in his voice.] "It's an interesting con-
> nection, because we can see how Milton's mind is working."
> [After a few more exchanges:]
> J: How many of you have had to memorize lines for a play?"
> Sts: [No one raised hand]
> J: "See, people don't memorize anymore. In the seventeenth century,
> people *did* memorize. Lawes as 'attendant spirit' is also *prompter*
> for the ladies. The part of Sabrina may have been played by an
> older married sister of the kids."
> J: (Developing analogy): "What might be your reaction if a relative
> were in play?"
> Sts: [Extended and increasingly animated discussion of those possi-
> bilities.]
> J: "Who were the main people in this audience?"
> Sts: "Family; the rest of the audience was involved in mirroring the
> family."
> J: (Recalling a student answer earlier about the masque being mainly
> for people of the court): "People in the play are also those outside
> the play—and that adds to the fun. The play exists on two differ-
> ent dimensions: the people (characters) in the play are also the
> people outside the play (members of the Edgerton family)."
> J: "What else does a masque have?"
> St: "Lavish costumes."
> J: "Why lavish costumes? [Making an contrast]: What is Thyrsis's
> job?"
> St: "(He is a) shepherd."

J: "What is he to wear?" [J then jokes in what has become in the last few minutes the beginnings of an engaging narrative]: "He doesn't wear a shroud, like Lycidas."

Comment: At this point the energy of the class has picked up considerably, due mostly to Prof. J's patient and persistent questioning—balanced with a joking and light attitude—which *provides the class with an energy they cannot provide, this day, for themselves.* The turn seems to come at the point when J asks them about their own families in a masque, and the students begin speculating (often to each other privately, with winks and smiles not on camera) about such a possibility. Perhaps one must reconsider ideas of being on-task during a whole-group question-and-answer. There are times when a private association will make the public discussion connect to a student in a way the material alone could not. Brief, shared insights and social interactions may add to the class interaction, and should not always be viewed as merely a distraction or being "off-task."

After a few more exchanges:

J: "What else [do you, the student, see in *Comus*]?"
St: "Pastoral themes."
J: "What else by Milton has pastoral themes?"
Sts: "'Lycidas,' 'Morning of Christ's Nativity,' 'L'Allegro' . . . [J supports a review of the connections between *Comus* and many other of Milton's works studied earlier in the class.]
J: "Anything about staging? [Was there] elaborate staging machinery?" [Repairs]: "At the beginning, how does the attendant get on stage?"

J draws attention to **textual evidence as support** for any answer to his questions, then continues:

J: "Where else are mechanized things are needed? How does/can Sabrina come up from the river?"

These apparently simple questions, relating the words in the text to the limitations of stagecraft, set in motion an engaged and (given the earlier part of this class period) even intense discussion of what was possible as a mechanical device in the seventeenth century, and what was likely given the words in the text:

St: "[The] characters could hide [them]selves . . ."
J: "Where? Behind the 'bushes'?"
St: "Sabrina comes up from the river . . ." [develops answer but indistinct on videotape.]
J: "Yes. How could you do that [arrive unseen]?"
St: "Stand behind something . . ."
J: (Jokes): "Ok, you could have elaborate stuff or let's say that this is the "CMC" (Cheap Milton Company). No wires or gimmicks. How could she come up from river?"
St: "Actors coming up from the trapdoors."
J: "Right. Good. Lots of trap doors in (for example) Shakespeare."

"[We] have to stop, ran out of time. I would like to do some reading and I need fifteen volunteers." J passes out a list of lines, character names, and line numbers.

Summary

At the end of class, J's mood is joking and lighthearted as it has been through most of this period. One would hardly know from his outward demeanor that this has been the "class from hell." Despite the patience needed to cope with a class struggling with the unfamiliarity of a seventeenth century masque, Prof. J remains unflappable. He does not demonstrate overtly any frustration with the students' reluctance to engage in what, in other classes, have been a series of lively exchanges. The students (for the most part) have done their assignments, but the strangeness of Milton's themes of chastity and virtue wrapped in a genre like a court masque has made their own personal connection with this material very difficult. Prof. J has applied his usual moves: joking, drawing on students' personal experiences, and providing analogies to other works and ideas previously discussed, in order to keep the talk flowing.

One other adjustment was made by Prof. J today. In the previous class, J's spontaneous requests to get students reading out loud (with no chance for prior preparation by the student) was not very successful. Today (five days later), J corrects his approach of the previous class period by **assigning roles and lines for the students to prepare.**

SESSION 10: CONTINUE PART FOUR

J takes roll and continues the discussion of *Comus*, focusing this period on the readings and dramatic movement on the "stage" in an English country house.

He puts everyone in a **circle for reading out loud** and begins by reviewing his lecture on the masque and asking report-level questions:

J: "What items constitute a masque?"

Sts: [Variety of answers.]

J: "What else (does a masque have)?" [J answers his own question]: "The masque usually delivers a moral lesson—it's an allegorical-type play with little elaborated interaction among the characters."

St: "Isn't this a little like *A Midsummer Night's Dream?*"

J: "Exactly." [Follows up student's literary analogy to Shakespeare's *Midsummer Night's Dream*]: "Can you elaborate?"

St: [Elaborates on similarity of magic, spirit worlds, etc.]

J: "How many have seen *A Midsummer Night's Dream?*" [J adds to student commentary and reminds students that both plays involve audience.] "At the end of the play, for example, Puck and audience are alone, and in this way Shakespeare, like Milton, makes his audience a part of the play. What else?"

St: "Beasts."

J: "Beasts do a wild kind of dance."

J: "How does he end?"

St: [Puzzled looks. It is clear the class is still having trouble with this genre, in spite of their memory of Shakespeare's fantasy play.]

J: "When all else fails, look at the text." [J models what experts do with literary texts.]

J: "Ok, so how do you [as a character] get in [to the set]? Fly or walk?"

St: [As student exaggeratedly mimes flying in, whole class applauds.]

J: "Wouldn't it be fun if you were a third grade (not a third-rate) teacher (and tried to put on a masque like this)?"

Here, J spends some time discussing directorial cues and the entrance of Comus—with his "charming rod" (rod of charms and spells) and his glass of spirits. J tells them about the magic

of the stage imagination: "If a chair becomes enchanted, it is because you say it's enchanted." Then he continues: "Let your
body loosen up; don't be embarrassed. Heck, I get up every Tuesday and Thursday and make a fool of myself. So, if you mispro-
nounce a word, just keep going." (At this moment the whole
class is engaged, and J has illustrated again the fact that students,
young and old, enjoy the sheer pleasures of live performance and
the opportunity of standing before their classmates and being
semi-serious, semi-silly while reading from a classic text.)

After fifteen minutes of beginning questions and setting up
the situation, Prof. J moves students to start readings. The first
student, David, reads and responds well. The second student,
Randy, is not quite as good a reader but is equally enthusiastic.
After ten minutes of reading, J stops the students and begins
questioning them about the particulars of what they have read.

J: [Relates reading to Shakespeare]: "The general law of many play-
wrights: The whole story (of *Comus*) is here at the beginning in a
nutshell, just as in *Midsummer Night's Dream*.
St: [Jason reads. J stops him and takes him back to some key lines,
119–25.]
Sts: [Several students read.]
J: "What does 'going into the woods' signify?"
St: "(It's) allegorical—(the woods are where) people get lost."
J: [Draws a connection to *PL* and defines "*prevenient* grace," the
kind of grace where God helps before being asked.] "So, Comus
shows up in the guise of a shepherd (the world isn't always as you
see it is, and the Lady will be tested)?"
Sts: [As Katie and Joe read, J tells them that their reading pattern is
called *stichomythia* [WDJ], alternating lines back and forth be-
tween two characters, one Comus, the other the lady.]
St: [Picking up on J's cue]: "Is there a scripted space in line 304
(where the character points)?"
J: "Yes." [Explains voice and different rhyme pattern per character.]
Sts: [Selena and Melanie read; J reminds them that in real life, the
characters are eleven and nine years old.]
J: [Posing questions]: "If the lady (who is stuck in a chair through
Comus's spell) has virtue, why can she not get up?" [J again uses
words du jour to remind students that "virtue" means "power."]
St: "(It would mean) the end of the play." [Placing the issue in relation to authorial intention, or what Phelan[4] calls character motivation that is textually synthetic rather than mimetic.]

J: "Yes, and it's not that you're not tempted, but you have the strength to resist."

[As they read and discuss, J **edits the text and moves students** to key areas.]

J: "Let's all get up [pointing to three students] and do the seduction scene. I'll ask you to put the seduction scene in your own words." [Students begin a college-language type "seduction" scene.]

Prof. J stops his readers at this point, and refers to the homework assignment and the Tuesday and Thursday handouts.
"Nice job. I applaud you all (for your performances today)."

Summary

Much of the success of today's class went to Prof. J's willingness to ham it up and to gently let his students know that he expected them to ham it up, too. The seventeenth-century masque, for all the glib analogies to *Midsummer Night's Dream* made by a couple of the students, is still *very* far removed from most students' experience—especially if it is read as a closet drama. By insisting that students make their understanding and reading of the lines approach the British country house atmosphere of the play's original setting, and by cracking jokes and laughing at even the bad ones, J suggests to his students that Milton *can be enjoyable,* especially the youngish Milton—in his twenties at this writing—who must have sensed the humor in a fifteen-year-old girl and two young boys playing parts for a family outing. Albeit funny the subject matter (chastity) is to contemporary readers of the young Milton, it may have been the only subject of which the elder gray-beard Puritans approved, and they did so without a hint of irony.

SESSION 11: CONTINUE PART FOUR

J begins Class 11 by announcing modifications to the syllabus and by giving students notice of upcoming work. He says that after thinking about *Comus* and the actors memorizing lines, he will ask the students to memorize the first two sentences of *Par-*

adise Lost (actually a kind of joke since the first two "sentences" run some forty-plus lines) and will give them a month to do so. (This is Prof. J's first request for what used to be, in an earlier generation, a standard literary skill—committing to memory important lines from a major work.)[5] He then reminds them to use the *Milton Links*, even though he says he won't be looking at them himself. These are designed to get students to reflect on the connections between their own lives and class work.

Prof. J asks the students to move into their small groups.

J: "[Let's hear] Sabrina's voice: 'She of few lines but of lovely lines.' Starting with ll. 890ff.; What does Sabrina do? What is happening? If you were staging this [masque], what are the built-in activities?" [Here, J is trying to get students to see the masque in three-dimensional space, visualizing and then moving through the blocking of the scene.]

J: "What does she do before she leaves?"

St: "She goes to the Lady [of virtue] who is the one who can break the spell."

J: [Paraphrases Sabrina's lines and indicates that Milton mixes the fantasy of the masque and the reality of the actors' (and family's) movements.]

Comment: Prof. J cuts and splices parts of the text on the spot, moving the class from line 921 to line 958 ff, and continues the questions. Only a master of the text could know it so well that he could "edit" (or select) a passage for **thematic emphasis on the spot.** It is an expert skill that, in the eyes of some, often gets overlooked (in practice) as "too directive," although such editing by directors is commonplace in the theater.[6] On-the-spot editing is an expert skill that *is* directive in the service of larger goals and a useful skill both for novice readers and teachers, especially teachers who must *know well* the text one teaches.

J continues the questions below:

J: "What are the actions in this last part? If you were the attendant spirit, where would you go and what would you do?"

St: "Milton leaves that open again; he (attendant spirit) can run or fly." [This student has picked up the skill of visualizing action in three-dimensional space from the words on the page.]

J: "Where is he going?" [Refers to student's comment in last class on *Midsummer Night's Dream*—very long-distance **up-take**]: "The Attendant Spirit gives us the message—in case the other 'long' speeches missed us. Remember, a masque ends with a moral. Virtue will help get us to heaven."

After almost thirty minutes of question-and-answer, Prof. J now asks the student groups to find structural and thematic information in the text. He insists that students turn Milton's language into words and phrases of their own understanding as they explain why Comus denies the value of chastity and the Virgin affirms it. When J stops the small groups, he asks them to report their findings. Below are some typical exchanges:

J: "Let's see where you are in terms of these major arguments. What's one of the major arguments *in your own words?*"
St: "To submit is nature-al" (natural.)J: [Paraphrases] "This is the 'nature-al' or *natural* way of life. What else?"
St: "Use it or lose it."
J: (Jokes about age): "Right; who's going to want you when you're thirty-five." (Pause; jokes) "Ok, forty-five"; (pause) "Ok, seventy-five or eighty, whatever!" [Whole class laughs since Prof. J is over fifty and consistently profiles himself as "ancient" to this relatively young class.] "Any other reasons?"
St 1: (Referring to l.737): "Virginity isn't that great; you must share the wealth." [This student does two things simultaneously: she refers to the specific line in the text that supports her reference, and she immediately translates it into contemporary English.]
St 2: "Don't they also say if you don't use it, won't the people be gone?"
St 3: (Paraphrasing Lady): "You're (Comus) out of my league, buddy."
J: (Repeats; students laugh.) "In a sense, Milton lives in a world of absolutes."
St: (Reads lines about virtue.): "Wasn't she saying he [Comus] was deceptive?"
J: (Paraphrases argument of Lady): "If you were virtuous enough, you'd know, but since you're not, you couldn't know." (To students generally): "It's a wonderful rhetorical device. Like, [to specific student] Melanie, 'You're smart enough to know that I'm the best-looking guy in the room.' Disagree, and what does that say about you?"

> **Comment:** Here, J introduces **paraphrasing on two organizational levels:** (1) The translation of a character's actual speech and meanings; and (2) the translation of a "narrator's" voice (not necessarily Milton's) who presents, as W. Van Peer suggests, the "character's actions or words in a specific way: neutrally, emphatically, ironically, and so on."[7] This latter paraphrase is directed toward "uncovering the 'deeper' layers of meaning, which are not apparent at first sight."[8] This first type of paraphrase (translating the Lady's words) is at a lower textual level, placing the Lady's words into a more inclusive textual context and then translating Milton's larger meanings (e.g., the rhetorical device the Lady uses on Comus about virtue as a replication of Milton's rhetorical strategies in the "Prolusions," ahead).

At this point J summarizes the end of *Comus*, as many of the themes, techniques, and issues point to *Paradise Lost*.

> J: "[*Comus*] has dancing, staging, and blocking of scenes, rather like the set Milton envisions for the angels in *PL*." [To students:] "Any [further] questions about *Comus* ?"
> End of *Comus*.

Summary

J reinforces his emphasis on the students' connections to *Milton as lived experience* by (a) reminding them to employ the strategies in his *Milton Links*; (b) asking students to paraphrase *in their own words* and *on two levels of textual organization* the rather arcane thoughts and language in the debate between Comus and the Lady over chastity and virtue; and (c) constantly joking while using the language of undergraduates to *translate a seventeenth-century masque into accessible thought* for his students.

In addition, he prefigures some of the elements in the major work ahead (*Paradise Lost*) by discussing stage directions for *Comus* as they become relevant. He pushes the students to visualize the actors moving in three-dimensional space by extrapolating action from the words on the page. Prof. J uses such imaging to give students practice for doing the same thing in Milton's heroic epic, *Paradise Lost*. It is one thing to visualize *actors* in motion, because the dialogue often acts (as in Shakespeare) as the primary cuing mechanism. It has been much more difficult to get students to do so for an epic poem, even if the author was rather theatrically minded.

SESSION 11: CONTINUE MILTON'S PROSE

After a quick review of selected elements in the masque, J moves the class to consider Milton's next great genre, *prose*. In what follows, his somewhat targeted questions serve to prepare for the class reading of material that, like *Comus*, initially appears very far from their experience. Unlike *Comus*, however, these "Prolusions" are merely a sophisticated version of typical freshman debate, complete with very young students practicing their newfound rhetorical abilities on nonresolvable and fairly abstract issues (like choosing between "day" and "night"), complete with all the classical allusions and rhetorical flourishes expected of seventeenth-century Cambridge undergraduate rhetoricians.

> J: "Let's look at the prose: the 'Prolusions' and 'Of Education.' The 'Prolusions' were (page 595 in our text) written in Latin. A *prolusion* is like a freshman composition paper, but meant to be performed—not just a dramatic reading, but a performance. *Prolusion* means *oratorical performance. [WDJ]*
> J: "Where have you seen something similar?—Helena?
> St 1: "'Il Penseroso' and 'L'Allegro.'"
> St 2: "But there's a difference between them, because Milton praises both 'Il Penseroso' and 'L'Allegro.' But in 'Day vs. Night,' one half of his argument is attacking Night."
>
> J: "Milton attacks the person who praises Night; think of Milton as an actor, performing this exercise that's meant to be playful. Put yourself in this setting; remember what Milton was called in college?"
> St: "The lady of Christ's [College]."
> J: "So he knows he's not popular. Milton does this exercise tongue-in-cheek. Afterwards, his peers will vote (Milton is seventeen or eighteen years old at the time). It's a formula. Think of this as a

performance to be read aloud. It must be playful; read it seriously and it sounds stupid. What's the bottom-line argument here?"

St: "Day is better than Night."

J: [Introduces term, WDJ] "*Dialectic*, from *lectio, a reading*. A dictionary is also a lexicon; a priest's readings are called a *lectionary*."

J: "What does Milton do to help capture his audience and win the argument?"

St: "He butters up the auditors [audience]."

J: "How does he do this?"

St: "He tells them they are a 'Great assembly.'"

J: "How else?"

St: "He apologizes immediately to his audience (for possibly offending them)."

J: "Right. 'If I have offended you, I don't mean to . . . .' What else?"

St: (Tells them how smart they are . . .) [Specific words inaudible.]

J: "Remember earlier, in *Comus*, the rhetorical trick: 'If you're intelligent enough to know that I'm the best-looking guy,' and so on . . .'"

Here, Prof. J reminds students, intertextually, of the rhetorical devices Milton uses in *Comus* during the argument between the Virgin and himself. In both cases, classical rhetorical tricks are used in the service of debate, although in one case these tricks are used by a character *inside* a masque, while in the second they are used *in propria persona* by the debater.

Prof. J then continues the class conversation:

J: "Any other things? Amanda?"

St 1: "[He] cuts down the other guy's argument even before he starts."

J: "Tell us where you [St 1] are (in the text)? Given what he is doing here, how seriously would those in the audience take him?"

St 2: "Seriously?" [Student sounds unsure and is totally wrong.]

J: (Disbelieving and asking others in class): "Would these students take him seriously?"

St 3: "They're all having fun."

In this exchange, Prof. J re-involves a student (St2, above) who is clearly not in the flow of class conversation and so misses the crucial element in Milton's adolescent "debate": the playful tone. J doesn't criticize him, but merely redirects the same question to another and allows peer response to "correct" the student.

> J: "The others (in Milton's audience) are aware of devices. Do you see (now, St 2)?"
> [Here, J returns to student with the wildly incorrect answer to soften its impact.]
> St 2: "Milton's colleagues would know all of these devices."
> J: "Yes. All of them know all the rhetorical devices and Milton does a slew of things they all recognize."
> In this next exchange J does something he has done before: salvage a student's ego by giving him or her a fairly easy question to answer, or by praising a correct answer.
> J: "Any other devices?"
> St 2: [Student who gave the really bad answer a few minutes ago]: "(This debate is in) so excellent a cause."
> J: "Yes, good! It's [The 'Prolusion'] so dumb an assignment."

End of Class 11.

Summary

As Prof. J changes genres, he is faced with preparing students for the new demands that this next genre will make upon their reading and interpreting skills while demonstrating the continuity of various Miltonic **literary techniques across genres.** The most obvious is that which connects the rhetorical argumentative device—praising the auditor's (or reader's) intelligence—with the forced choices the rhetor pushes on the reader to display that intelligence. J says Milton first demonstrates that particular argumentative skill in the mouth of a clearly reprehensible character, Comus, in a verse masque, and then requests that the reader notice the same usage again, this time in a largely comic vein by the speaker in the prose "Prolusions." J creates a comfortable, repetitive pattern in the class through his attention to the etymology of **relevant vocabulary** (*words du jour*), his attempts to help students recover from earlier gaffs, and his warm and consistent sense of humor.

SESSION 12: MILTON'S PROSE CONTINUES

> J: "Let's finish up the 'Prolusions.' Please take out your worksheets."

Prof. J begins class with a **quick review** of the basic issues addressed last class period and starts a question-and-answer session involving report-type questions. Note, however, that since the fourth or fifth class period J has been following up responses to factual questions with *requests for further elaboration* or *specific textual evidence.*

J: "Remember, these were 'academic performances' (like verbal term papers). Milton is displaying skills with lots of humorous elements as part of the performance. What were some of the humorous elements?"

St: "A lack of sincerity."

J: "Good. Give an example of that (lack of sincerity)."

St: (Stephanie) "(He) butters up his friends."

J: "Another element?"

St 1: "(He) insults other speakers; if they don't agree with him, they're just stupid."

St 2: "Anyone who'd defend 'Night' is a lower life-form."

J: "Can you find the passage?" Then J asks a student to read out loud. [To student]: "Read it dramatically. Come on, stand up!"

St: [Reads from 'Prolusions' with mock-dramatic voice.]

J: "Well done!" [Whole class applauds with enthusiasm.] "Another—Amanda?"

St: "[He] goes after myths. On page 598, second column." [Reads.]

Comment: Here, students are following the patterns that Prof. J has modeled, pointing to specific lines, sentences, etc., to illustrate their claims. They now do so as automatically as J, and with much of the same gusto.

J: "Right—lots and lots of amusing devices in the 'Prolusions.'"

J: "[Do you] recall the word for arguing both ways—it's a *word du jour: dialectic.*"

St: "Dialectic—Milton was trained as a dialectician, as were ancient Greeks."

J: "Someone read Milton's dramatic second to last and last paragraphs? [To student about to read]: "Stand up, loosen up. He's [Milton] literally made a spectacle of himself. So [you] be a spectacle!"

St: [Reads with mock dramatic flair; involved class members smile.]

J: "Recall the word ending this speech: *benediction,* or *bene dictus!* Literally, 'good word' [WDJ]. Who does [Milton] call upon?"

St: "Phoebus Apollo."

J: "Phoebus Apollo—where have we seen that reference before? Come on . . . it's on the tip of your tongue."

St: "'L'Allegro' and 'Il Penseroso.'"

J: [Continues narrative to conclude]: "These 'Prolusions' are (1) a 'fun type of academic exercise,' and (2) it's a view of Milton we don't get from reading only the serious stuff. Milton knows how to manipulate his audience; he can work the crowd . . .What else is different between the first and second 'Prolusion'?"

St 1: "Milton is not arguing a point; it's not as 'fire and brimstone.'"

St 2: "Milton doesn't end it as same as no. 1; [it] ends more abruptly."

J: "You're right. He ends this one 'and so I shut up.' No *bene dictus* or benediction."

St 3: "I didn't find as much wit or humor in it [as the last one]."

J: [Smiles, then summarizes so far in one continuous narrative]: One ['Prolusion'] is argumentative, one descriptive."

St: "Was this a speech he gave, or did he just write a paper?"

J: "I haven't read how these were presented; however, in academic conferences, papers are still read to this day."

J: [Describes how Milton works in names of friends into Latin speech]: "For example, if your name is 'Earl,' he'd say: 'I'm addressing all the Dukes and **Earls.**' These 'Prolusions' are examples [of the writing of] of the bright young Milton who can *argue well and play on his audience.* These will be qualities he will perfect later in life and use to his advantage."

In this first section of class twelve, J pushes students to look back at words and concepts used in earlier classes and then prefigures Miltonic concepts that will be useful in later classes.

J follows with a mini-lecture on Milton's college life: He finished college in six years, spent five years at home, then did the Grand Tour. Milton loved Italy, and visited Galileo (who wouldn't recant). J says watch later for a statement about blind people. (Galileo was stalwart and blind!) Diodate had died so Milton returned to England, which was on verge of civil war for class, economic, and religious reasons. The Church of England was also at war with the other churches in England. Milton's first job was at age thirty. He met a fellow from the Continent (Comenius) who was trying to reform education; Comenius wanted girls to be educated, and the middle and lower classes as well.

J: "Well, that's the background on this piece. Why would they [students] have to be upper class, twelve to twenty-one years old? Costs: Tuition, boarding, servants, etc."

J: "How many want to be teachers? I asked you to outline the essay. **In groups,** let's look at Worksheet Question no. 3. Looking at the faculty, [we notice that] Milton doesn't talk that much about faculty. This [process of reading] is learning to read through the text [i.e., *inferential* work]. Learning to read in the margins, too [*tacit knowledge*]. What else is assumed in the margins?"

J: "What were Milton's goals for education?"

St: "More virtuousness and becoming acquainted with God."

J: [Reprises *didactic*]: "Which means what? Milton was typical of the Renaissance."

J: "What else?"

St: "[Milton] emphasizes practical matters."

J: "Why? Because the boys are going to be leaders. Milton is strong on leaders."

St: "Boys would control estates."

J: "Boys will be leaders; how do you best be in charge of other people? Because you have done it yourself." [J delivers an anecdote of telephone hierarchy]: "All Bell Telephone executives started out as linemen."

St: "MacDonald's does that, too." [and then elaborates.]

J: "*Virtue* (in Latin) means 'strength.' [Goes to page 632]: (Look at) two major descriptions. *Key phrase:* 'I call therefore a complete and generous education allows a man . . . peace and war.'"

J: "Look at word *magnanimously; magna* means 'great'; *animus* means 'spirit.'"

J: "Now go back to page 631. What's the goal for education? What's the reason for doing this [getting an education]?"

St: (Reads): "[To] get closer to God."

J: "What did Adam and Eve do? They blew it! Great! This is why Milton says we do it [get an education]. We do it to repair the ruins of who our first parents were. To know is to love is to imitate is to demonstrate virtuous faith; virtue was important for our fellow man; faith is important for God."

J: "Who is going to learn to participate?"

St: "Milton assumes we all learn the same way."

End of Class 12.

Summary

This day is simultaneously devoted to continuing the development of appropriate mental patterns and to the introduction of some major cognitive skills required of anyone reading Milton. J continues his ongoing classroom patterns: a quick review at the beginning of each period and word-level attention via *words du jour*. Most interestingly, Prof. J continues the pressure on his students to cite specific and relevant textual evidence to support their generalizations about Milton's writings. In an earlier class (no. 7) he made eight requests for elaboration or for further information, whereas in this class there are twelve such requests. Thus, J's work on students' detailed textual awareness is both ongoing and intensifying.

That J is succeeding in inculcating this habit of mind in students is illustrated by their responses in class. Prof. J, in turn, has shifted from an emphasis on textual evidence to the beginnings of students' inferential analysis. Now students begin to answer questions and make comments with textual evidence, using specific page and line numbers. In response they are also urged to "read through the text," to use their tacit knowledge base and inferential thinking (built up from lectures and personal reading) to examine what is *not* mentioned in the text. In playing with abstractions, this class is nearing the top of the game.

Finally, I note again the atmosphere of good humor and joy in this class, appropriate to the intelligent but still juvenile "Prolusions" of Milton's college years. Scholars devoted to the "student-centered" classroom attempt to vilify the straw man of the dull lecturer. Harvey Daniels, for example, speaks of the "same old curriculum" that is "more structured, memorization-oriented, [and] teacher-dominated."[9] In Prof. J's class, students *are* initially "dominated" by the professor's structure, but *structure is required* for students to master the complexities of reading literature from a distant culture and era.[10] The atmosphere of the current class, however, is anything but dull and rote, and therein lies the key: Prof. J's goal is to create a joint adventure between a master guide and amateur explorers.

SESSION 13: STEP FOUR CONTINUES

J shows a newspaper article with references to a sonnet, reviews earlier work, contextualizes through lectures, and sets up the context for *Areopagitica*. [To students]: "We've covered a great deal thus far and we've now come into the 1640s. We've seen in [Milton's] early prose works [i.e., "Prolusions"] the kinds of argumentation and the kinds of playing with audience that he uses in serious prose works in the 1640s. By now, Milton gets involved in national politics; education is terribly important to Milton. Writing *Areopagitica* enters Milton into politics in a radical way. At same time, he marries Mary Powell and publishes a divorce tract. Milton writes lots of prose works during this period, that is, roughly around the English Civil War."

> J: "Take out your materials on 'Of Education.' Please move back into the same groups of the other day. What kinds of students did Milton assume would go to a private boarding school?"
> St: "Milton doesn't mention it, but they have to be able to afford their education." [Here the student is expressing the *tacit knowledge* J mentioned that was so important in the class before.] "They needed a moral education."
> J: "Say more. Wouldn't we would call it 'holistic?' How do we teach students a 'moral education'?"
> St: "Teachers live with students and live model lives."
> J: "Milton's idea of education doesn't deal with just the mind. [One is] teaching the whole person . . . So, what are they going to be when they grow up?"
> St: "Leaders."
> J: "As a leader, the more you know about the people you are leading, the better a leader you will be. Milton has a twin focus: how to get along with people, and how to deal with God."

Small Group Work

After several brief exchanges of the "report" variety (memory questions), Prof. J asks each group to discuss one aspect of the tract:

> J: "Go back to mission statement." [Response to a student question: "It's on page 632."] "Recall 'magnanimity'—*word du jour*—*great spirit.*"

> J: [Divides tasks among groups]: To Group One, he asks: "What is the public life in 'On Education'? How does their education prepare them? Next group, Private life? Next: Influence of Peace? Next: Influence of War?"

Students are required to search throughout the text, looking for answers to the questions posed on their worksheets. After about

fifteen minutes of small-group work, Prof. J stops them and begins whole-group question-and-answer, requesting reports on
what was found in their small groups. Much of what follows is
report-type question-and-answer, until the last ten minutes of
class:

> J: "How is he going to prepare these boys? How do you teach them
> about morality?"
> St: "Read the scriptures."
> J: "How often do they get scriptures?"
> St: "Every day."

After one of the more routine practices of the traditional
teacher (whole-group question-and-answer), J asks students to
express their opinions on Milton's view of education, explicitly
drawing attention to their own responses in their homework
writings. He begins by reading at length from the end of the tract
where Milton says that God has chosen England to lead the
world, and will do so by training its young people.

> J: "The papers you've written [those chosen for review via J's *Cards
> 'o Doom*] have some interesting comments on them [about Mil-
> ton's tract]. Is there anything Milton does *not* mention?" [Another
> example of reading inferentially—or "reading in the margins of
> the text."]
> St 1: "Milton never talks about specializing." [Student develops an-
> swer.]
> St 2: (Disgustedly) "There are no family for these boys, no mothers."
> [Elaborates about absence of women generally.]
> J: "They might not have good relationships with women. However,
> when you're between twelve and twenty-one don't your friends
> become your family?"
> St 3: "They seem to be drawn from only one social class. Not every-
> one has the money for (a private education)." [Speaks briefly of
> students' financial-aid problems.]
> J: "Yes. Milton's theories perpetuate the class system. The boys are
> members of the leisure classes."
> J: "What happens to boys who don't like Greek or Latin? Milton
> doesn't talk about the drop-out rate either. Who's going to deter-
> mine who becomes the leaders in society?"

[J alludes to Thomas Hardy's *Jude, the Obscure* and the distance between the ordinary citizen's dreams (of the spires of Oxford) and those of the leisure classes.]

St: "[They're drawn from] those who go through this curriculum."
J: "(Your) point is well taken."
St 4: "Milton doesn't talk about artists—music, dance, and so on [elaborates]."
J: "Right. They get music as background while they're studying. The performing arts aren't part of the curriculum."
St 5: "(These) students aren't well educated in social interaction with the other classes—the poor, the . . ."

(9:14 a.m.; J stops class): "We will do *Areopagitica* next."

Summary

This class is admittedly one of the more traditional of this semester. Prof. J moves through a homework review and discussion on Milton's "Of Education" to further the students' understanding of the educational philosophy of John Milton before approaching *Areopagitica*. Despite the format, he makes the coverage enjoyable by drawing on his vast knowledge of the details of Milton's life and his own use of wit and humor, as well as an insistent narrative style that keeps the class alert and on-task.

The proliferation of strongly felt student opinions at the end of class makes it clear that they *are* following the progression of Milton's argument. They have internalized J's request that they read "in the margins" of the text, and are forming their own opinions. These opinions are based largely on the contrastive nature of their own educations in their own culture and Milton's ideals of education. Prof. J patiently agrees with them, while subtly suggesting that Milton's educational philosophy is from another time and culture. Hence, students learn that to argue with Milton they first "must understand him and his intentions."[11] They were free to argue with those intentions from their perspective, three hundred years in his future. Historians usually call this an "act of the historical imagination," moving novice readers (to the degree possible) from considering only their own perspective to considering those from another time and place as well. It was the blending of the two that made watching this class exciting.

SESSION 14: STEP FOUR

In this last of the regular classes before their Midterm Opportunity, J gives the students a brief quiz on *Areopagitica* (1644). With good humor and lots of "ham," J gets students to pronounce *Areopagitica:*

> J: "Why is it called that?"
> St: [After some stumbling around]: It's a Greek council."
> J: "Makes connections between wise men (jokingly corrected to "wise *persons*") and Parliament."
> J: "To whom was he writing this?" [Answers his own question]: "He was sending this to Parliament. *Parla-e-ment* means 'who speak together.'" [J's etymologies].

For the next thirty minutes or so J lectures on the context of *Areopagitica* and, intermittently, conducts a question-and-answer session. Prof. J combines and blends lecture, occasional question-and-answer, and frequent allusions to texts read previously in the class. All of this is delivered with wit and humor and in a conversational, informal narrative.

> J: "What happened before this [*Areopagitica* was published]?"
> St: "The Licensing Act was passed in 1637."
> J: "Who did the licensing, or gave the *imprimatur?*"
> St: "The Archbishop of Canterbury and three others."
> J: "Wonderful! Very good [summarizes student's imperfect memory]. There were four people for entire country: Archbishop Laud of Canterbury; two councilors, and someone from Oxford who happened to be the archbishop. Milton refused to get an *imprimatur* and had his tract privately printed; at the time, Milton was an unknown school teacher."

As he begins, J reminds them how difficult this tract is to understand. "(This) particular tract . . . is so tightly argued—and I know you were outlining it; it is difficult stuff—one of the hardest things you'll ever have to read. Do you have a note about Parliament changing its mind? [He then asks them to place the text into some sort of structure or genre.] Remember, this is an 'Oration'—somebody *speaks* it."

He contrasts Milton's "Prolusions" and *Areopagitica,* and sees connections in terms of audience manipulation. J tells them that there is no record of this tract ever being discussed in Parliament. "Milton never went to Parliament to argue this and Parliament did nothing [about it]. For years, the tract just laid there . . ."

> J: "What kind of picture does Milton draw of Vice? What kind of movie star might be [cast in this role]?"
> St 1: "Vice is a woman."
> St 2: "(Jokes) Like Sharon Stone."
> J: "Now look at the picture of Virtue on page x." [J defines Virtue.] "Milton says that he 'cannot praise a fugitive and cloistered virtue.' What's the image he uses here?"
> St: "[This virtue] is like a nun's."
> J: "We've [heard] this before. Where?"
> St: [Immediately] "In *Comus*—the Lady in *Comus.*"

Thus far, J has reinforced the intertextual connections among Milton's ideas, his ongoing personal life, and the various genres in which his ideas are expressed.

In what follows, Prof. J plays the devil's advocate regarding censorship. The give-and-take begins in a fairly routine manner, but quickly escalates:

> J: "How many [of you] have children? Can you think of books children should not read? He doesn't talk about the children, does he?"
> St: "Depends on the age."
> J: "(Give an) example of a book ten-year-olds should not read?"
> St 1: "Stephen King's . . ." [indistinct].
> St 2: "*American Psycho.* It's controversial for many adults."
> St 3: "Lust and romance novels."
> J: "What about a twenty-year-old? You're all at least twenty. Are there books you honestly think adults should not have access to in our society?"
> St: "NO. They should chose whatever they . . ." [indistinct].
> J: "What about *The Unibomber's [Manifesto]?* If you had children killed by him, or were the spouse of one who . . ."

St 1: [Interrupts] "I just happen to have the *Unibomber's Manifesto* (here)." [Holds it up; loud laughter.]

J: "Are you kidding me? I don't believe it!" [laughter.]

St 2: "Milton says, 'To a pure man, all things are pure.' People can figure out anything; I'd rather take my chances and read whatever I want."

St: "If you ban how to make the bomb, then [could] you also ban deadly grips in the martial arts?"

J: "[Jokes] Deadly grips; I have no problem with that. [Aside]: Sounds like a date I had once. [Returns]: I have your best interests at heart. Trust me, I am a good guy, but the other teachers are not. Trust me, but ignore the others."

St 1: "(I would) censor the media and so limit the paparazzi."

St 2: [Skeptical] "Limit therefore [only] elements of the media?"

J: "How many of you live within the boundaries of Chicago? Would you be in favor of people having a hand gun?"

St 1: [Shakes her head in disbelief; J smiles over his own attempt at specious rhetoric.] "People can still get them (handguns), whether you regulate them or not. People can still get cigarettes, alcohol. We've all had drinks in here before we're twenty-one."

J: [In mock disbelief] "Not in *here?*"

St 1: "Regulate all you want; people are still going to do it."

St 2: [With *ah-ha* tone]: "It says here (in *Areopagitica)* that you'd have to regulate everything before 1637 [date law was passed] as well, and all the knowledge we've learned before."

J: "(Should we) censor everything that's written beforehand?"

St: "Who watches the watchman?"

J: "Yes! Who censors the censor! We know the government regulates smoking. [To student]: Let's say that St1 here is our [hypothetical] censor—he has the power to say yea or nay and I want to make sure my book, *Bill's Guide to Making Bombs,* gets published. What am I going to do? I need to get past this guy or get his *imprimatur.* [Jokes] I could bomb him? What am I going to do?"

St 1: "Send expensive gifts, trips . . ."

St 2: "A nice (boat)."

J: "Sure. Tobacco lobbyists give parties to influence people. All of that is in the psychology of politics. If the cause is really good, why not? We all have our prices, how do you do it? How do we know what the agenda is of Bishop Laud? (Milton says) how do I go about censoring the censor? A little later . . ."

St: [Interrupts] "If they remain censored, England will slip back on the evolutionary scale and will become ignorant again, slavish to others."

J: "What's made us the England we are?"

St: "We had so advanced an educational system."

J: "Literacy rates really high. What else?"

St: "Great kings and leaders"

J: "Yes, God-fearing people, we English. We're doing God's work."

J: [Connects to *PL*]: "In *Paradise Lost*, in the Garden of Eden, why doesn't God just get rid of the snake [Satan]? If he did, that would censor man, thereby taking away his freedom. I hope you all see his rhetorical tricks, (same kind of arguments as) in the 'Prolusions'?"

St: [Develops her own analogy]: "It's like, teach a man how to fish and he . . ."

J: "Absolutely—give man choices, teach him how to make choices."

End of class.

Summary

At the halfway mark in the semester, Prof. J sees the fruits of his labor in the "literary" behavior of the class today. J starts off with a brief "reading quiz" followed by fifteen minutes or so of orienting lecture material, discussing *Areopagitica* as yet a further example of Milton's basic political and civic concerns—stretching back four classes to *Comus*, the "Prolusions," and "Of Education." Furthermore, as he builds this model of Miltonic civic virtue, J also gives the class a glimpse forward to *Paradise Lost*, the capstone of the course.

In this recursive context, he repeats his familiar *words du jour* pattern detailing the etymologies of the words employed during class and also conducts a debate on censorship as he covers the material. Prof. J has trained students to begin with Milton's arguments, understanding *Areopagitica* well enough to be able to use it—at times word-for-word from the tract—in their own discussion surrounding Prof. J's mock advocacy of censorship. Once they have internalized the issues from the text, they become capable of criticizing that which a moment before they were employing in defense of their own position. In that context—both understanding and criticizing the tract—his students become able to translate the formal properties of the argument for use in their own contemporary life. In effect, they have begun to act like situated learners and *do* most of the activities that a professional reader of Milton would do.

6

Step Five
Milton's *Paradise Lost*

O voi ch'avete li'ntelletti sani,
mirate la dottrina che s'asconde
sotto'l velame de li versi strani.

O you possessed of sturdy intellects,
observe the teaching that is hidden here
beneath the veil of verses so obscure.
                    —Dante, *Divine Comedy*, Canto IX.

In STEP FIVE, WE BEGIN THE OPENING HALF OF THE *PARADISE LOST (PL)* unit—the next six classes. Prof. J has set the groundwork through discussions of Milton's earlier and smaller verse and prose selections. Now he moves to the poet's masterpiece and spends considerable time acclimating the class to its major characters, themes, and unique problems. It seems, therefore, fruitful to divide our discussion of *PL* into two sections: the first six classes, where J tries to help students to understand the basic issues before them, and the second five classes (the last two were merely summaries), where they pick up speed and are sometimes able to anticipate what is needed to successfully complete their reading of Milton's epic creation.

CLASS SESSION 16: STEP FIVE

As Prof. J introduces *Paradise Lost* he confesses to a sense of "trepidation," because the class's journey to complete this masterpiece is such a long one. He therefore begins with an exhortation to see *PL* in the larger framework of all of Milton and to

148

consider the reader's place in that over-three-hundred-years' tradition:

> "We are . . . with Milton, looking at a context; Milton as a person, his life, his times. The things Milton writes about are things that concern us, too—they're our own concerns: How (for example) the outside world views you when you know things about yourself that the outside world doesn't know; (concerns with) with death, jobs, happiness, how Milton (seeks) to manipulate his audience, to 'work the crowd.'
>
> "All (of these) have a bearing on what turned out to be his major accomplishment, *Paradise Lost,* a major work in all of English literature. Whether or not you come to like *Paradise Lost,* it has been recognized (by educated readers for over three hundred years; indeed) from the beginning, and of everybody in England, in America, every literate person and any good writer who has read Milton for three centuries, most found it astounding, filled with bits of information. People have responded to it in human terms, and (so) you're sharing in something that for three hundred years every educated person has been involved in. You may still want to decline, but we're English majors, so . . ."

After this initial exhortation and motivational speech, J begins with a **brief overview** and some memory-type questions regarding the plot and the techniques required to read the epic successfully.

> J: "We'll journey, through Milton, the scope of the universe. When does *PL* begin and suddenly end? What has come before? Before the expulsion of fallen angels? Do Adam and Eve exist before (or after) the war in heaven? When you were a kid, (did you) ever hear of a war in heaven? [At this point, several students cough.] J jokes: "War brings that out, doesn't it?"
> St: "It begins in the pre-time, before the world begins."
> J: "Where does the 'Morning of Christ's Nativity' begin? When does this timeline end?"
> St: "[With the] Apocalypse."

J opens the classroom door to illustrate the timeline and points to the position of "Hell" out in the hallway.

> J: [Asking students to take out sheets done for homework]: "(The real) focus (here) is to read *PL,* and to read it out loud because it's

great *oral* poetry. What is the rhythm [scheme]? [To student] Give
us the first line, please."
St: [Student reads line badly.]

Prof. J models reading, emphasizing Milton's *synereses* (drop-
ping a syllable in 'disobedience,' making it four syllables instead
of five for the sake of the sentence meter) in Milton's first line
of iambic pentameter. J also emphasizes *enjambment*, reading
through one line into the next.

J:"What about rhyme scheme in the first six lines? It's heroic verse,
or blank verse: unrhymed iambic pentameter."

It is interesting here to look back on J's teaching of the sonnet
form in Class 3, Step Two, where he does *not* discuss such poetic
qualities as enjambment and synereses.[1] He believes that such
details come *after* students are more acquainted with the basics
and have had time to practice them.

At this point J moves the class into small groups and asks
them to share their homework assignment, proposing: "What
are the elements of an epic?"

> **Comment:** This *focus on genre* is very important because it
> sets up textual expectations in the reader, what Peskin[2]
> calls "structure as cue (grammatical units; stanzas; reso-
> nance between structure and content)."[3] Peskin contrasts
> novices with experts who were able to contextualize
> quickly—"to place the poem in a general context *con-
> strained by certain conventions pertinent to the genre* of a
> poem."[4]

After five minutes or so of group discussion, J leaves the students in their groups and draws their attention to line 1. He then
models reading *PL* out loud, the first twenty-six lines (or two
opening sentences). After reading for a few minutes, J begins a
whole-group question-and-answer in a manner called a "close
reading" of the poem's opening lines, simultaneously teaching
about the *beginning of this epic* and how to read *any poem's initial lines* by careful attention to images, word choice, and tensions among specific words and images:

J: "Fruit from *that* tree; what does "mortal" mean? The answer's right there in the text. Death (root of mortal)! Why do we die?"

St: "Because we took a bite of that fruit."

J: "It's the forbidden tree; we're all going to die, What do these seeds (of mortality) carry? What's all of our woe? One element—"

St: "That we die."

St: "That sin is inevitable."

Sts: "[We're] cold, dark, hungry, in pain . . ."

J: "[If] we know where the story is going to go, that allows for what?"

St: "[We do not] necessarily [have to] follow the plot."

J: "Right, [we can] focus on other things."

St: "See *Oedipus Rex* [relates intertextually]: the Greeks knew the plot beforehand and so that [knowledge] allows us to . . . [develops]."

J: "Right! (Makes another analogy): Before reading *Paradise Lost*, what did you know about the Bible?"

St 1: "I knew details of Adam and Eve."

St 2: "(I) knew the story of Christ . . ."

Following this intermixing of close reading and pointed questioning, J summarizes by saying that the "first twenty-six lines give us the subject of the whole poem."

Assigning Students as Teachers

Near the end of class J gives out topics for each of the several groups, who are to report their findings to the whole class. These topics include such things as examining characters' descriptions, analyzing Satan's persuasive rhetoric, a physical analysis of places such as "Pandemonium," looking up key words in the *OED*, and preparing a "close reading" of some lines in Book II. J suggests students consider a method of delivery "other than lecturing." He hopes they'll use a kind of "discovery learning" both as they teach the material and as they learn it themselves *to* teach it, so that it is, in Hammer's terms, "largely discovered and *emergent*."[5]

Summary

This class's pace is deliberate. Prof. J alternately lectures and asks memory-type questions during the first fifty minutes of the seventy-five-minute class. He uses now-familiar techniques: an overview of what is ahead during reading; a gloss of the epic's genre concerns; a quick review of Milton's poetic devices; a list of the speakers in Book I. He outlines the physical settings of heaven and hell and also places *PL* in relationship to Milton's other writings.

During the last fifteen minutes of class, he models what the (old) New Critics call a "close reading"[6] of the opening twenty-six lines of the poem and indicates that in these opening lines, Milton encapsulates the basic story. Indeed, Prof. J considers these first twenty-six lines so important that he asks all his students to memorize and recite these to him (privately)—a now-classic component of his Milton class. During the last ten minutes, J passes out assignments for next class and discusses general classroom procedures.

SESSION 17: STEP FIVE

During the opening few minutes of class, Prof. J reminds students of pending conferences. He offers choices for English papers and asks them to come up and confer.

> St: "Can we do our (first two sentences of *PL*) recitations then?"
> J: "Yes!"
> St: [Anxiously]: "What if we can't remember some of them?"
> J: [Joking]: "I'll prompt you."

As he tries to alleviate his student's anxiety level, J also reminds them to narrow their topics for the upcoming term paper.

J now begins the new material by lecturing and modeling close reading. Reminding the students that group work is ahead, he turns to *PL*'s first two sentences. J starts with close readings of lines 29 ff. and tells them about the Epic Question, saying that Adam's seduction reminds one of Comus's seduction: Comus's character *prefigured that of the devil*. J also discusses the status and motivation(s) of the chief actor of the poem (the infernal serpent, Satan), who causes things to happen. J draws an analogy to the motivation(s) in *The Odyssey* and *The Aeneid*. J alludes to the *embedded-ness* of the word *fire* (*fer*), in the word *infernal*.

> J: "Who gets deceived? Eve, the Mother of mankind? Why is Satan's seduction a vain attempt?"

St: "Satan's pride; but the battle is in vain. We know how it ends because we know the plot ahead of time."

J: "Milton gives us a teleological picture and an ontological picture as well." [To students generally]: "Watch for directions—heaven, hell, etc." [J mentions penal fire and discusses the root word for "punishment"].

J: "Line 50: what do the fallen angels fall into, literally and metaphorically, from Heaven to Hell? How do we see what's going on there?"

St: "From flames, it's "darkness visible."

J: [With relish]: "Great stuff, isn't it? Once you get to Hell, there is no hope; Beelzebub becomes Satan."

Here, J pauses in his lecture/discussion mode and asks, first hesitatingly, and then more forcefully, the **key question** of the morning:

J: "How could God make something good out of that terrible destruction? Can anything good come out of that? *And yes, that's a real question!*"

A long pause follows this question. Prof. J may have not allowed enough of a transition between the memory-type questions interspersed through his lecture and this more complex one. The silence of the class appears to reflect confusion rather than ignorance of the material. However, after one tentative answer, the class starts to respond with its regular energy:

St: "[God wanted to] prevent future uprisings?"

J: "What else?"

St: "[They will have to go about] rebuilding heaven."

J: "How will they fill in gaps? Where does man come from? When does this part take place? When does man arrive?"

St: "Man doesn't exist [as the angels are falling]?"

J: "Then when does man exist? What is God doing when they're falling?"

J: [Answers own question] "God's off creating the world and the people who eventually fill in the gaps and take the place of the fallen angels. God is making good out of bad. However, Satan is the ultimate deconstructionist, taking everything and undoing it."

One notices immediately how directive J is here as he asks "questions." What is of interest, however, is less the questioning technique (one that assumes the student's lack of familiarity with *PL*), and more the *motivational* statements, overtones, and outright exhortations. J's own enthusiasm for *PL* becomes *the* major topic of class conversation.

> J: "Moving quickly to ll. 192 ff.; if this were a play or a movie, how would you stage these two actors (God and Satan)? Are they sitting in chairs, talking?"

Repeating a technique used in teaching *Comus*, J asks students to visualize—in three-dimensional space—the characters speaking their lines.

> St: "They're on the lake, floating."
> J: "Yes, Satan is astonishingly big." [J reads appropriate lines] "In l. 282, how big is Satan's shield?"
> St: "Like a moon."

J recites lines and indicates Milton's allusion to Galileo; once again, the professor's relatively low- cognitive-level question becomes an instance for extratextual enrichment.

> J: "Look at lines 330 ff.—I love these lines!" [J reads with relish.] . . . "Listen to these lines," as he recites Satan's words; "Satan called so loud that . . ."
> Sts: "How loud did he call . . .?" [imitating late-night comedian's *schtick*.]
> J: "So loud, that . . ." [raises voice to high decibel levels and recites the lines loudly.]

This kind of joking and obvious *love for the text* itself is both an instance of a person enjoying his work and the *modeling for students of how English teachers behave* in the context of the literary materials to which they have devoted their lives.

J now moves to small-group work, asking each to report on the materials assigned since the last class session. He asks the first group, "Do you want to stay where you are or move up front?"

> J: [Draws student to ll. 615–20ff]: "Follow the reaction to Satan."
> St: "You [Prof. J] asked us to come up with two metaphors (see ll.

594–97). Note the contrasts between light and dark." [Students from group give relatively lengthy, strong, but often indistinct answers.] "Milton uses words like 'faithful' (1. 611) to describe the fallen angels, even though it's a disaster."

Student's *thinking* moves from single words to higher-level concepts like character analysis. As this student speaks, J writes the etymology of the word on the board: *Disasters* = *bad star*, or *bad sign*.

> St 1: "Second metaphor—614ff. [The other] angels have been burned but will still follow him (Satan)."
>
> St 2: "Even though (605–12) Satan is leading them to Hell, he is remorseful that they followed him."
>
> St 3: "In l. 620, is he crying?"
>
> J: "Does Satan say, 'I want to be your king'?"
>
> St 1: "No, [Satan lets] them choose."
>
> St 2: "Satan never says, follow him; better, [he] lets the fallen angels [decide] to choose him."
>
> J: "For next week, work on Book II. The rest of the groups will work on Tuesday of next week. I need five volunteer readers?"

Summary

This class continues Professor J's introduction to Milton's major epic. Although J largely controls the conversation in this class, leading students to specific textual passages and helping them to develop answers to his very pointed questions, his purpose is to build a solid foundation for one of the masterpieces of Western literature. J spends a considerable amount of time modeling *how* to read the passages from the poem, relishing the words and phrases in a way that shows (*by doing*, rather than by exhortation alone) how interesting and poetically powerful Milton's verse can be. J also asks the students to use dramatic visualization—to picture in three-dimensional space, the physical representation of major characters—as when they read *Comus*.

Then, J asks the small groups to report on the homework questions assigned. While tentative at first, students quickly become more authoritative in their answers as they employ such well-rehearsed J-type techniques as: (1) movement from word to high-level abstraction and back down to word again: (2) close attention to specific images and words as markers of a particular character; (3) the use of metaphors to create patterns of recognition in characters.

Finally, J promises the class that they would spend "all of next week" on Book II of *PL*. Thus, he will have spent four class periods and almost three calendar weeks on the first two Books. This time expenditure ensures a solid grounding in the basics of the epic before the students are allowed to push ahead to more difficult and complex matters.

Class Eighteen, scheduled for the previous Thursday, was canceled in order for Prof. J to present his scholarly paper on **Comus** *in Atlanta, Georgia. He bases this work on an idea derived from an earlier Milton class [See Interview # 2].*

Class 19: Step Five

Professor J. begins class with some of the usual housekeeping matters, then asks:

J: "Any questions about your reading?"

St 1: "I am confused about 'chaos' in *Paradise Lost*."

J: "For Milton, Chaos is a *place* between earth and hell. Where *else* is Chaos?"

St 2: "Where God is not."

J: "When God is not there, what happens in Chaos? Warring elements where there is unrest. It's a place *and a person*, a character. Satan has a wonderful line: "The mind has its own place, and can make heaven of hell or hell of heaven." Satan carries Chaos within himself."

St 3: [Challenging tone]: "Is there some reason *Chaos* is female?"

J: "Yes." [J is rather hesitant here.] "We noticed that there are few female characters in *PL*. We connect Satan and Adam whether you're male or female. We make the connection between Eve and the other female characters—Chaos, Sin, and Night. They are all part of Eve and *so are we*—all part of all literature—including Dickens and Lear. We know why Adam gives in—because we [must] as well. Your question is a good one."

St 3: [Argues]: "A friend's mother has a bumper sticker: 'Eve was framed.' Aren't women subordinate in Milton?"

J: "Yes and no. Think carefully about structure. Who's at the top of the universe? Where is the Son in this hierarchy? Satan is jealous that God moves the Son to be an equal of himself. (Lots ahead about Satan. Hierarchy in heaven.) Lots of people have written how misogynistic Milton was. But it's not because Eve is lesser, but what she has to do is just different. Following from the Bible, following one thousand years of tradition . . . in Milton's universe, he is quite liberal—but still hierarchical." [Nonverbal cues indicate student is not totally convinced.]

J: "What's one thing Adam is supposed to do?"

St: "Take care of Paradise."

J: "They are gardeners; they work because all Puritans work. Else?"

St: "Adam names all the animals . . ." (develops idea in detail).

J: "What's Eve's job?"

St: "She will procreate—terribly important. Sex in Paradise."

J: "What else does she do?"

St: "She serves Adam—the role she is given."

J: "But not subservient, Milton says. We have to separate our [contemporary] view of gender from Milton's (in the mid-seventeenth century). Adam [speaks] directly to God; Eve [goes to] God through Adam. To 'wait' on someone is respectful. One more quick question!"

St: "No death in paradise, right? What do the animals eat?"

J: "Milton never tells us—this is fantasy, a story, a myth. [Maybe] they're vegetarians. Does that help you to understand where women are in the universe? You have to have a hierarchy . . . Adam feels inadequate without Eve, and she is inadequate without him. Where does Eve come from?"

St: "Out of Adam's rib."

J now moves the class into small groups to complete the reports begun the previous class period. "Let's get back to where we were; get back into groups."

J: [Continues lecture]: "(There were) so many angels sprawled in hell, they looked like leaves." [J then asks groups about Satan's angels.]

St 1: Group 2, Meredith reports (concerning ll. 641–43) in detail.

St 2: Amanda reports and reads out loud from text (l. 654) in detail.

J: "Good comments from your group." [Reads from ll. 630 ff]: "Look how picturesque these lines are. What's going on here? Tone shifts?"

St: "It's a riot!"

J: "Yes, it's a riot of swords. Physically, what do they do?" [Here J insists that students see these scenes in their *dramatis-tic* aspect.]

"This is how they're cheering Satan; when all the devils riot, you have *Pandemonium.*"

J then connects Milton's description of a "fabric huge" to the description of St. Peter's Cathedral in Rome (part of Milton's antipopish sentiments). Most students would not make the connection to architectural styles, so here Prof. J inserts this topic:

J: "What is Milton describing?"
St: "Like the Pantheon in Rome?"
J: "Yes—I was there this spring: What big cathedral is in Rome?"
St: "Saint Peter's."
J: "Why does Milton use St. Peter? [Pause] What would be your guess?"
St: "Laughing at the pope (and at Catholics generally)."
J: "What else?"
St: "ll.795 , Milton, uses word 'conclave'—like the Bishops in Rome—a further parody of the Church of Rome."
J: "What does this word *conclave* mean? *Con* is 'with'—like *chile con carne*—and *clavia* means 'keys.' When the College of Cardinals elects a new pope they're locked in a room to which no one has the key, and [they] cannot come out until they've elected a new pope. What's electing a new pope have to do with devils?"
St: "Satan is campaigning to be elected by the College of Devils."

Prof. J has used his *words du jour* to provide students support in making an analogy from one element of Miltonic literary parody (*pace* those who are members of the Roman Catholic Church) to a textual problem in *PL*. Thus, J moves his students up the ladder of abstraction, from the word *conclave* to a crucial element of Milton's larger textual parody of the church: Satan and his fellow devils act (or wish to act) just as Milton imagines (that a member of the Protestant Anglican Church would imagine) a group of Catholic dignitaries acting.
End of Class.

Summary

J is slowly building his students' knowledge of the cast of characters, the setting (both physical and metaphysical), and some of the important themes in *PL*. J builds students' baseline knowledge through a focus on individual words (his *words du jour*). These words lead students to consider much more complex issues at the level of character, theme, and genre. He also continues to model how English professors build their interpretations of a text by accretion of single words and phrases and speculating; by trying out how the poet intends the reader to move his mental focus from the smallest (word) level to image, to character analysis, to theme, to genre, and so on.

Session 20: Step Five

Professor J asks if everyone has signed up for next week's recitation of the first two sentences of *Paradise Lost*. Following various class announcements, J (as always) **sets up the context** of what will happen in the beginning of this chapter of this epic poem:

> J: "Now we move to the beginning of Book II and take a look at 'hellish politics.' This is a great political debate, and Satan subtly lays out the platform of 'what Satan wants.'"

In a brief two minutes J sets out Satan's basic argument, consisting of three major points: (1) The war isn't over yet; we can fight again and hope to win; (2) If we stay here, maybe God will forgive us and at least it won't get worse; this land is ours by rights and maybe we can cultivate Hell; (3) There *is* mankind on earth.

> J: "Turn to page 232 [in *PL*; l. 42–43]; we have three major speakers, Satan, Moloch, and Belial." [J sets up a stage in the front of the room for a debate.] "Let's move the speakers to the front of the room."

In this class, **speakers are prepared,** as J builds on the exercises done with the "Prolusions" earlier in the semester.

> J: "Milton gives us stage directions." [J asks a student to read Moloch's speech.]
> St: [Reads lengthy passage. The student still is unable to enjamb appropriate lines and so garbles some.]
> J: [After the student finishes his reading]: "In a nutshell, he says what?"

St: "It can't get any worse than now."
J: "[Repeats]; We have nothing to lose. So what?"
St: "It's a 'do or die' situation."

Following this discussion, J **bridges** to the next (Belial's) speech, which a student reads aloud while standing in front of class.

J: [To class]: "In a nutshell, what is Belial saying?"
St: "If we stay out of trouble, maybe God will forgive us."
J: "God will forgive us—at least it won't get worse. *Why* does Belial argue like that?"
St: [Objects and selects lines. J asks for line numbers.]
J: "You're right, but read the rest of the line—we don't want to tick-off God."

Here, J insists that students avoid the temptation to embrace immediate impressions, encouraging them to look at the whole context and argue from that position. Impulsive analyses are a major problem with novice readers.

J: "What's the effect of Belial's speech? The effect of his going second is that he undoes Moloch's speech. The most important part of this argument is . . . where?"
St: "[The] last."

J then draws attention to Milton's argumentative tactics in the "Prolusions," in his essays, and so relates Book II of *PL* to students' prior knowledge. Thus far, J has repeatedly alternated between his *bridging* and student's *reading*. He then asks the student to read additional lines; following that reading, the text indicates that the devils give the speaker much applause. J asks students to applaud (lots of laughs, joking). He continues:

J: "Describe the elements of Hell. Physically; it has a wall—just as Heaven and Eden. Go to line 629; [to student] read 630—35."
St: [Student reads.]
J: Satan never takes a straight path, always wondering, 'casing the joint' . . . [There are] nine gates to hell. It's foreboding."

Through the end of this period, J reads and explicates the text. He mentions the following **wordplay:** the left side means sinister; the right side is called *dexter.* "Sin is perfect image of Satan." J explains the allegory of Satan producing sin.

Summary

During this class students read out loud, in front of the whole class, the debate by the devils. The devils' chief concern was what to do next, and Milton captures the vagaries of political debate, including the give-and-take of arguments (issues presented as open for discussion when in fact those in control have already made a decision) and the relief that the devils feel at the end of the chapter when a decision is finally made.

In many ways this chapter of *PL* is enjoyable to read out loud. By having **prepared to read,** most students are prevented from garbling the fairly subtle political satire. Several students take turns, some reading for just four or five minutes and others for almost ten. J provides "bridges" between each reading, by asking questions related to the material or by reading and interpreting the transitional material himself. As ever, J's good sense of humor—"You're not *grave* enough," he offers to the one reading Satan's later, "grave" lines—keeps the class engaged and occasionally laughing.

J draws attention to the relationship between Milton's satiric, argumentative style in the "Prolusions" and his nearly identical use of it in *PL*. This weaving of a rich fabric of **prior knowledge with the newer threads** of the current chapter give students not only a better sense of the chapter, but of the whole that is Miltonic literature. Prof. J also continues his use of *words du jour* as an extension and embellishment to class conversation.

At this point, I still see little student-to-student debate. Much of the disputation about the meanings of lines and the nature of the various characters is still between individual students and Prof. J. He has been socializing them. Now may be the time to let some of that socialization work without overt direction.

<h2 style="text-align:center">SESSION 21: STEP FIVE</h2>

J **sets the context** of the last quarter of Book II, *Paradise Lost.* By reading aloud from selected passages and by asking a series of memory-type questions, J briefly characterizes the major figures in Hell who will travel to earth to confront Adam and Eve and discusses the trip Satan makes from inside the bowels of Hell to Earth via the famous "Closed Gates of Hell."

J: "As Satan is moving toward the Gates of Hell, he speaks to the guardian of the Gates, his own daughter, Sin, referring to her as his 'daughter dear.'" [J goes on to talk about incest with Sin, producing Death.] "This is a complex family tree. What does Death do (son of Satan and Sin)?"

St: "Death is the father of the hell hounds—Satan's grandchildren."

J: "Right. Who is the mother of the hell hounds? Sin! [794 ff] 'Dear'in this context also means expensive; how is sin costly to Satan? What has it cost him to have a daughter like Sin?"

St: "He lost his place in heaven . . ."

J: [Correcting statement he made last class period]: "Last time you asked the gender of Chaos; what I told you was wrong and I apologize. Chaos *is* male; 'dark night' is female. [Repeats]: Chaos is male; dark night is female. Look at page 254, lines 927–28, where Satan spreads his wings. What's the course of his flight?" [J reads lines.] "Satan never goes straight. He winds up, falls down, since Chaos is filled with warring elements. He is not alone [see l. 1025] and doesn't know this."

St: "Sin and Death go with him—they pave a . . ."

J: "Road of bricks, a broad highway: why the *broad* highway?"

St: "So lots of people can follow."

J: "Finally Satan gets to glimpse 'empyreal Heav'n,' that was 'once his native seat.' He is weather-beaten by now. Notice the rhythm of these scenes!"

J: "In Book III, the first fifty-three lines, the narrator gives an 'ode to light.' We move, in l. 56, to another place in the universe—heaven (where) we find interesting things about the Father. (Let us) list the attributes of God—(and do it in small groups of) twos and threes."

After about fifteen minutes of writing and talking the students have over twenty items listed. J then moves back to a mix of bridging, lecturing, and memory-type questions:

J: "We hear little about the Holy Spirit. Satan parodies these; recall in Book II that Mammon wants to make hell a cheap imitation of life in Heaven."

J: "What does God know?"

St 1: "[Isn't He] setting us up to be sinners?"

St 2: "If He's all-knowing, He has known about the battle in heaven."

St 3: "Why send his Son?" [develops this question.]

St 4: "If He values free will, He is nevertheless judging . . ."

> **Comment:** This is one of the relatively few times so far that
> the **students take over the questioning** in class. The stu-
> dents are having a difficult time understanding the issues
> and paradoxes surrounding the concept of "free will," as is
> elaborated in Milton generally and in *PL* in particular. J ac-
> knowledges their concerns and attempts to answer them
> with analogies—moving from difficult discussions in verse
> to more comprehendible examples.

J: "This is most difficult part (of) Milton's theology. [J uses the comparative metaphor of grades]: Milton is predestinarian. [Imagine]
if I say to you, 'Six of you will receive As and six, Fs, no matter
what—do what you will—and you will not know until you're dead
which you received and why.'"

St: [Quizzical] "If He (God) knows all, (there's) no such thing as free
will?"

J: "Then, if there is no such thing as free will, we're stuck, given how
Milton values free choice."

St: "Depends on the perspective, doesn't it? 'I know you'll get an A
because of your merits' is different from 'I make you get As (or
Fs).' He (God) just watches you do what you would have anyway."

J: "Yes!"

J reinforces the student's answer by jumping up and standing on
top of the desk, joking and waving to someone walking by outside the room. He has everyone's attention! From his new van-
tage point, J uses the metaphor of watching while students no. 1
and no. 2, each being given a car, race around the bottom of a
mountain and crash. From the perspective from the desktop (the
metaphoric mountain), he can see an accident coming.

J: "That's the position of Milton's God. Look at all the warnings
from God to Adam and Eve throughout *PL*. Remember *Areopagitica*'s 'I cannot admire a cloistered virtue.'?"

St: [Articulates J's analogy and lecture in her own words.]

J: "We'll pick up on page 268, Books III and IV for Thursday."

Summary

Professor J and his class are now deeply immersed in the gritty
details—including character building, plot movement, and difficult thematic concerns—that make up this master epic in the

English language. In this class, the students took charge of class
conversation by **asking authentic questions** about Milton's ideas
of free will. As Arthur Applebee has said, this "is the way we
gain knowledge-in-action in any arena, through gradual immer-
sion in new conversations rather than by standing alongside and
being told about them."[8]

Session 22: Step Five

Prof. J begins by commenting on the beautiful day.

J: "We have a long way to go and some really, really good stuff [to
cover] this morning. I'll recap Book II and then we'll move to
Books III and IV." [J asks a student to remind the class what happened at the end of Book II.]

St: "Satan learns about his children and grandchildren; he takes his
trip through chaos where Satan never goes in a straight line. The
narrator then encounters the light and, at the beginning of Book
III, gives the famous 'Apostrophe to Light': 'Hail Holy Light.'" [A
student interrupts with a single word, "God."]

J: "Yes, God is always watching and listening. Let's return to the
speculation of the previous class. Why does God allow this (Satan's flight to earth, etc.) to happen? What's the answer?"

Here, J is not merely reviewing assimilated materials, but actively **resuscitating the debate** from the last class. He moves
them to recall the debate, and reinforces the class's conclusions.

St: "Free choice—a la *Areopagitica*."

J: "Yes. Adam and Eve were warned over and over, but it's still their
choice. Just think, a few months ago you didn't even know what
Areopagitica was—some awful after-shave lotion."

J rewards them by mentioning their collective in-class history
and how much they've learned in a short period of time.

J: "Without [God's hands-off policy] we wouldn't have free choice."

Then, J asks them to "reprise" what Group One said in the previous
class period:

J: "Who can give us some information about the opening of Book III
and some things stated by Group One last period"?

Sts: [Students list items.]

J: "(This is a) major point in Milton. Everything you do has cosmic connections."

J: "How about Group Two? Let's look at comparisons between the Father and the Son. Summarize what you're learned so far."

St 1: "Satan uses power differently from the Father" [and develops ideas further].

St 2: "Satan and God are each the head of a hierarchy."

St 3: "Satan is going to trick human beings."

J: "These are all good." [J refers to leadership models, God and Satan; each have different modes of leadership.]

J: "Question: Does the end goal justify the means?"

St: "I (noticed) the different relationships of father and children. The Father and the Son have a mutual and loving relationship, like a [human] father and son. Whereas with his daughter, Sin (l. 345), Satan wants something from his daughter, and his incestuous relationship with Sin is different from that of the Father and Son."

J: "Good! *I hadn't thought of that.* Those relationships—you're quite right, the way they function [differently] with their offspring."

J appears honestly surprised and impressed. The tone of his response to this student is genuinely pleased—as if J had just learned something from a teacher. At this point, the class's response pattern shifts from the previous memory-driven question-and-answer sessions to one of mutual investigation. J still leads the class discussion, but his **willingness to have his own thinking modified** by the student's answer, beyond "uptake," signals **mutual collaboration** and what Nystrand calls "high level responses."[9]

J: "Let's move on. Why doesn't Satan know where to go [on his trip to earth]?"

St: "The earth wasn't created yet."

J: "See line 498 (Book III); Satan glimpses the light of heaven. [Does this] remind you of another gate?"

St: "The Gate of Hell."

J: "How big? 'So all the universe can pour in,' the Nine-Fold Gate of Hell. Is Heaven's Gate that wide? (L. 516). In Heaven's Gate, the ladders are drawn up, like . . .? What's the biblical story?" [J is genuinely searching for the allusion.]

St: "Jacob's ladder."

J: "Right—I knew it had a "Jeeh" sound. Group 3: 'Satan sees the world (earth) for the first time.' I asked you to look up in this passage the imagery of sight."

St: "[There are lots of] references to what Satan can see."

J: "Right—lots of terms for seeing; what else?"

St: "[Vision] leads to insight (see 1. 635): Satan [lands] on the sun."

J: "What's he referred to when he lands there? A sun spot, a blot on the sun. From Satan's place on the sun, he sees Uriel and Satan changes form."

St: "Nothing that we've seen is exactly what we expect it to be."

J: "Right. The fire on the lake is not fire; Satan gives a great speech, but later we see he is lying down."

By now, the **students are well-socialized** to use the text, for answers and to help settle disputed issues. They do so as regularly and as naturally as J, and with as good effect.

St 1: [To J] "Look at 1. 542."

J: "Isn't that a wonderful passage—reminds me of that shot of the Earth from the Moon. Satan discovers something unaware—a new 'prospect' . . ."

J: "Other things; [To students] you're on a roll. How can Uriel be fooled by Satan?"

St 2: "Lines 680–85; neither man nor angel can discern hypocrisy."

J: "What line are you on?"

St 2: "Line 680–85."

J: "Say more about it."

St 2: [Reads lines and explains]: "The ability to see evil is unknown to angels and man before the Fall. Only God sees evil because He alone knows it. The Tree in the garden is a tree of good and evil."

J: "Tricking means being seduced by hypocrisy. It is part of free will: Uriel is the sharpest-sighted spirit of heaven." [Reads lines.]

St 1: "This passage reinforces how God sees all."

St 2: "I got the sense that Satan wasn't acting; just observing."

J: "Right—he's prospecting; what Satan does a lot of—now think of this: [He] stands on the outside and watches."

St: "He's like a stalker, a voyeur."

J: "All right; we need to move quickly. Near end of Book III . . ."

St: "[Interrupts]: Satan wants to see what God created."

J: [Repeats line out loud.] "Uriel! Why don't you (Satan) know about it? What's Satan's response to Uriel?"

St: "He wants to see for himself because he wasn't there at the creation."

Prof. J. begins Book IV of *PL* with a quick summary of the opening, and mentions the process of moving from Book III to

IV. He connects the tone of the narrative voice to an audience of children at a horror movie; J **constantly translates the text** into areas students would know from their own knowledge.

> J: "What is and what makes a *soliloquy* a soliloquy?"
> St 1: "It's a speech, like Hamlet's—speaking alone."
> J: "What can you do in a soliloquy that you can't when others hear [you]?"
> St 3: "[You get a better] sense of how a character's mind works."
> J: "Look at lines 32–132—almost a hundred lines."

In what follows, J and the students are now **trading line numbers and insights.** In at least one of these exchanges(*), the student anticipates J's question and answers it even before the question is completely asked:

> J: "Wow! Input line. He hates the word, 'submission.' But there's also his 'dread of shame.' Satan has seduced other spirits—in [this] century, we always talk about seduction and . . ."
> St: "Sex."
> J: "Yes, sex is in there too. Does anyone recall how he gets into the garden? Satan's seduction of Eve is like his penetration of the Garden of Eden. He goes over the wall; what else?"
> St: "Satan knows he is evil (l. 110)." [Student reads]: "'Evil, be thou my good.' See also lines 642–43."
> J: [Responds with delight at the rolling around of the words in the student's mouth and repeats the line.] "Satan can't stop—he's addicted, and when you're addicted, you've lost [your] free will. Ok—what else—if I [Satan] repented, what would happen?"
> St: "See l. 39. [Satan's] pride and ambition threw him down."
> J: "Yep—even if I repented, I (Satan) would do it all over again. Thus, Satan is an absolute prisoner of his own character and he doesn't have a choice because . . ."
> *St: "See ll. 81–84. [Satan] would never submit because he knows that he's a Seducer and wouldn't be [willing to share with] lesser spirits."
> J: "Yes! We can admire his admission of all these things—but he continues what he's going to do anyway (l.125–30). Uriel sees him disaffirmed; his [Satan's] force (light) is dimmed."

The end of the class is worth noting. After discussing the geographical and allegorical elements in the Garden, J takes them to the word, "insinuating," used to describe how Satan navigates into and around the Garden. He has the class read, **in choral form,** the specific lines connecting Satan, his mode of travel, its meaning, and its future allegorical import.

> J: "Where do Adam and Eve spend most of their time?"
> St: "Their bower" [class laughs].
> J: "Yes, their sexual relationship is very important. Looking at ll. 393–535, we move further into the Garden. Milton develops Eden. Look at the kind of animal Satan becomes ('four-footed kind'). He turns into several and it isn't until l. 333 that he becomes a serpent."
> J: [J has students read lines out loud and in chorus]: "' . . . close to Serpent sly insinuating.' What's this called? *Onomatopoeia.* (Book IV, l. 347) Look at the word *insinuating.* Anyone ever had a sinus headache? Sinuses coil, and the word, *insinuate,* means 'coil.' Note the word inside: *sin.*"

J hands out a short assignment and collects the *Cards o' Doom.* He tells them, "Nice job, all of you," as students leave class.

Summary

This is the most interesting class of the opening *Paradise Lost* sequence. Rather quickly, and for almost the whole period, the discussion increasingly resembles the give-and-take of an ordinary conversation. The students are clearly learning to discuss Milton by staying very close to the text—by using the actual lines and making reference to specific line numbers. Student interviews suggest that their "reports" are largely based on their homework rather than from small group interaction. Nonetheless, the whole group class conversation is fast-flowing, very detailed, and stimulating. It clearly represents J's socialization. By the end of Step 5, J has taken six of the allotted eleven class periods to introduce students to *Paradise Lost,* to socialize them into reading it well, and to continue to weave into this new fabric all of the earlier learning his class achieved about Milton and his writings.

One should note the typical learning patterns that are by now ingrained in almost every class: (1) a casual, friendly attendance that moves seamlessly into the class's work for the day; (2) J's review of key elements from the last class period; (3) liberal use of *words du jour,* with repetition during the period; (4) small-group work alternating with whole-group conversations; (5) J's use of "priming"—a focusing of students' attention and the use of motivational exhortations—as he assigns work for the next class; (6) J's apparently casual feedback via the "Cards o' Doom," a randomized homework check that uses humor to soften what is essentially a policing activity.

The next and last Step will be to finish *Paradise Lost*.

7

Step Six: Completion of *Paradise Lost*

> Subjectivity may change the way the world looks, but it does
> not change the world. Conversely, objectivity limits what
> there is to see, but it does not determine how the mind will
> see it. [If] one takes it for granted that subjectivity and objec-
> tivity are intrinsically related, that this is the natural rhythm
> of thought, there is nothing in the distinction between them
> to be particularly worried about. The trouble begins when it
> is supposed that subjectivity means that we cannot know the
> object at all, or that the reality of the objective must at all
> costs be defended against subjective distortion. And it is pre-
> cisely along these categoric, winner-take-all lines that the
> battle over what the university can presume to teach with in-
> tegrity has come to be waged.
>
> —Charles W. Anderson, partly quoting Juliana Hunt

SESSION 23: STEP SIX

As THIS CLASS BEGINS, THE STUDENTS IMMEDIATELY ASK QUESTIONS
about the term paper, formatting, citations, and so on. Dr. J responds, discussing citations and the format for referencing *Paradise Lost* (*PL*) in research papers. He then prepares the class by
indicating plans to finish Book IV and go on to Book V. For the
first fifteen minutes, J conducts a drill-like question and answer
on the geography of *Paradise* based on questions asked in the Assignment Sheet no. 3; the students seem generally on-task and
able to answer. After a few minutes of these questions, however,
one of the students asks a question (immediately below) *that
sets off an interesting exchange* about imagination and realism:

St 1: "Is the Garden of Eden in Paradise, or is it Paradise?"
J: "Both; Paradise is on earth—supposedly in Mesopotamia in the
near-East."
St 2: "Doesn't the Crucifixion take place on a hill also?"

J: "Right; good connection. Where is Pandemonium?

St: "In many myths, there is a tree connecting earth and heaven."

J: [Alluding to a previous class where students provided this answer]: "Does this remind us of Jacob's ladder—the staircase from Heaven to Earth? Milton and poets generally keep putting the tree on a hill and God on a tree on hill, and so on."

St 1: "Why do we learn about the creation in Book VII?"

St 2: "Because God created the earth, etc., in seven days."

J: "Remember we discussed how epics are structured? They're not in chronological order, but begin—what's that phrase?—*in medias res*. Hence, we don't fully get to the seven days of creation until Book VII. Answer your question about Paradise? Where is Hell?"

St: "Satan is hell."

J: "Satan carries Hell with him. Where would you guess (parallel with Hell) Paradise is?"

St: "Wherever God is—is heavenly."

J: [Recites from *PL* lines students had to memorize to illustrate these points]: "'Inside (the soul) is far more important than outside.'"

At this point, many **students know enough background information to contribute** material to the discussion and so collectively build upon the description and organization of Paradise in Book IV.

J: "Why is Satan watching? How does Satan respond to what he sees?"

St: "They're [Adam and Eve] happy; Satan wants to see what they are."

J: (Ref. lines 395–96): "They are blissfully happy, all the things he (Satan) is not; if you dwell on it . . .?"

St: "He's jealous."

J: "Yes. It's the same emotion that got him into trouble in Heaven. See Satan's first soliloquy."

J: "Which side of the Garden does Satan enter?"

St: "(From the) West."

J: "Yes. The East is associated with good, light, sunrise, God; the West with death and the setting of the sun. What's Gabriel waiting for?"

St: "Waiting? What are you asking?"

J: "Gabriel is waiting for Satan." [J continues his running narrative.]

St: [Corrects J]: "I thought Satan tricked Uriel?"

J: [Apologizes]: "I'm sorry; you're absolutely right." [Makes joke]:

"It's good you're paying attention. I did it on purpose!" [Students laugh.]

Clearly, these students are following J closely. They are immersed in the particulars of both *PL* and Miltonic knowledge; they have also been socialized into disagreeing with J when he makes a slip of the tongue or presents an issue with which they disagree. They are not merely receivers but *legitimate participants in the ongoing conversation*, albeit at a lesser level of expertise.

Following a brief discussion of Gabriel guarding the Gate of Paradise, J uses his w*ords du jour* technique during the next exchange to describe Milton's controversial ideas of Adam's supremacy and Eve's willing obedience to the hierarchy of God, Adam, Eve, and the rest of creation:

J: "Look at line 610: Adam says to Eve, 'Let's to bed.' Line 635, Eve replies to him as her 'author and disposer.' Adam sets her schedule; she's aware of the order of things; God rules Adam; Adam rules Eve: 'To know no more / Is woman's happiest knowledge and her praise': line 637. Ironic, given what's coming." [Here, J jokes about differences between Miltonic values and the more "enlightened" present.] "Eric. Wipe that smile off your face!"

St: "Since she does nothing of her own will except by Adam's permission, *he* is in a sense responsible for the Fall." [She develops this further.]

J: [Genuinely pleased] "Yes!—It's a tricky situation; her responsibility is to be submissive, her role is to obey Adam. She provides the sensitivity he doesn't have. Granted, these are stereotypes, but Milton suggests their (complementary) nature."

Mini-lecture: "Look at line 687; 'Hand in hand, they go to their bower.'

[J's aside]: "Remember, in *PL*, hand images are important."

[He continues]: "In *PL*, when things are going well they go *hand in hand. [WDJ] Alone* means 'all one' (all together); *atonement* means 'at-one-ment,' a variation on this. Eve is more lovely than Pandora. Recall? *Pan* means 'all'; *dora* means 'gifts.'

"Adam and Eve then enter their bower and, like good pre-Christians, praise God for His gifts before they make love. They are unanimous. This means what? *un* means 'one'; *animus* means 'spirit'; hence, *unanimous* means 'one spirit.' Milton says that sex is a beautiful part of their relationship. Eve is Milton's idea of a perfect wife; Adam, the perfect husband; their marriage is a perfect marriage. Remember, in the opening of Book III, 'Hail holy light?' Well, here it's 'Hail holy marriage.'" [J's prompt recalls relationships between earlier knowledge and current issues via Milton's lyrical passages.]

J: "Group Six: Given the above, what changes do you see in Satan?"

St 1: "Satan must take a step back, [knowing] the battle with Gabriel's lost."

St 2: [Lengthy answer] ". . . Satan becomes enormous; and becomes dimmer [since] Lucifer means the 'light-bringer.'"

St 3: "Satan is angry with God and wants to fight God."

J: "Book V takes different tack; we'll see more on Eve as character. What is her dream about?"

St 1: "She dreams she takes a bite out of the forbidden fruit."

St 2: "A toad whispered in her ear. It wouldn't have occurred to her on her own."

End of Class # 23.

Summary

J has socialized his class *to participate in the weaving of class-room dialogue* by (1) questioning J's authority when they disagree with his statements; (2) contributing their own substantially growing knowledge to the discussion; (3) laughing or indicating via nods and body language that they follow his jokes and his self-deprecating asides. J uses *words du jour* to help students see interpretations via analogies and etymologies.

SESSION 24: STEP SIX

J: [Moves class into small groups.] "We were just getting started on Book V and we have to whip through Book V. We open with Eve's bed (or premonitory) dream, a good literary device. Eve tells Adam—and in doing so tells us, the reader."

J: "Let's draw this [small group work] to a close. Ok, Book V, lines 136–208, the morning prayer." [To student 1]: "You who caught me in error the other day [jokes]; look at line 139 ff. How do these lines describe [why] prayer is important?"

St 1: "They're Puritan-like; Milton pokes fun at Catholics."

J: "If you learned formal prayers—that's not what Adam and Eve do."[1]

J: "I asked Group One—what did you find similar to the Book of Psalms?"

St 1: "[The real] question is, what's not like the Psalms." [Student reads ll. 205ff., and describes contents of prayer/psalms.]

J: "Other people in Group One! Anything to add?"

St 1: [jokes] "No—I've said it all!"

J works through the groups' findings in response to their hand-out sheet from the previous class. The most notable exchange follows:

J: "What are the concerns Adam has?"

St: "Doesn't he wonder if angels really eat?"

J: "Raphael is a sociable angel. What do the angels do about bodily functions?"

St: "Raphael says that heaven's fruit is different from others, from mankind's food."

J: "See line 519! [Reads]: 'Be happy—all you owe is to God.' What does the word *immutable* mean? Think about this in literary terms; what does this allow Milton, the writer, to do?"

St: [Jason]: "[This strategy] allows him [Milton] to do whatever he wants to do [with naturalistic detail]." [Student elaborates.]

Comment: As this exchange makes clear, students have been following the idea of the epic poem as an artistic construct, containing details not necessarily amenable to rational or naturalistic logic. As Jane Hirshfield has pointed out concerning (mostly) American students and readers: "Americans distrust artful speech, believing that sincerity and deliberation cannot coexist. The sentiment has root in the last century: 'A line will take hours, maybe; / Yet if it does not seem a moment's thought, / Our stitching and un-stitching has been naught,' Yeats wrote in 'Adam's Curse.' Romantic temperament, he knew, equates spontaneity and truth."[2] This romantic temperament does not apply to Milton himself, of course, but it is worth noting that such is the mind-set with which most contemporary American students start reading him.

In the next exchange, the student explains his answer with a specific textual reference in mind:

St: "Who speaks? Does Milton say this?"
J: "Well, it's the narrator." [He delivers] a long description . . ."
St: "I see a comparison between the way Satan talks to his companions (l. 673) and the way he talks to Eve."
J: "EXCELLENT!! Sin! [to student]: Your point is excellent! Satan is envious?"
St 1: "Of Adam."
St 2: "[There were] similar lines in Book II, when Satan talked to Beelzebub about corrupting man (ll. 703 ff)."
J: "We're reminded (in ll. 720 ff) of that, even as Satan is plotting."

After another exchange and near the end of class, J reads a lengthy passage. His students react as second-graders listening to a storyteller:

J: "This is one of my favorite parts of *PL*. Look at l. 873." [J reads aloud to end of Book V.] "We'll stop with that. We're only one Book behind. For Tuesday, the Battle of Heaven. Great stuff!"

End of Class no. 24.

Summary

Professor J's last words this period "prime" the class for the next period's readings. As with the last class, students continue to exhibit active listening and active participation, whether the teaching technique is lecture, class discussion, or small-group reports. For most of this class, the reports have an **interactive quality.** As J asks questions of the groups' reporters, they in turn ask him for clarification of certain items. Beyond mere exposition of details, students are *developing an interest in Milton's artistry* and the strategies he uses to explain what could be problematic: angels are not corporeal, but students still wonder what they ate and how they eliminate waste. The class members' collaborative sense continues.

SESSION 25: STEP SIX

J begins this class with a discussion of reference citations in student term papers, then turns to Book VI of *Paradise Lost:*

J: "Do you recall the last character from the other day? I've thought a lot about him. Do you remember what we focused upon in the sonnets [at the beginning of the semester]?"

St: "Milton, himself."

J: "Think of Milton's personal life. [Do you] recall the peer pressure?"

St: "He was called the 'Lady of Christ's.'"

J: "I really think that Abdiel is one of Milton's heroes. Milton projects himself into Abdiel." [Moving to another topic]: "Remember, there is no break between Books V and VI. God's will forces them into battle; this is a seventeenth-century battle, and the battle scenes are based on actual battles as well as on classic battle theory."

Dr. J follows this lead-in with a somewhat lengthy combination of lecture and reading aloud from the text, with a few memory-questions thrown in. Students seem slow today, perhaps because J controls much of the class tempo and information direction. An example follows:

J: "[Look at] lines 344, 355: Gabriel fights with Moloch. How many days are there in an epic battle?" [Answers own Q]: "Three days. So, at the end of the first day, [it's] good guys, 1; rebels, 0. What happens after first day's battle?"

St 1: "Satan goes over the battle."

J: "Then what does he say?"

St 1: "The devils need better equipment."

St 2: "I have a quick question—can you tell which name is on whose side?"

J: "Good Question! It's not easy, because some of the angels still have heavenly names." [After giving some answers, J returns to his earlier question]: "What can he [Satan] do [get] for really good equipment?"

St 1: [Unsure] "A tank?"

J: [Not the correct answer.] "(It's) more than a . . ."

St 2: "[He gets] a cannon."

Now J moves to the homework assigned from the previous class (with explicit directions that students were to explicate ll. 825–912 for today's class). Discussion improves in these last few minutes, as students are better able to speak their minds about this or that element in the text.

Prof. J opens with a mini-lecture:

J: "In every epic, there are three days of fighting. During this second-day battle, the angels start throwing boulders, and even mountains [out of] real frustration [with the power of the cannons]. See line 671; the Son is the victor of the third day, as God ordains the third to be His (line 713)."

St: "See line 833; is this reference to the Son or to someone else?"

J: [Answers by reading the text aloud. Student sees the answer.]

St: "Isn't this a connection to the *Four Horseman of the Apocalypse?*"

J: "There's the number *four* again. Other things learned here?"

St 1: "Line 854: I thought it was interesting that the Shepherd [image of Christ] heads a flock of Goats [devils], not Sheep [people]."

St 2: "Yes, shepherding the Goats to the wall (surrounding earth)."

J ends the period (after a few more memory-questions) with a brief summary of Book VI, and then prepares students for the next class where they will be reading Book VII as well as parts of the Bible, in order to compare the Creation story with Milton's version. J reminds students that term papers are due at the next class.

Summary

Slow class this day. Perhaps because J controls the discussion and pacing for the first forty-five minutes, students seem to have lost their participatory enthusiasm from the previous class. The few good exchanges with students appear to suggest that when the class is called upon to perform they can and will, but like many university students they are perfectly willing to let the professor do all of the talking at times. This session is one of the very few where J's need to "cover the material" takes precedent over his concern for student interaction and engagement. However, as Do and Schallert have recently pointed out, when "students' general affective response to the current context was positive, they paid more attention to what was occurring in class at the moment, moving immediately to deep listening."[3] Anyone viewing the video recording of this class would find most students in a "deep listening" mode.

SESSION 26: STEP SIX

J: "I'll collect your papers today and return them by Tuesday next [a quick turn around]. I asked you to bring bibles and Book VII of *PL.*

Milton was only three years old when the King James Bible was first published. A committee of over fifty wrote it. What happens in first [chapters] of Genesis? The Creation stories. Which does Milton use? Milton used the second version of the Creation story [in *PL*].

"I'll read, then someone else jump in for a couple of verses." [Reads out aloud, followed by several students, for almost fifteen minutes.]

J: [Exhorts class]: "Isn't this just beautiful language? You've done enough Milton analysis; now just *feel* the language. Notice?"

St: "There's a real slow cadence."

J: "Why couldn't you read faster?"

St: "You'd lose the solemnity [of it all]."

J: "[Given this language], you'd have to read a grocery list slowly, too. So, one reads Milton slowly; what else?"

St: "The reiteration of it was good."

J: "What else?" [J is asking students to explain their own experiences via authentic-type questions.]

St 1: "[You] repeated the word "and" over and over."

St 2: "Some of the words . . . there were random italicized words."

J: "Not the same in all texts; there are no original texts left. Some words have disappeared. And, there are no vowels in Hebrew. Why was this written? For the tribes of Israel?"

St: "(It also describes) where do we come from."

J: "Comparable to what life was like in the old country. This is a *good* translation [emphatically] . . . This is what we get in *PL*."

J switches teaching techniques from the last two class periods. For Class 26, he **starts them with an experience, and then asks them to reflect upon it.** Following his exploration of their reading experience and after a few report-questions, he asks the class to turn to *Paradise Lost* itself. J then asks students to read out loud again. Following a lengthy reading, J guides the class in a close reading of the story of the creation in *PL*, contrasting and comparing it to the version in Genesis. After a brief discussion of the days of creation, J wraps up Book VII and previews Book VIII:

J: "[God] rested on the Sabbath. Adam and Raphael then have a conversation in Book VIII, lines 204–8. What doesn't Raphael know?"

St: "While man was being created, Raphael went to Hell to make sure the gates were open."

J: "So then Adam tells his story; first thing he remembers?"

St: "Waking from a deep sleep, and a dream . . ."
J: "After the creation of Adam, line 363, God is playful. Ok, Tuesday, finish up VIII and do Book IX, the center of the action."

End of Class no. 26.

Summary

Much of this class is taken up with slow and lyrical reading of elements from Genesis with comparable passages in *Paradise Lost*. J models the joy of **slowly reading** some beautiful prose, and then asks the students to read aloud as well. There is evidence of great pleasure and rapt attention during J's and their colleagues' readings. Although questions are more often structured question-and-answer mixed with mini-lectures, students answer confidently and with good comprehension of the creation elements presented in both Genesis and in *PL*.

SESSION 27: STEP SIX

J puts the students into small groups and asks them to look closely at Book VIII. He asks them to consider, generally, the "perfect spouse." What would he or she be like, and what is the problem Milton has to resolve here? Getting more specific, he discusses the organization and structure of Paradise:

J: "Why was Eve created?"
St 1: "Procreation."
St 2: [A male student. with obvious relish]: "To serve him!"
J: [Joking]: "With all the women in this class, you'd better be careful."
St 3: "[Female student]: A helpmate for him."
J: "Yes—she has equality with him. What does Eve help Adam with?"
St: "She tends the garden with Adam."
J: "Isn't that hard work? Why not hard labor?"
St: "Because it would not be Paradise."

At this early point in the class, J reads aloud from the epic and asks members in the three small groups to discuss the differences between the creation story in Genesis and the ones in *PL*. Some exchanges:

> St 3: "There are differences in who is telling the story."
>
> J: "Right. In Genesis, one is a third-person account—just telling us what happened. In *PL*, the further we get into the Book, the more we get character's motivations and get into their minds. Indeed, closer we get to Book IX, the closer we get to motives. Any other differences?"
>
> St: "In *PL*, the Son is doing the work of the Father."
>
> J: "Yes, in the Bible, it just *is*. Look in Book VIII, line 521 ff. 'Bliss' came up before 'woe.'"
>
> St: "Adam was told that he loved Eve way too much and God not enough."
>
> J: "*Carne* means meat, as in *chili con carne*" [meaning repeated from earlier class]. "Adam asks Raphael what angels do in heaven. Raphael says they embrace. What else? See line 618 ff; Raphael *blushes* when Adam asks him about sex in Heaven and tells him that it transcends the physical."
>
> St 1: "Raphael cuts off the conversation so he didn't have to answer more."
>
> St 2: Isn't it a great literary device on Milton's part? Then he doesn't have to get into details he'd rather not?"
>
> J: "Remember, the whole point of Raphael's visit is (once more) to warn Adam and Eve (given what's coming in Book IX)."
>
> St 3: "Yes, there's another warning on line 635."
>
> J: "Right. This is one more example of the moral passion relating to 'inside' the soul versus 'outside' it."
>
> St 4: "Isn't this like *Comus*?"
>
> J: "Sure. [God says through Raphael]: You have been made perfect, but it's up to you to stay that way. The chapter ends with each going to their separate places: Raphael flies back up to Heaven and Adam walks over to Eve.
>
> "Now we go to Book IX, *the crucial* book in Milton's poem. Lines 1–47, we get a list of epic subjects. Look what the narrator says: "I must now change those notes to tragic and foul distrust . . ."

In the exchanges above, we see more examples of **student responses within the context of a teacher-led discussion.** Most students are engaged (in part because of the homework assignment from the period before) and following along carefully, asking for page numbers and contributing appropriate commentary.

J begins Book IX with his usual exhortations. He then reads

from Chapter III of Genesis, comparing and contrasting it to what Milton wrote in Book IX, in order to *set up what students are to expect* in the Book they have just started, focusing on the *genre aspects* of the narrator's opening, and changing the scene. Several examples follow, as J describes Eve's attempt to persuade Adam to split up and work separately during the day. Students question the validity of Milton's characters and the epic's structural qualities, and bring in relationships to works studied earlier in the course:

J: "Good responses on Eve's part; anything else?"

St: "She sounds like Milton, in *Areopagitica.*"

J: "Right; how does Adam respond to all of this?"

St 1: "Be strong; (line 351): God left them free will." [The student **reads from text** and continues lengthy answer.]

St 2: (Lines 316–17): "He (Adam) allows her to make decisions even though he's the thinker . . ." [Lengthy answer; much is indistinct.]

J: "Right. (cf. line 290): It's last time he can call her "immortal Eve." Unless you've tested your virtue, it's not based on experiences."

St 3: "One of her mistakes is in line 383."

J: "Yes, she thinks 'a strong foe won't go after a weak woman.'"

St 1: "I took that line as sarcasm because she only calls him Adam. Maybe she is irritated?"

St 2: "How come all of a sudden the Garden needs all that work? Why does she change . . .?" [Lengthy speculation.]

J: "You're right. [It's a device Milton uses] to move the story along."

St 3: "I think it's kind of good that he [Milton] does, because it doesn't show Eve as this weak and stupid thing. She's feeling like low that Adam doesn't trust her and along comes Satan and says that *she* could be the sovereign . . ."

J: "She does have a voice; she can argue, and even weeps a couple of times. This is terrible for a guy . . ."

St 3: "Adam reiterates what we talked about before about inside/outside . . . [indistinct]. The whole thing about him being in charge and cloistered virtue. In line 366, he says if she really wants to test her virtue, she should be loyal to him (Adam)."

St 4: "Adam reiterates what Raphael warned them of in line 366: If you want to test virtue, love me."

J: (Lines 472, 473): "Satan is formulating his final plans; it's all sneaky and tricky."(519): It's *tortuous:* from text, it means *twist, winding.* (553): Eve is amazed that the serpent can talk; recall what fruit means in Latin? It means *malum.* The root is 'mal' and that means . . .?"

Sts: [Recite in unison]: "Bad!"
J: "That's Good!!" [Moving to Group 3]: "Satan makes a number of points [in his logical argument]. What are they?"
St 1: "Satan ate it—and he didn't die."
St 2: "God would praise her for using her mind."
St 3: "If God hurt her, He wouldn't be just."
St 4: "Just as a snake, she'd moved up the great chain. She would be as the gods."
J: "Before we discuss this further, we need props."

J **passes out red apples** (although Milton merely says "fruit," he reminds them) and, after reading line 781, he says to the class: "Ready? Bite!" J takes a big bite out of the apple as do the members of the class. Everyone chuckles . . . and eats.

J: "What are the other consequences of eating the forbidden fruit?"
St 1: "Eve starts to worship the tree."
St 2: "God becomes the *great forbidden* to Eve and Satan."
St 3: (Line 791): "She's described as being greedy."
St 4: (Line 821): "Isn't there a possible pun on co-partner/carpenter?"
J: "I hadn't thought about that; let me give that some thought."
St 1: "She's becoming another [kind of] Eve . . ."
J: [To Student # 1] ". . . which you mention in your term paper."
St 2: "She wants to be better than Adam at times."
St 3: (Line 825): "She sounds a lot like Satan."
J: "Deceit is coming in. Ok, we have to stop now."

J passes out next week's assignment sheet (Tuesday after Thanksgiving), returns term papers, and collects the students' class notebooks.

Summary

As is typical of many of J's classes late in the semester, this session starts slowly with J's initial technique of mostly lecture and report-type questions. Students appear somewhat lethargic during the first thirty minutes of class, but the energy level picks up when J prompts them using the small-group report format. Then students demonstrate that they are paying attention, ask and answer well, make references to Milton's earlier works with comparable themes and techniques, discuss the subtleties of characterization, and use *words du jour* to make their points. Students have begun to use their fairly substantial knowledge of Milton, his other works, and *PL* to answer questions with a considerable air of sophistication. They are **participating in a literary conversation.**

SESSION 29

J begins this class with a fifteen- to twenty-minute *review* of the previous day's work. Given that this is the next-to-last class and the two final Books of *PL* remain, these final classes are more tightly controlled by J, in a way quite different from any previous this semester. His narrative is designed to tie together all the various elements of the story line (up to Book X), and he exhibits little patience with any student answer that deviates from the forwarding, in order, of the narrative line in these last two Books:

> J: "Last class period [before Thanksgiving], we discussed the pivotal point: Eve's taking a bite of the apple. The full act of original sin is in the biting of the apple (actually, the fruit of the tree of the knowledge of good and evil). Why does Eve eat the apple?"
>
> St 1: "She thinks she'll be a goddess."
>
> St 2: "She'll be wiser than Adam."
>
> St 3: "Noontime; she's hot and hungry."
>
> J: "How does one describe the *perfect* marriage and the *perfect* mate?" [Repairs]: "What is Adam's response?"
>
> St4: "Out of love for Eve. He chose her because she has chosen 'death.'"
>
> J: "Adam is weaving a rose garland. What happen to the garland?"
>
> St 2: "The flowers die and he drops them."
>
> J: "[It] reminds us of first lines of the poem" [memorized by students.] "What's the first thing that happens [after both eat of the forbidden fruit]?

Mini-lecture: Have we used the term, *prelapsarian?* It is the time before man has fallen; it's now past happiness. We're so far out of the Garden that we can't perceive prelapsarian life. What's the mark of their imperfection? Keep your eyes on their hands [images of hands]. List the consequences of the Fall."

> St 1: "Lust."
>
> J: (Line 1011 ff): "'In lust they burned their carnal knowledge, til

they fell asleep after their amorous play.' It is a mark of their fallen nature—their sexuality. Eve sees things differently. What do they see? Compare to the opening of Shakespeare's Sonnet 129, 'Th' expense of spirit in a waste of shame / Is lust in action.'" [Intertextual allusion.]

St 2: "They are aware they are naked."

St 3: "They begin to cry (line 1121)."

J: [Quoting]: "'And of the fruitless hours of their vain contest there is no end.' Book X and part of XI describe the consequences after the Fall. Everything is connected—one never sins alone. What else happens in Paradise?"

St4: "The angels are sad."

St 5: "They pity Eve and Adam and the angels leave Paradise."

J: "What's the Father's response—who is responsible?"

St: "Adam and Eve—they had choice. They could have said no."

J: "It's not the angel's fault. These are consequences in Heaven."

St5: "They hide when God approaches."

J: "Let's wait on that—it comes a bit later." [J asserts a *tighter control of the pattern of conversation*.] "The consequences in heaven—best part of it all is similar to the Bible version. [J reads from Genesis.] Isn't this a wonderful psychology? (Book X, ll. 85–228. Now, notice that Adam and Eve are going into forest to hide; it's a kind of interiorization of their emotions."

Most of this class is devoted to J's reading passages from Book X and conducting his narrative to finish the semester with the epic complete. After several more exchanges, the following takes place, unusual because of J's determination to finish the poem before the end of the next class period:

J: "Note the changes in Satan."

St 1: "See line 500 (something)." [Indistinct.]

J: "Actually, that comes a little later—let's look at L. 450."

St 2: "Satan at the dinner of all the devils tells them the story of Adam and Eve's Fall."

J: (Line 485): "Satan speaks of seduction. What is their response?"

St 3: "The devils laugh."

J: "Satan says, 'I did it with an apple.' Now we get to the line Melanie mentioned—line 564. How would you want your audience to respond if you were Satan?"

St 1: "With applause."

J: "Look at what does happen—lines 485–519. They all hiss and slither, like serpents. This is the law of the jungle—Paradise is lost and death comes in."

After a few more exchanges, J reintroduces the concept of *prevenient grace*, which the class had discussed in *Comus* and other Miltonic works.

This ends the class; J gives them a short assignment for Thursday (last class of the semester), their take-home final examination, and collects their course notebooks.

Summary

This period is relatively unremarkable but for the near-complete control Prof. J exercises over the discussions. Students are on task and both students and professor appear focused on completing the epic within the time constraints. J's narrative weaves passages from Book III of Genesis and Milton's version in *PL*, and J presses his students to recall the details of the consequences of the Fall.

SESSION 30: STEP SIX *(FINAL CLASS OF THE SEMESTER)*

Opening lecture and review:

J: "Open Book XI of *Paradise Lost*. Milton calls Adam and Eve our [readers'] grandparents. Notice how the pace of the Book has picked up."

Following this introduction, J's questions function more as filling-in his oral reading and mini-lecture rather than authentic exchange:

J: "What is *sin* in Milton? We get it in the beginning all the way up?"

St 1: "Disobedience to God." [**Pronounces it in syncope,** as the first line of *PL* is pronounced.]

J: "Whatever we do connects to everything else. Even as they speak their repentance, they're forgiven. Recall *prevenient* grace? God already prepared to forgive them, even before they'd asked. I asked in today's assignment about the Son and the Father, Book XI ll. 30–60. What's going on there?"

St 2: "Is this like Book III, where the Son says 'I'll go and help man?'"

J: "Right—now its in chronological order. [Line 72.] I asked you to consider these lines. What's God doing with Michael here?" [Reads out loud.]

St 3: "Is he telling Michael what to say to Adam?"

J: [J sets up scene at length.] "Yes. What does the Father tell Michael, the Archangel?"

St 4: [After J reads passage aloud]: "Tells Adam and Eve to leave Paradise."

J: "Right, but it's not a vicious or mean kind of thing; this is justice. It's an eviction notice; but first, give them some information. What is this—all of Book XI and half of XII?"

End of Class no. 30

Summary

As with the previous class, almost the whole of this one is taken up with J alternately lecturing, reading from *PL*, and asking memory-questions (almost like a drill) to increase momentum to the end of the poem. Most of these exchanges involve students not so much building on a common narrative, but rather answering some pointed and very specific questions. J (and the students) are clearly enjoying the pace and summary-like nature of this semester's conclusion; they listen attentively as he relishes reading some of the great final lines. At the end of the period, J asks the students to "write a letter to Milton, telling him [Milton] anything you want to say: I hate you! I loved the poem, etc." Students laugh. J asks them to bring this "letter" to the final examination.

8

Study Discussion

THIS STUDY WAS FUELED IN PART BY MY CONCERN THAT IMAGINATIVE literature is often not taught very well at the university level. My purpose, therefore, was to observe an expert professor who *does* teach very well, and to identify his values, his behaviors, and his teaching techniques during a full semester in order to generalize about the possibilities for our teaching of literature to the next generation. This study explores how Prof J, a widely acknowledged expert university professor of literature, apprenticed novice students into the practices of authentic literate reading and interpretation. I particularly focused on how he assisted students in negotiating the "snakes and ladders of abstraction," an activity necessary for novice readers to understand complex, often not-realistic texts—especially texts unfamiliar in content, formal properties, and historical context. Throughout this process we are able to observe these students building a more complete, relevant, and well-structured knowledge base to support their interpretations, principally by evoking their increasing prior knowledge to make sense of new literary material.

I was also interested to see which important and recurrent patterns the professor helps students to recognize and use to support literary interpretation and, in doing so, how the professor assists students in self-regulation regarding their own learning, which included monitoring their understanding and evaluation of their own ideas as well as the ideas of others. I watched to see which specific literary practices the professor introduced into the class and how he went about integrating these into his teaching.

Finally, I observed how Prof. J socialized students into a community of professional literary practitioners. In keeping with Jean Lave's insistence that learning is most often done through this process of socialization,[1] I watched how the professor engaged and fostered students' personal identities as apprentices to literary practice. I witnessed how he helped them both participate in and, ultimately, *own* these practices. I also noted that his teaching methods evolved over the course of one school semester as a function of his sensitive attunement to these particular students' literary growth and development. His fostering of the class identity as a community and encouraging individual students to become capable readers of complex literary texts were as important to Prof. J as the students' ability to pass tests via decoding textual passages.

I have argued that many of the current investigations into the teaching of imaginative literature at the college level do not focus squarely on *teaching*. Those that do tend to be flawed, because they focus exclusively either on a belief that the professor's main task is evoking readers' cognitive and emotional responses to the text, or that the text instantiates Platonic-like themes or cultural examples that must be identified. Each emphasis distorts the process of *getting students to read literature expertly*, since one tends to ignore the author and merely tolerate the teacher; the other elevates the teacher to a "keeper of the sacred text" and largely diminishes the reader's engagement with the text.

What I have displayed in this study is one teacher's means of avoiding extremes, moving away from both the *Scylla* of Reader Response and the *Charybdis* of the (old) New Criticism, by weaving them together in a tapestry of reader *and* text *and* teacher. My task has been to show how, when, and why this teacher makes the moves he does; in so doing, Prof J develops novice readers of Milton into proto-experts who have internalized most of the tools and techniques used by the grand masters of the text. What then characterizes an *expert* teacher of imaginative literature at the university level?

CLASS STRUCTURES

Prof. J structures his semester's work on Milton into six *Steps* or sections, each corresponding to a combination of texts studied, literary skills to be mastered, and historical/biographical information to be added to the students' knowledge base. In each section, he builds upon students' textual knowledge, mastery of biographical details and skill practices, and also aids the students in displaying what they had learned and interpreting their encounters with the literary and historical materials. Each section is structured around a text or set of texts, initially organized chronologically according to the period in Milton's life when each was written. Further organizational structuring devices include the genre(s) of each text as well as their increasing complexity.

This carefully orchestrated organization stands in contrast to "student-centered" classrooms where student curiosity is the prime generator of class agendas. While student-generation may, at times, work in classes devoted only to students' immediate experiences with very contemporary literature and culture, it is less useful for those texts from another time and place.

By structuring the opening of each class with specific review questions, Prof. J continuously models for his students a careful attention to the text's language—in general, via his *Words du Jour*—a goal achieved in part by asking them to consult the *OED* as well as to consider the evolving meaning of specific words. This modeling of basic literary processes is particularly important for anyone teaching a literature far removed in time and space from most North American students' experience, but the procedures could as easily be applicable to a class in any contemporary literature. Hence, a well-structured and intricately woven class routine is one major component of English professor expertise.

The Snakes and Ladders of Abstraction

Another of J's emphases throughout the course is to assist students' negotiation up and down the "snakes and ladders of abstraction." The skill of moving from the single word or image level through intermediate character and plot developments and ultimately to the highest levels of character analysis, genre, and theme, may well be one of the major accomplishments of any sophisticated reader of imaginative literature. Although most college students are able to find textual fragments of meaning, they are often not capable of emerging from the details into a clear view of the whole sonnet. Conversely, neither is it likely that they would then look back to details to support higher level assertions and claims.

One also notes how slowly J moves his students through this trajectory of the abstract. Only after developing typical patterns of picking out images and giving students both local and contextualized meanings within the whole poem, only after discussing root words and etymologies and then contextualizing the responses further by embedding them in extratextual sources (the Bible)—only after all of this does J move to larger issues like theme. Unlike what James Phelan says many "thematizers" do,[2] J does not expect students to jump from textual details to an abstract statement of overall design without having had this enormous amount of specific preparation. Although Purves[3] and others may believe that in a student-directed class conversation, participants should be allowed to "find and develop their own topics for discussion,"[4] Prof. J finds that approach highly problematic when learning about a writer as complex as Milton. A second characteristic of professorial expertise, then, is the ability to help students move with growing ease up and down the "snakes and ladders of abstraction" in literature.

Students' Knowledge Base and Prior Knowledge

In order to develop a general sense of the class's baseline knowledge, on the opening day of the semester J directs his students to take a piece of paper, draw a line down the middle, and write everything they know about the seventeenth century on the left side and everything they know about Milton on the right. Then J contextualizes this information, beginning with what students know and adding an oral narrative background in seventeenth-century history.

Hence, one of Prof. J's earliest and most important tasks is to expand his students' knowledge base of vocabulary and syntactical rules to *support the process of decoding a text* written in an unfamiliar (early modern) type of English,[5] set in a past (1608–74) remote from their own experience, and exhibiting values distant from students' own assumptions. Since the original King James Version of the Bible was so deeply embedded in all that Milton thought, said, and wrote, contemporary students needed to become familiar with that version—a parallel text to complement any reading of Milton. J often starts with the literal meanings, eventually moving into Milton's linguistic and imagistic borrowings from it. He does this, in part, by *reading out loud*, allowing students to hear the sounds of the language from an excellent reader. He also *encourages active listening* by asking questions, comparing sound patterns, and posing suggestions for alternative interpretations.

Emotional Identification in Building a Knowledge Base

In addition to building students' knowledge of language matters, J creates associations by regularly yoking many new concepts to students' prior knowledge (in one instance, to elementary-school campfire experiences). As he helps to socialize students into acquiring new knowledge by making explicit links with their prior knowledge, J also develops the students' emotional identification with Milton as a *prelude* to analyzing the text. Prof. J considers the first twenty-six lines of *Paradise Lost* so important, for example, that he asks all his students to memorize them and to be able to recite them back to him (privately). This memorization helps students to "own" that piece of the poem, and so quite literally make it part of their conscious and even unconscious thinking. As Alice G. Brand has suggested, it is "naive and inaccurate to believe that all ways of knowing may only be represented intellectually."[6] For Prof. J, *emotional identification* is an integral part of the larger mosaic called *learning*. Hence, another characteristic of professorial expertise is the constant enhancement of the students' knowledge base by helping them to identify emotionally with that which they are learning.

IMPORTANT AND REOCCURRING PATTERNS

How do such professorial characteristics help student-learning over the lengthy time-period of a semester? J does not merely talk "at" his students, nor does he give assignments that require "busy work." J's tasks are often patterned after Milton's own early-college assignments, such as a rhetorical exercise exploring "Which is better, day or night?" This assignment prepares students to understand Milton's experience as a young author.

In the next *Step,* J asks his class to examine "L'Allegro" and "Il Penseroso" as companion pieces, moving students from considering only one poem to two, and considering more complex poetry than the sonnets. Both poems are textually interrelated and both, while containing elements of Milton's early poetic practices, are a step in complexity above his students' previous academic exercises.

The daily homework assignments are crucial to successful student socialization and learning. J emphasizes that since Milton's texts and ideas are vast and there was so much to cover, students *must* do daily written assignments or they would quickly fall behind: the "assignments are geared to help you get into the text [since most students] don't know what to focus on, because there is so much." He tells them that these assignments are "to give you a start; to give you help," allowing students to incrementally develop an intimate familiarity with the text. In particular, these assignments are designed to attune students to "pattern recognition of high significance."[7]

Many times, as J and the class simultaneously review yesterday's thematic material and analyze the current work in the context of report (or memory) -type questions,[8] J suddenly asks a "class-stopper," a higher-order thinking question (HOT) to which no one has an automatic, preformed answer. One example of this is when J asks, "But *why* does God (who is all-powerful, all-knowing) need you to do . . . *X* (anything)?" When no student answer is forthcoming, J leaves the query hanging there—a question to keep in mind as students continue to read Milton, but one to which he could return, repeatedly if necessary.

Milton's Language into Student-Speak

J also insists that students turn Milton's language into a calculus of their own understanding. During the *Comus* summary, for example, J reinforces his emphasis on the students' connection to Milton as lived experience by (a) reminding them to employ the strategies in J's *Milton Links* (a handout asking for specific personal information relating to Milton); (b) asking students to paraphrase *in their own words* the rather arcane thoughts and language in the debate between Comus and the Lady over chastity and virtue; and (c) constantly joking and using the language of undergraduates to *translate* the seventeenth-century masque

into accessible thought for his students. As the semester progresses, students' earlier one-line, semi-coherent responses to J's
questions become more articulate—even using the language of
the seventeenth century at times—in part, because J's rather
generalized prompting now requires students to create a mix of
Milton's language and their own speech in order to clarify their
comments.

FOSTERING PERSONAL IDENTITIES WITH THE MILTON CLASS

Early into one of the first sessions Prof. J refers the class to
the handout entitled *Milton Links*, a set of three yellow sheets
explicitly asking students to connect elements of their own lives
to the issues in Milton under discussion. He begins by asking
general questions, such as "What makes a good friend?" After
initial conversation, J makes it a point to weave their answers
into a reflection of those qualities which Milton found in his
best friend, Diodati. "One trusts one's friends with intimate details, and this letter is like two guys writing inside jokes." J takes
great pains to interrelate his students' own lives and the text
under discussion.

Also early in the semester, Prof J begins each class with a
lengthy roll call (some fifteen minutes), during which he memorizes student's names and faces, joking lightly while exchanging
small anecdotes and stories. The casual and leisurely pace of
these roll calls masks their serious purpose: one must first "develop trust and familiarity between individual students and the
professor," as well as among the students themselves, to conduct a class of active participants.[9]

J also asks his students to write an exercise similar to one from
which Milton drew his inspiration and honed his poetry-writing
skills. This *experiential method* that J uses suggests part of his
educational philosophy: students can neither appreciate nor understand the work of a major figure like Milton without seeing
him, at least in part, as being *someone like themselves*. One way
to do this is by giving students an academic exercise comparable
to the type that informed Milton's own poetic inspiration.

When J moves specifically to a text—in this instance *Eligia
sexta* (Christmas 1629)—and begins what amounts to report-
type questions, these contain new information and, most impor-

tantly, emotionally charged motivational statements. Hence, his questions are unlike a traditional *drill* (that environment where questions are exercised primarily to retrieve information from students' memory) and *require student engagement.* J also models his delight through *words du jour,* recognizing the text's excellent choices in language; he ends his explanation of the word, *mnemosyne,* with "Isn't that neat." J's periodic exhortations are one of his major heuristic practices meant to involve his students in genuine aesthetic experiences.

By midpoint in the semester, the proliferation of student opinions during many discussions makes it clear that the class is following the progression of Milton's argument, that they have internalized J's request that they read "in the margins" of the text, and that they have formed their own opinions. These opinions are based largely on the contrastive nature of what they have liked or disliked in their own educations and culture vis-à-vis Milton's ideal education. Prof. J patiently agrees with them, while gently suggesting that Milton's educational philosophy was from another time and culture. Hence, students learn that to argue with Milton, they must first attempt to contextually understand him, his intentions, and his times. To do that requires a slow but steadily growing acquaintance with Miltonian works and thoughts.

Hence, from the first day Prof. J begins a *reciprocal* process of learning through both emotional identification *and* textual analysis. In addition to having students talk about Milton as a young man, and thereby identify themselves with what he was doing, they are also developing the technical expertise of sonnet analysis; all three processes, simultaneously. Prof. J specifies, "the bigger picture [is] that we're softening that hard, frightening view of Milton they (students) may have heard of."[10] His building on the students' knowledge of and identification with Milton is accomplished, in part, through the medium of daily writing assignments wherein students follow (granted, in a modest way) Milton's own educational experiences of regular written exercises.[11]

Bridging Mechanisms

Since one of the major tasks for J early on is to connect the materials from a distant poet and culture to the students' own lives, he constantly searches for *bridging mechanisms;* methods of helping students see the relationships between the seventeenth century and their own time and interests. One effective example J employs (in Class no. 7) is to invoke the students' raw emotional experience from the shock of Princess Diana's untimely death, then only three weeks earlier, as a connection to the genre of the eulogy in the specific example of Milton's "Lycidas."

In sum, professorial expertise displayed over time requires (a) the use of an initial "tying-in" strategy, *before* reading the more complex texts in the course; (b) continuing movements toward personal identification while the students are struggling with textual analysis; (c) identifying bridging mechanisms that *may emerge opportunistically* from daily interaction with the students' environment and then using these to move students from their world to those of the text(s) under consideration.

ATTUNEMENT TO STUDENTS' LITERARY GROWTH AND DEVELOPMENT

J constantly reinforces the sense that mistakes are part of students' learning. As he reminds students that the schedule is a map, not an inflexible blueprint, J draws attention to his own mistake on a handout, and uses this as a tool to teach a *word du jour:* St Augustine's *peccata forte* means "sin boldly" if one is going to make a mistake. In this way he implicitly signals to students another connection between the ethos of the subject matter and their own education. Milton was fiercely independent, yet could produce high-level, traditional poetry. So too, J's students might question the value systems in the texts they are reading and perhaps never agree with Milton (on his treatment of woman, for example), but to do so effectively they need to bring well-thought-out arguments to class.

J also uses Bartholomae and Petrosky's technique of getting students to list and consider their own agendas first, and then examine a professionally written text for comparable patterns.[12] After the students had done this own self-examination early on, Prof. J suggests that they trace several themes in "Morning"— specifically light/dark, time, music /sound/silence, and nature. J asks them to contrast the more traditional nativity scenes, some of which they might have written down themselves, with those in the poem. In effect, J encourages students to begin specifying the big issues in the poem, starting with their own experiences.

Narrative Collaboration

With this exercise, the students and J collaborate on weaving the class narrative line. In a short time, teacher and students *jointly* begin to weave a class narrative, albeit the Loom-*master* is still Prof. J. By late in the semester J's focus shifts again, from questioning techniques, to motivational statements, overtones, and outright exhortations, all woven into the fabric of succeeding classes. J's own enthusiasm for *PL* becomes *the* major topic of class conversation. Experience indicates that U.S. college students would have a difficult time coping with an old-fashioned epic like *PL* without a strong boost from the teacher. Clearly, his love for the text and his ability to fold cultural humor into his lessons exemplifies how English teachers should behave in the context of the literary materials to which they have devoted their lives.

By late in the semester, J is often still leading the class in discussion but openly welcomes modifications from students, signaling to the class that their insights have triggered new thoughts in him, the expert, and that if they can do *that*, then the conversation has become a *mutual exploration* of an extremely dense and difficult poetic masterpiece. This blend of J and the students *questioning and being questioned* signals a very interesting give-and-take which fosters a class well-socialized in using the text for answers and in settling disputed issues. Hence, professorial expertise displayed over time includes an initially well-structured scaffolding, but provides for the gradual dismantling of the teacher's sole control over knowledge.

WEAVING ON THE LOOM OF LEARNING

What ultimately identifies an expert professor of literature at the college level? To paraphrase an old popular song, the professor is a "dream weaver." One descriptor of Prof. J's teaching skill employs the metaphor of *weaving*—ideas, motivations, historical information, student learning, as well as energy and exhortation—into the fabric of class learning. In an early class, J includes the meaning of Sonnet no. 7 in particular, genre considerations of sonnets in general, Milton's biographical data, and the larger abstract connections among all these with the students' own experiences with parents and teachers who want to know "what they're going to do with their lives." J often uses metaphors from both *Paradise Lost* and Milton in general to illustrate his points, modeling through his attention to specific language matters the activity of "systematically integrating descriptions and references from multiple levels of the text(s) referenced."[13]

Another regular part of the weaving process is J's relating Milton's Puritan ideal of *ethical choice* to his own continuing evaluation of students' behaviors in class. J acknowledges the students' workload in other courses but asks them to give the assignments in this one an honest try: "Be honest—to me, to the profession; to yourself . . . don't 'fake' assignments, 'cause you're the one who loses. We'll only have time to survey this material—it's too much otherwise." He reminds them that it is "part of [his] job to assess; I'm doing it all the time." He reveals that the highest percentage of the final grade is the "J factor" because he "constantly interact[s] with students as we work together in small groups, larger groups."

The end of one later class typifies, in tone and substance, all of these attitudes. After discussing the allegorical elements in the Garden, J focuses the students on *insinuating,* a word used to describe how Satan navigates around the Garden. *Insinuating* comes up in discussion via the technique of *Words du Jour;* J asks the class to read, in choral form, the specific (and important) line tying together Satan, his mode of travel, the line's meaning, and its future allegorical import. Because *words du jour* have become so woven into the internalized fabric of class conversation, the students make a joke of its meaning in the context of an interpretation:

J: [Reads lines 472, 473] "Satan is formulating his final plans; it's all sneaky and tricky. Look ahead at l. 519; it's tortuous: from text, it means twist, winding. (Now see l. 553)—Eve is amazed that the serpent can talk; [Do you] recall what "fruit" means in Latin? [It means] *malum.* Its root is *mal* and that means . . .?"
Sts: [recite in unison]: "Bad!"
J: "That's good!"

STUDY: STRENGTHS AND WEAKNESSES

Strengths

The strength of this study rests on the detailed information, gathered from a wide variety of sources and recorded over a complete semester taught by a (previously acknowledged) master professor. This study has captured the history of a student-aggregate representing a wide variety of abilities and backgrounds within a particular major. Since the course was merely one of several choices with the cluster known as "major authors" and was offered at the difficult hour (for many students) of 8:00 a.m. (thus, "Red-Eye Milton"), those enrolled were not a homogeneous group. Thus the study captures both the history and (most importantly) the development of a fairly typical class of U.S. state university undergraduates. It examines the process of their development rather than merely studying periodic and relatively static snapshots of the products of Prof. J's teaching. Since this focus on process comes within the purview of one of the three most often taught writers in the canon (Chaucer, Shakespeare, and Milton), the content of the class is central to anyone studying English in contemporary North American universities.

Given Milton's centrality, this study challenges the practical pedagogic delivery model(s) of many (if not most) classes devoted to the study of the current canon in literature: variations of both Reader-Response and what has come to be called the (old) New Criticism. After examining the evidence presented above, I argue that neither direction alone—neither the primary focus on the students' response nor on the authority of author and text—is in itself adequate for a heuristically useful method for the teaching of imaginative literature from a time and place remote from most students' experiences.

What is required is a master teacher, who can weave the threads of the students' motivation, their developing curiosity, their occasional frustrations and subsequent "ah ha!" illuminations when textual problems brighten into solutions, and their willingness to follow a classroom leader—weave all of that in and around the life and writings of a classic author worthy of their labors. The model I suggest, therefore, is that of master teacher as *dream weaver,* able to connect the *warp* of student intellectual development and the *weft* of ancient history and culture by shuttling both into a seamless pattern of classroom learning.

This weaving combines many activities and sources of information. The professor begins by focusing on the student as a person, trying to get to know each of them both in and out of class. He spends energy finding out what they know about Milton and the seventeenth century and then organizes activities around his growing knowledge of what they bring to the class, both intellectually and motivationally, and what they need to leave it successfully. He imparts his own breadth of information about his subject matter judiciously, requiring students to gather information on their own first, then sharing it with their classmates; only after their own research has been exhausted does Prof. J impart *what else* they need to know. He invites students to challenge him as their store of information grows, and the end result of these invitations is a collaboration among students and professor to unravel the mysteries of the literary text(s) under discussion. In sum, the model of expertise illuminated by this study is the professor as *Master of the Loom of Learning*.

Weaknesses

The weaknesses of this study are those typical of the case-study method in general. Since this study examined only one professor in one school, other investigations may look to alternative methods of successful literature teaching in other types of universities with different authors. What are the pedagogical ramifications of distance learning, for example? Another study may wish to examine a course where an entirely different type of literature (or subject matter) is featured. One could investigate then how "excellence in teaching" is less or more intimately tied to a specific subject matter. This study could have been strengthened as well by observing the class as a whole. What sorts of systemic issues would need to be addressed if one investigated simultaneously the professor's expertise and the students' detailed learning curves? Indeed, the next step may be to take the knowledge gained from this study and examine another professor in another area of literature, as well as to conduct a micro-analysis of all the students in the class. Such longitudinal investigation of teacher and learner could prove highly informative.

Finally, one could research the same group of students and their expert professor as the students move from an undergraduate to a graduate course in the same subject area. What changes take place when such detailed student learning is then separated by two, three, or more years? What effect does both intellectual and emotional maturation have on the interactions and learning among a collective of students and their professor, who is, him/herself, consistently in the process of change and development. Systems analysis[14] would suggest that in classrooms, as in life, neither professor nor student is static. As each element changes, as either the warp or the weft elongates or shortens, the effects on quality learning would need to be further examined.

Appendix A: Course Materials

ENGLISH 409:1 MILTON
T/Th 8:00–9:14 RH 205
Office: [number] [location]
Hours: 10–11: 15 T., Th. and by appointment
Fall Semester
Prof. William C. Johnson
[email address]

Expectations, concerns, comments, caveats

We will give our attention in this Milton course both to surveying the Milton canon and to improving our skills in reading (in larger contexts of that word)—both Milton and ourselves. We will look at many of the "major minor works," both poetry and prose, and then focus on *Paradise Lost*. There will be some lecture, some discussion, and considerable question-and-answer (from student to professor, and vice versa, as well as student-to-student). In class it will be impossible to discuss thoroughly, sometimes even adequately, all the works; however, it is each student's responsibility to keep up with the readings as assigned **and to come to class prepared for daily discussion.**

I have high expectations of you as advanced students in this upper-division class; I don't expect that you necessarily will have read Milton prior to this course, or even that you know how to read his works, but I do expect that you will be willing to throw yourself into a serious study of one of the world's greatest writers. I also expect that you will be willing to work hard, knowing that things worthwhile take time and effort. There is no way around it: Milton is not an "easy" writer. But you will be surprised, perhaps, at how you can gain a knack for knowing what to look for and how to look for it, and you'll be surprised as well at how much you'll find of yourself in what he writes.

I also expect that you recognize the value of solid, honest, scholarly questioning; learning never takes place in a vacuum, and your questions (as much as your answers) to me and to one another are an invaluable part of the learning experience.

In short, <u>above all else I expect intellectual and personal honesty</u>. I am assuming you are here to learn, to challenge and to be challenged, and to grow. I will help you as often and as much as you wish—and sometimes even more than you wish.

CAVEAT: Those unwilling to participate in discussion, to be actively engaged in group work, or to be involved in a considerable number of "ungraded" (although assessed) course activities, should not take this section of the course.

Text

Hughes, John. *Milton: Complete Poems and Major Prose.* (Odyssey)
(You might also find having a Bible—especially a King James version—helpful.)

Course Objectives

(a) to explore some of Milton's major poetry, the more significant minor poetry, and selected prose works;
(b) to develop skills in understanding how, why, about what, and for whom, Milton wrote;
(c) to trace some major themes running through Milton's works;
(d) to apply those themes to our own lives and personal development; and
(e) to develop critical thinking facilities, using Milton's poetry and prose to stimulate these.

Course Requirements
Examinations

(a) a midterm opportunity, covering everything on the syllabus up to that time;

(b) a comprehensive final opportunity; and

(c) (possibly) a number of brief quizzes.

Papers and Other Assignments

(a) successful completion of an 8–10 page investigative paper on a topic mutually agreed upon by the student and professor;

(b) compilation, completion, and submission of a course project notebook (to be explained in class); and

(c) successful memorization of selected lines from *Paradise Lost.*

Attendance Is Required

English 409 is in great part a discussion course; you are expected to work with others in discussion groups and on various assignments. Discussion and teamwork simply are not possible when one is absent. Three absences will result in the final grade being lowered one full grade; four absences will lower it two full grades, etc. This action is not meant to emphasize the importance of grades; it is intended, however, to emphasize the importance of active participation and engagement in the class as well as in one's own education.

Grading

The final grade is a composite of many factors; it will be comprised of the following approximations: 15 percent for the midterm, 20 percent for the final examination, 30 percent for the investigative paper, and 35 percent for the "J Factor" (for "Johnson," who will assess the quality of quizzes, class involvement and, especially, the course project book).

All assignments must be typed, submitted at the specified time, and may use the standardized abbreviations for Milton's works as listed in the Hughes text, pp. xv–xvi.

Investigative Papers

Students must make an appointment to discuss, and to get approval of, the topic of investigation; this must be done no later than October 21. Papers should follow the format distributed in class. For your protection, keep a copy of your paper until the original is returned to you.

Schedule

(A general map; not an inflexible blueprint)

Begin your first reading of *Paradise Lost* immediately; we won't read it in class for many weeks, but you will need considerable time for a first and a second reading **before** we begin discussing this work.

Week 1	August 26–28	Introduction. Also, sonnets 7, 18, 19, 23. Plus chronology of M's life, xiii–xiv
Week 2	September 2–4	Minor poetry, pp. 42–50; 67–76
Week 3	September 9–11	Minor poetry, pp. 116–25
Week 4	September 16–18	*Comus*, pp. 86–114
Week 5	September 23–25	"Prolusions," pp. 595–604; "Of Education," 630–39.
Week 6	September 30–October 2	"Areopagitica," 716–49; "Tenure of Kings," 750–80.
Week 7	October 7–9	"Second Defense," 817–38; "Doctrine and Discipline," 696–715
Week 8	October 14–16	Midterm Opportunity October 14; begin *Paradise Lost* on October 16.
Week 9	October 21–23	*Paradise Lost.* October 21 is the last day to have the investigative paper topic approved.
Week 10	October 28–30	*Paradise Lost.*
Week 11	November 4–6	*Paradise Lost.*
Week 12	November 11–13	*Paradise Lost.*
Week 13	November 18–20	*Paradise Lost.* Investigative papers due on November 18.
Week 14	Nov 25	*Paradise Lost.*
Week 15	December 2–4	*Paradise Lost* and term wrap-up.

Our final examination is scheduled for Friday, December 12, 10–11:50 a.m.; no early or late examinations will be given.

ENGLISH 409

COURSE ASSIGNMENTS AND
COURSE PROJECT NOTEBOOKS

The weekly assignments, as well as the traditional "exams" and papers, are a **very** important part of this course. **All the weekly work must be typed, prepared before the class during which the materials are being examined,** and used as the starting point of your investigations. Class discussion should help you fill out the studies and your notes may be added in the margins or on separate pages.

The (almost) daily projects give you some specific things to explore as you work with Milton's works, allow you various ways of entering the texts, broaden your knowledge of and ability to use literary tools, and encourage you to see connections among Milton's works and between the works and yourself. These notebooks will provide you a good source of review of these materials, will allow you to see your own progress through the course, and will permit me an opportunity to see where you are doing your best work or where you might be needing assistance.

The Notebooks

Please use a simple two-pocketed folder. Make sure your name is printed clearly on the cover. These notebooks should include **all** of the assignments, in numerical order. Include, as well, various other items: the midterm opportunity, investigative paper,'"words du jour," etc., as these become available. I realize you very well may have additional handwritten comments and notes on the typed pages; that's as it should be. If you have running class notes among these pages, that's OK too—although it is not necessary for me to see these.

I will ask, several times during the term, that you submit these notebooks so that I may see if we're on the same page (in terms of what is going on in class, what is happening in the small groups, and how you're doing with the various assignments).

Milton Update

We've made some changes in the syllabus; let's all be clear on where we are, where we're going, and what we're doing:

1. You will read "Areopagitica" for October 7. You will **not** be reading "Tenure of Kings and Magistrates." There will be a short assignment for October 9 concerning the "Second Defense"; you will **not** be reading the "Doctrine and Discipline of Divorce."

2. On October 14 we'll have our midterm opportunity, the purposes of which are (a) to review and pull together the many things you've already learned and (b) to express (*express;* to press out of yourself) some of that material.

3. The exam will be essay, open-book, and will cover all the works that we've read thus far (including the sonnets we didn't discuss in class). You may also bring, and use, your class notebooks if you wish. I expect that you will know the works well and that you will be able to work with *how* Milton does, as well as *what* Milton does, in these pieces.

4. We will begin our reading of *Paradise Lost* on October 16; you should have completed if not all then at least most of your first reading by that time.

5. I've asked you to "learn by heart" (a nice phrase, that one, when you think about it!) the first two sentences of *Paradise Lost.* The best, the easiest, way to do this is to read the passage aloud many times and to pay attention to what it says. Savor the words, the structure, and the sounds of your own voice reading. You may recite your lines to me, in my office, at any time **before November 6.** Call [office phone], just come up [office location], or e-mail for an appointment.

6. You will need to consider very soon the topic of your investigative paper; by October 21 (at the latest) you need to discuss this topic with me. You have already learned *many* approaches to reading Milton and have already learned to respond to many different kinds of assignments. This project will allow you to apply, if you wish, much of what you've already learned to the reading of *Paradise Lost.* Do start thinking of this very soon!

7. Don't hesitate to see me if you feel you are having difficulties. I am here to help—and want to do so.

MILTON LINKS (I.E., YOU AND MILTON)

Your Age:

When, in recent history, and during your lifetime, was the event you consider most intellectually or historically exciting?

When, in recent history but **not** during your lifetime, was the event you consider most intellectually or historically exciting?

If you could have lived at anyone time in history, when would it have been (or, you could opt for the present time)? Why?

Consider your Education

Your year in school:

List the three main reasons you chose to go to college and prioritize them:

Why should there even be colleges, or educational systems, at all? What is the purpose of education?

Your major:

List the three main reasons you chose this major and prioritize them:

If you could chose any other major, what would it be? Why?

How do you know your current major is the right one for you?

If you could choose any profession, regardless of salary, prestige, or preparatory time, what would it be? Why?

If, at your age and at this time you weren't in school, what would you most like to be doing?

Consider People In Your Life

Who is the most important point of inspiration in your family?

If you could change the relationship between you and your family members, what would you have it be:

Friends: name your closest friend. How would you feel if you lost their friendship? How do you feel about being a friend to this person? What is your greatest strength as a friend?

Consider Religion

How important is "organized religion" in your life? Would you consider yourself a "religious" person?

Do you feel there is a "divine" purpose for your life/being? If so, what is it?

Politics

For whom did you vote in the last election? Why? (Be precise)

Should government have no, little, some, or considerable say in an individual's life, if that person chooses to live in this country?

What should be the three main criteria for being elected president?

We proclaim ourselves "one nation, under God." Should the government be involved in religion?

What are the arguments for/against such involvement?

Should our national, state, and/or local government protect people from "moral dangers" such as pornography and "treasonable" materials?

For Tuesday, November 25

Submit **Notebooks**

Please use a simple, two-pocketed folder. Put your name on the outside of the cover; if you are "into" design and don't want to inscribe your name there, for the time being you may put it on the cover with a removable tag.

Your course notebook should include **all** of the assignments, in numerical order. Include, as well, any quizzes you have and the midterm opportunity. I realize you very well may have additional handwritten comments and notes on the typed pages; that's as it should be. DO NOT retype just to "clean up"; these are assignments of the mind and heart—*not* of your typing abilities. If you have additional running class notes among these pages, that's OK too—although it is not necessary for me to see these.

Additional request: As a last sheet, include a typed note of not more than one paragraph in which you indicate which work read thus far—other than *Paradise Lost*—was to you the most meaningful (as a work of art, or personally, or historically—whatever you make of "most meaningful"). And why?

QUIZ NUMBER 1: SEPTEMBER 9

Name: _____

Both poems begin with the word *hence:*
1. What is L' Allegro "hencing"?

_____

2. What is Il Penseroso "hencing"?

_____

3. List anyone kind of person (occupation) the L'Allegro narrator meets when going out during his day:

_____

4. Melancholy is. described as looking like a figure dressed like a

_____

5. What kind of plays does the narrator of Il Penseroso like:

_____

QUIZ NUMBER 2: SEPTEMBER 16

Name: _____

Morning/Mourning Exercise on "Lycidas"

1. Milton's dead friend, about whom this poem was written, is (circle one) Charles Diodati   John Donne   Edward King
King James   Philip Hassinger

2. The *persona* here is (a) a college student, (b) a clergyman, (c) one of Paul's Pigeons, (d) a sailor, (e) a shepherd.
3. In the poem's middle, the persona attacks (a) college students, (b) clergymen, (c) sailors, (d) shepherds, (e) the monarchy.
4. The person commemorated died (a) by drowning, (b) in a religious massacre, (c) from the plague, (d) in a duel, (e) during the great Civil Wars.
5. At the end of the poem, what happens to Lycidas:

MILTON
INVESTIGATIVE PAPER ASSIGNMENTS

Due November 18

For this assignment you have a choice (Milton would like that) of the kind of paper to prepare. **Select one of the following:**

I. For those who like considerable flexibility, you may select any topic which is (a) solely on *PL* or (b) on *PL* and some other work of Milton's. This project may be, e.g., the exploration or tracing of a theme, the argument concerning Milton's use of some idea(s), an examination of Milton's developing or changing opinions—or some other topic of that nature. If you select this option, you must **get approval** of the topic before October 21; unapproved topics/papers will not be accepted.

Your completed paper should be ten to twelve typed pages (excluding the Works Cited page); it must have a clear and precise title, a readily recognizable thesis statement (preferably in the first paragraph), and should be carefully and fully documented. You may use either the MLA or the Chicago Style for your format, endnotes, and/or Works Cited. See the directions below under number 5, "Bibliography/Works Cited."

Although this option leads you to doing a "traditional term paper," I urge you to develop your own thesis before you go to the library for your research. There are massive amounts of material on Milton; you will learn to appreciate the value of a good title when you try tracking down information! Bear that in mind when you title your own paper. You will probably want to have a minimum of six to eight different sources; these should be from journals as well as books. For the purposes of this project, please make sure that the majority of your references were published after 1980 (there is nothing necessarily wrong with earlier material, but it is important to know what is going on in more recent times too). At least one of your sources should be from after 2000.

-Or-

II. For those who like something very precise, very "handleable," you may select approximately fifty to seventy lines from *PL* (excluding I. 1–125) **for an incredibly, fascinatingly, painstakingly, exuberant explication.** If you select this option you will need to select a "block" of poetry which forms some kind of unit (that is to say, your lines should not just start in an arbitrary place and stop 50 lines later). The format of your paper will be as follows:

Part 1. Indicate which lines you are explicating and provide a brief (one paragraph) statement about why you selected these lines.

Part 2. Here you need to provide the setting/context of your lines. That is, what is going on in the narrative at this point in *PL*; what, e.g., is Milton doing with his "justification of God's ways" at this point? This section probably need not exceed two to three paragraphs.

Part 3. This section will pertain to the criticism which relates to your passage. For this you will do the necessary library research in order to locate those articles and books which, either in part or in total, pertain to your passage. What you are doing, in essence, is providing a brief essay on what the critics say about this section. The question you are addressing is, "What is important here?" I expect you will look at more books and articles than you actually use, but you probably will use at least 10–15 different articles and books. Your Bibliography/Works Cited at the end of the paper will give the full bibliographic information; in Part 3, however, you may merely cite the author's name and page numbers of the book or article. This section should be kept to two to four typed pages.

Part 4. The explication—and the main part of your paper. My best advice to you here is to SHINE. Your object is to become the cosmic expert on your lines. Analyze your lines rhetorically, etymologically, thematically, theologically, and philosophically. Do them in every way you can think of. Go ahead and be as pedantic as you wish. Make connections everywhere you can (between these lines and other parts of *PL*, other works of Milton's, other things you have read in other authors, etc.). The explication will take the reader through the passage with as close a reading as you can provide; remember, though, that it is a reading, not just a line by line list of things you are thinking. Ask yourself, "what does this passage mean?" The answer will provide the general thesis which controls the reading you are providing. This section should not be less than eight, nor more than twelve, typed pages.

If you select this option, you must **get approval** of the topic before October 21; unapproved topics/papers will not be accepted.

Part 5. Bibliography/Works Cited Citation, printed copy.*

* For I and II: "Typed" means typed or word-processed clearly, cleanly, using a good ribbon or printer. It also implies very careful proofreading. You are educated, cultured adults—no matter what your major, no matter what situation you are in, no matter what you are doing. It is expected you will make your best presentation—always. This means careful presentations, careful proofreading, care-filled concern, so that the reader sees your paper in its best possible light. Paperclip the pages together, and make sure your name/course/date are on the first page. And be SURE to keep a photocopy or disk copy for yourself (who knows when a publisher might rush in and want to have the rights to your work?).

Use MLA or Chicago Style for your Bibliography or Works Cited page; do NOT mingle the two style sheets; do not make up a creative form of your own.

Citations from Milton: Every citation of the text needs to be referenced. It is acceptable, for this paper, to use the abbreviations listed in the front of the Hughes text. For *Paradise Lost* merely use *PL*. For the book and line, the format is: PL IV.31–4. Keep in mind that short quotations (one to two lines) are included within the text; longer ones are double-indented and given their own space.

NOTE: These directions pertain to *this* assignment in *this* class; the directions are not intended to be generalized for all papers in other classes. Feel free to (and I encourage you to) discuss your topics, share your writing and toss ideas around with others in the class; this is part of the *shared learning experience.* Above all, **proofread your paper** several times—then have a colleague or two proofread it for you again.

ENGLISH 409
MIDTERM OPPORTUNITY

Name : _____
Fall Semester

This is an *open-book, open-note,* open-minded exploration timed for one hour and ten minutes. Please watch your time carefully; pay attention to the relative value of the parts. **Write clearly** and do all your work in the space, or on the pages, provided. Pepper your essays with quotations from the text; impress your reader with your vast knowledge!

Part I. Short Identifications (20 points)

Identify the work from which each of the following is taken. (Works may appear more than once.)

1. Sometimes with secure delight
   The upland Hamlets will invite,
   When the merry Bells ring round,
   And the jocund rebecs sound

To many a youth, and many a maid,
Dancing in the Checker'd shade.

---

2. Virtue could see to do what virtue would
   By her own radiant light, through Sun and Moon
   Were in the flat Sea sunk . . .
   He that has light within his own clear breast
   May sit i'th' center, and enjoy bright day,
   But he that hides a dark soul and foul thoughts
   Benighted walks under the midday Sun . . .

---

3. From hence, and not till now, will be the right season of forming them to be able writer and composers in every excellent
   matter, when they shall be thus fraught with an universal insight into things. Or whether they be to speak in parliament
   or council, honor and attention would be waiting on their
   lips.

---

4. He than can apprehend and consider vice with all her baits
   and seeming pleasures, and yet abstain, and yet distinguish,
   and yet prefer that which is truly better, he is the true warfa-
   ring Christian. I cannot praise a fugitive and cloistered virtue,
   unexercised and unbreathed, that never sallies out and sees
   her adversary . . .

---

5. For so to interpose a little ease,
   Let our frail thoughts dally with false surmise.
   Ay me! Whilst thee the shores and sounding Seas
   Wash far away, where'er thy bones are hurl'd.

---

6. The Shepherds on the Lawn,
   Or ere the point of dawn,
   Sat simply chatting in a rustic row;
   Full little thought they then,
   That the mighty Pan
   Was kindly come to live with them below . . .

7–10. Briefly identify four (not five) of the following, making clear
      that you really know who/ what you are identifying, and also

noting a work by Milton with which the person/figure might
be identified. Cross out the one you are not identifying:

Bridgewater; Edward King; Samuel Hartlib; Waldensians;
Charles Diodati

Part II. Brief—But Specific (10 points)

1. What hath night to do with sleep?
   Night hath better sweets to prove.
   Venus now wakes, and wak'ns Love.
   Come let us our rites begin,
   'Tis only daylight that makes Sin,
   Which these dun shades will ne'er report.

Poem: _____

What is the significance of these lines **in the whole poem?**

2. The hungry Sheep look up, and are not fed,
   But swoln with wind, and the rank mist they draw,
   Rot inwardly, and foul contagion spread.

Poem: _____

What does "foul contagion spread" mean here?

Comment on the significance of these lines in the context of entire poem:

3. Then to the well-trod stage anon,
   If Jonson's learned Sock be on,
   Or sweetest Shakespeare, fancy's child,
   Warble his native Wood-notes wild.

Poem: _____

What is the speaker doing at this point in the poem?

4. . . . God doth not need
   Either man's work or his own gifts; who best
   Bear his mild yoke, they serve him best . . .

Poem: _____

To what question is this fragment the answer?

What is the famous last line of this poem?

> 5. And then at last our bliss
>   Full and perfect is,
>   But now begins . . .

Poem: _____

When is "then"?

What is happening "now"?

What is the significance of these lines in the whole poem?

Part III. Essays (70 points)

Select **two** of the following (**not three**). Prepare a concise essay on each of your selections, using frequent citations to the text. **Indicate clearly which essays** you have chosen on your paper.

1. Milton's ideas concerning "liberty" are multifaceted and complex; they appear in one form or another in almost all the prose works and in many of the poems. Discuss "liberty" as Milton uses it in the works we have read thus far. You will find it helpful (although it is not necessary) to begin with an outlining sentence such as "Milton uses 'liberty' in [x number of] ways in his early poetry and prose: (a)., (b), (etc.)."
2. Discuss the uses of irony in the following works: *Comus* and "Lycidas." If you see irony in any other of Milton's poems or prose, note that as well.
3. In many of the works read thus far, Milton writes as a concerned citizen, a devout Christian, and a "seeker for truth." Focus on three works of your choice and discuss in what ways Milton's sense of being an Englishman is expressed.

ENGLISH 409
FINAL OPPORTUNITY

Name : _____
Fall Semester

Our "final opportunity" is scheduled for **FRIDAY, December 12, 10–11:50 a.m.** There will be no early or late examinations.

As you requested, the exam will be *open book;* you may use whatever notes you have in your book—plus you may use one 3″ × 5″ note card for each question below. No more; be honest. The exam will have two components: (a) an objective section (very short, only on *PL*); and (b) an essay portion (about sixty minutes). You will write for a maximum of one hour, fifteen minutes; we'll use the rest of the time for a wrap-up and course evaluation. Additionally, you'll submit your *Letter to Milton,* as per other written directions.

I will provide the writing paper; you will need a pen **and** your Milton book.

If you wish to have your examination grade and/or semester grade before the university sends them, attach to your exam a stamped, self-addressed card on the December 12. I'll mail this as soon as the
   information is available.

Part I (objective) will be given on December 12; Part II follows:

Part II.

   At the time of the examination I will select three of the following questions; from those three you will select two on which to write, for thirty minutes each.

Note: The reason for having your textbook is so that you can use it; **provide support, support, support** from Milton's texts. Being able to back up your statements by citing Milton's text is of **major** importance. For convenience sake you may use standard abbreviations for Milton's works.

1. Milton's works (not just *PL*) are filled with creation stories. (a) Identify four or more of these (*PL* and other places). (b) What categories can you provide for these various kinds of creations? (c) Comment on the importance of your selections in their particular contexts.
2. Milton believes that evil is not merely (or necessarily at all) the absence of good; it is a very real, active force in the cosmos and something with which we must daily contend. Using examples from the prose **and** the poetry (other than *PL*) discuss Milton's application of that belief.
3. Using at least three works, at least one of which should be from the prose we read, discuss how Milton's early poetry and prose foreshadow *Paradise Lost*. (You may wish to consider such things as structure, theme, techniques.)
4. Milton writes about "the poet" and "poetry" in a number of his works. Discuss "the calling of the poet" as a sacred profession (or at least as a special calling). Use at least three of Milton's works to support your statements.
5. As you have read, one of Milton's chief ethical interests is in freedom. It is a theme that one may trace in both the poetry and the prose. (a) Categorize at least three kinds of "freedom" with which Milton deals; (b) Discuss the types as they appear in, and apply to, at least two of the minor works and *Paradise Lost*.
6. Assume that *Comus* has just been discovered—but it is anonymously published. You are a well-recognized scholar trying to prove the work was written by Milton. What is your evidence to support your claim?
7. The Father (*Paradise Lost*) provides Adam and Eve with everything they need—including their education. Compare, and then contrast, the education they receive with the educational program Milton outlines in "Of Education."
8. In Milton's view the Christian hero(ine) becomes heroic by making the hard choice of truth; the hero(ine) does this in suffering and in abstinence. This is clear in the minor

poetic works, the prose, and in the major poetry. (a) Indicate where we see this exemplified in at least three of the minor works (prose and poetry); (b) Discuss what are the consequences for the inclusion of such an ideal pattern in the structure of *Paradise Lost,* especially in the vision of the future (Books X, XI, XII) and in the details of the final scene.

9. Milton's concept (or "doctrine") of duty—whereby people are expected always to be doing some kind of service to God, to others, or to both—pervades his prose and poetry, and may be seen as a thread connecting the early with the later works. Discuss Milton's use of this "doctrine" both in his poetry and prose.
10. In his "Areopagitica," Milton argues against the licensing of books. Is he actually arguing in favor of total freedom of expression? If so, how? If not, why not?
11. Throughout our reading we have seen Milton draw heavily upon classical literature. How would Milton have justified all those classical references within his overtly Christian works?
12. In writing *Paradise Lost* Milton not only drew upon the biblical story of Adam and Eve's fall, but he interpreted this according to his particular beliefs. Carefully now, as this is complex: for Milton, did Adam and Eve have to fall? If yes, why? If no, why not?

*   *   *

You have labored long and hard, not only through *PL* but through most of Milton's other poetry and a sizeable portion of the prose. And I need hardly point out that you've gone through a good number(!) of written assignments—from word searches to bibliography assignments, from outlining prose arguments to examining particular types of imagery, and others not yet attempted in prose or rhyme. You've done a midterm, have completed a research paper, have considered many "deep questions," and will do more pulling together of materials for this final assignment: We set out to survey the matter—and survey we did; each of you can be pleased with the amount you've covered, with the various approaches you've had to use to get into the subject, and with the intensity with which you've approached this difficult, provocative, splendid subject. You've worked me hard—and I have done the same to you. I think Milton would agree that we have not been slack!

For those returning in the Spring: have a splendid holiday (word du jour: *holy-day*) break! I will look forward to seeing you in the academic term(s) to come. For those completing their degree work now: I wish you well in whatever vocation (as Milton would call it) you select—or which selects you. Be diligent; be patient; enJOY.

ASSIGNMENT 1

Milton Sonnets—Assignment to be prepared for August 28

Your syllabus directs you to four sonnets. Milton worked with this form of poem throughout his early and midlife years; hence you will find them scattered among the works listed (pseudo-chronologically) in Hughes, pp. ix–x. For Thursday, you are asked to do the following assignments; please do them in the order listed.

Type your responses to these items, not in a fully developed paper but in such a way that you may use the responses for quick recall and reflection when we discuss the poems on Thursday. You will be expected to **keep this Assignment Sheet along with your response sheet in your Course Project Notebook;** the notebooks will be collected at various times during the term.

1. Locate and read each sonnet carefully. For the first reading just read through each poem; don't stop to look up words or read the footnotes. Read the poem(s) this way one or two times, slowly, *aloud.* Prepare a list of the criteria for identifying a poem as a sonnet; identify your source(s) for this information.
2. Now read footnotes; if there still are words you don't understand, look them up in the *Oxford English Dictionary* (hereafter *OED*) or another reliable source. Make sure you understand each word, and each word in context. Now you are ready to **analyze** the poems. Respond for each of the **four sonnets:**
   a. Who is the speaker? To whom is he/she speaking?
   b. What appears to be the purpose of the poem? (as best you can tell);
   c. Who might be the intended audience of each poem?
   d. In what ways does each poem "fit" the criteria you prepared for what a sonnet is supposed to do or be?
   e. Conversely, in what ways do these sonnets not fit the pattern?
   f. Make a list of the real *human* concerns, or real human desires, Milton expresses in each of these poems. In

short, why do you think he wrote these poems? Think
carefully about this—there are important issues here!
3. Finally, and importantly, given what you came up with in
number 2:
   a. How do these poems relate to **you?** What, if anything, in
   them speaks to you in your own humanness, your hu-
   manity, your quest for living? Your quest for living
   deeply? With which sonnet do you most identify? Even
   in those which seem to have little to do with your life,
   what are the issues, concerns, problems with which you
   can identify?

ASSIGNMENT 2

English 409

"On the Morning of Christ's Nativity," written when Milton
was twenty-one, is often considered his earliest significant
poem. One will find in it themes, devices, and techniques he was
to use later in his more mature works, yet they first are used
here in both meaningful and moving ways.

Before reading the poem, read Milton's brief letter to his friend
Charles Diodati (pp. 50–53); this provides the setting for the
writing of the poem.

1. From the following list of **themes and techniques,** one will
   be selected for you. Trace this, in detail, throughout the
   poem, and be able to discuss this intelligently in our class
   discussion of the work.
   (a) Light/darkness   (b) Time   (c) Music/sound/silence   (d)
   Nature
2. Consider, too: (a) the use of paradox and (b) the nature of
   the child. Write a brief paragraph on each.
3. Consider the narrator: Where is s/he in time? in space? in
   relation to the events described? How does the narrator
   draw us—as individual readers—into the poem? What is
   different about the narrator's presentation in I–IV from the
   narrator's presentation in "The Hymn" (I–XXVII)?
4. Consider the event being described. How is this different

from the "nativity" scenes you are used to seeing in traditional Christmas celebrations? How might you explain the
difference?

5. What connections do you find between the poem and what
   Milton says about the poem in his letter to Diodati?
6. Finally, what are the "big issues" M deals with here? What
   "unasked" questions might he be answering in this poem?

ASSIGNMENT 3

English 409—Assignment To Be Prepared for September 9

Here's a fun exercise in comparative analysis; it also shows us
how Milton works with contrasting themes and arguments.

Milton wrote "L'Allegro" and "Il Penseroso" as companion
pieces, possibly as an academic exercise. The works show Milton's ability to argue, compare, and contrast two sides of a topic.
If you **look carefully at the two** you will find that many elements
of the first are paralleled by similar, sometimes opposite, items
in the second. Look at the first **ten** lines of each, e.g., and you
will find that in each poem **three strong verbs** describe what the
respective subject is to do. Additionally, "genealogical" information about the two major figures ("L'Allegro" and "Il Penseroso") is provided, along with parallel descriptions of particular
loci. Such parallels—in theme, description and (to a point) structure—may be traced through the poems.

1. For this assignment you are to make a two-columned list;
   head one of the columns "L'Allegro" and the other "Il
   Penseroso." Go through a **comparative listing of paralleled
   items,** noting by word and line number the parallels you
   find (these may appear as similar—or even the same—
   words, opposites, parallel structures; anything that links
   the one poem to the other). The challenge is to find as
   many parallels/contrasts/etc. as you can.
2. Remember to ask yourself of both poems: (a) Who is speaking? (b) What is the speaker doing as s/he speaks? and (c)
   Why is the speaker telling us these things? We'll discuss
   your findings when we discuss the poem.

3. Summarize the **main arguments** for why the daytime ("L'Allegro") is preferable to the more contemplative, quiet nighttime ("Il Penseroso"). Then do the same for "Il Penseroso" (that is, why does that poem say that night is better than day?).
4. Do you feel Milton has a preference for the sentiment expressed in one poem as opposed to that found in the other? If so, to which? If not, why not?

ASSIGNMENT 4

English 409

Moving on to "Lycidas": we'll examine that poem on Thursday and Tuesday. Work through at least #6 before Thursday, and finish by Tuesday.

For Thursday

As we move on to "Lycidas," you'll find it **very** helpful to spend some time going back for a quick review of the main issues in the four sonnets, the "Nativity Ode," "L'Allegro," and "Il Penseroso." Ask yourself: What are the links you can see among these poems? And what, specifically, do you **learn about Milton**—as a writer, as a person, as a scholar, as a man-of-faith—from these poems? You needn't write out your responses, but given that we will address these in class, you might want to jot down a few responses so that you'll be prepared.

Then

Ask yourself those same questions concerning how, and in what ways, "Lycidas" links with the previous poems.

1. Make a list of as many ways this poem connects with the others you've read and
2. in what ways do we learn about Milton through this work.

"Lycidas" is one of M's finest "minor" poems. It is also one of his most complex. Read the introductory materials (116–20), then read through the poem a couple of times until you feel somewhat comfortable with the overall work. Note in particular item 3 on p. 116 concerning the three movements of the poem—and be able to point out where they are.

One literary critic writes of this poem that "Lycidas is the most poignant and controlled statement in English poetry of the acceptance of that in the human condition which seems to man unacceptable." Another critic suggests that the real subject of the poem is not Edward King but Milton himself. Consider these possibilities as you read.

3. **In your text:** You will find it helpful to outline the poem in the margin of your text.
4. Make a list of the **elements of "pastoral" poetry** and be prepared to discuss them; Make a note of where you found them; please **don't** just use a dictionary. This is a complicated and interesting subgenre; the more you know about it, the better you will appreciate and understand this (and other) literary work(s).
5. **In your book and on separate paper:** As you read the poem, select two of the following and trace them through the poem: (a) water imagery; (b) the pastor/sheep imagery; (c) the theme of fame; (d) the theme of affirmation. Don't just point out where the image or theme appears; mark those—and think, as well, of how they are tied together and how they mark movements through the poem.
6. Ask yourself: (1) who is the narrator?(be able to describe him in detail); (2) who/what is the narrator (not to be confused with Milton) lamenting; and (3) what ultimately happens to Lycidas?
7. At the library, look up two journal articles (published after 1985) on this poem. Give the bibliographic information (author, title, journal, volume, year, pages) and provide a four to five sentence **synopsis** of the contents of each article.
8. Finally, consider the "questions" behind the poem: (a) What do you think Milton is really "crying out" about? (b) What are the big issues of life to which he is responding? (c) And—importantly, but in only a few lines: What might

your responses be to these same issues? (d) In what ways can this poem be "relevant" to a reader in our time?

ASSIGNMENT 5

English 409

Reading *Comus* will be a somewhat different experience from reading the works examined thus far. It is longer, it has a very complex internal integrity, and reading it calls for patience as well as imagination. You will need to know that this is a *masque;* if you don't know what a masque is you will need to practice your library skills and find out. Please don't merely look it up and set the information aside; be able to apply the description—in detail—to what you are reading. Be sure to read as well the Introduction to the work on pp 86–89.

Consider (and prepare typed copy of) the following—**for Tuesday** (be prepared to submit this material following discussion; short answers will be fine):

1. What are the main elements of a "masque?"
2. List places where you find the masque elements in use.
3. List four themes you find in the play.
4. Rank these themes according to what you think is most important (number 1) to least (number 4).
5. Imagine that you are producing/directing this play; what stage machinery would be needed in the theater for a good performance?(make a list). Indicate where in the play you would need to use such machinery.
6. Also make a list of the props you would need (including costumes). Be sure to keep track of where and when in the play you would need these props.
7. Consider that we don't know if this play was first performed inside or outside. What differences would it make in the production of the play if it were outside and not inside?

For the following class (Thursday), do the following:

1. Important: examine carefully Comus's and the Lady's dialogue in 660–813; (a) What are the major points of his argument? (b) What are the major points of her argument?
2. Fun: Consider that the characters in the play are parts of the family and the household of the Earl of Bridgewater; the Lady in the play is his daughter, the two brothers are his two sons, the Attendant Spirit is his music master, etc. In what ways do you think this situation would affect the play—both the script and the performance? How might the play have been different if the family/household were not the intended players?
3. By now you've read several of Milton's "minor" works. What common threads—themes, devices, plots, patterns, whatever—can you find among them?

ASSIGNMENT 6

English 409

"Prolusions" and "Of Education": Prepare these for Tuesday and Thursday next

With these works we move into some of Milton's early prose. The first items give you an idea of what he was writing as a college student; the second, as an adult, about a topic of considerable interest to him.

A. The Prolusions can seem dry, difficult, and very remote unless you approach them as the clever rhetorical displays they were meant to be. As you read "Whether Day or Night" (etc.), keep in mind that he is a bright undergraduate presenting this orally to his peers; he is attempting to be clever, to win his listeners (his peers) over to his side in this argument, to use some "in" jokes appropriate to listeners his age and with similar interests, and ultimately to win an argument. Thus, this seemingly ridiculous topic (and perhaps that was part of the point of its being assigned) allows for humor, mock seriousness, clever argument, and rhetorical flourishes.

<u>Assignment:</u> Read through the first prolusion ("Whether Day or Night . . .") several times, reading it aloud and imagining the kind of reasoning and scenarios suggested above.

1. Prepare a paragraph-by-paragraph outline of this prolusion.
2. Write out: (a) the places you feel the speaker is being humorous; (b) the kinds of humor being employed; and (c) the strategies of argumentation you see. (d) What does the speaker assume of the listener?
3. Look at the two prolusions you were asked to read and see (e) what connections you can make between them (style, process, topics), and (f) what connections you can make between them and the previous works of Milton's that we've already read.
4. Given that you've found Milton's subtle humor in the first prolusion, where are examples of his wit in the second?

B. "Of Education," written when Milton was about thirty-six, describes an educational system which, on the surface, might seem a far cry from what we are accustomed to. Here's your chance to dip both into Milton and into educational theory—after all, we've all been part of this "education" business for the greater parts of our lives.

1. Start out by going back to the yellow "Milton Links" sheet you were given a few weeks ago; look at the section on "Consider your education." Take a few minutes—really, take a few minutes—to seriously consider the items listed there. Doing so will help you connect both with Milton and with the topic.
2. Prepare a detailed outline of the essay, going to at least 3 levels (I, A. 1):
   a. What are Milton's assumptions (make as long a list as you can) about students? about faculty?
   b. How does Milton present himself? That is, what can you say here about the speaker/writer of this piece? (Please don't just say "he's smart"; let's get deeper into it than that!) What can you tell about the speaker, his values, his views, his goals?
   c. Remember that in writing this piece Milton is responding to something; all problem solving does this. Ask

yourself: What are the "Deep Questions" which are behind Milton's proposal? That is, why should anyone be
concerned about education? (List and be able to discuss
at least three; after you've listed them, put them in rank
order with number 1 the most important).

d. All mission statements, vision statements, plans of action, have a goal; what—precisely—is the goal of the educational system Milton proposes? And what kind of
person does Milton expect to produce from his "system?" Use passages in the work to support your statement.

e. If Milton were to examine elementary/high school curricula today, what, **specifically,** might he find good about
them? And what, **specifically,** might he find wrong/bad?

f. Finally, importantly, formulate a statement (one paragraph at most) of what you feel/believe/think the purpose of education should be.

ASSIGNMENT 7

English 409—"Areopagitica"

Considered one of Milton's finest prose pieces, "Areopagitica"
contains both a tight argument and elegant prose. This exercise
will get you into it closely and carefully. This is a carefully written, carefully argued piece; **reading slowly is essential.** Give
yourself plenty of time. You may work in pairs if you wish.

For next Tuesday

1. Read the editor's Introduction on p. 716; this will give you
   the background of the tract;
2. Prepare a written outline of the whole essay (this does not
   have to be detailed, but should cover the whole piece);
3. What is the image Milton presents of himself in the essay?
   What are some qualities he attributes to himself? That is
   to say, the speaker/Milton wants Parliament to think of
   him as a certain kind of person—what are the attributes of
   that person(a)?

4. Make a list of the ways in which Milton links his ideas of censorship with his ideas of what it means to be English;
5. You've already looked, in other works, at various ways in which Milton argues a point. What devices—oratorical and rhetorical—does he use here to persuade his audience? Where else (poetry and prose) has he used these devices?
6. What are the major points of this argument? Mark these in your text, make a list, and be prepared to discuss them.
7. At the library (and to re-familiarize you with the *Oxford English Dictionary*): look up the word "license" (you must use the *OED* for this assignment). What **meanings** (plural) were available to Milton when he used this word? (Cite meanings, examples, dates, etc.)
8. Finally, if you were to find a major flaw in the argument, what would (and where would) it be?

MILTON—*PARADISE LOST:* ASSIGNMENT NUMBER 1

On Thursday we'll begin our in-class reading of *PL.* Although we may not get through Book 1 at that time, make sure you've finished rereading that carefully so that you'll have the context for our comments and work. **I urge you to read the poem aloud;** it will help you to better understand what you're reading, and you'll have some terrific voice-music in the process.

You should be working on your memorization of I.1–26; next week I'll set up the appointments to discuss your research papers and to hear your recitation of the first two sentences. Do give both your serious consideration.

For Thursday

1. Make a list of what comprises an "epic." Check this out in a handbook or book on such matters.
2. In the margin of your book, indicate who the speaker is of each of the speeches in Book one; be careful—not all the speeches begin and/or end with a verse paragraph;
3. Consider the poem's speaker: Who is he, where is he in time, to whom is he writing?
4. Look especially carefully at lines 1–191:

    a. What are the major images?

    b. What references to time do you find? to space?

5. What links do you find between Book I and the previous poetry/prose we've read?

6. Finally, examine lines 670–798, the wonderful description of Pandaemonium. We'll look at these lines very carefully; read through them several times, watch what pictures develop, and pay attention to those little devils. Of what does the "Great Consult" remind us?

Keep working on those first two sentences!

MILTON—PARADISE LOST: ASSIGNMENT NUMBER 2

For Tuesday, 21 October

In Book I we get our first glimpses of Satan; the physical descriptions are impressive—as are the kinds of things we hear him say. You have read enough of Milton's poetry and prose to know how to read through and around the words; things are not always as they seem!

Your group will be assigned one or more of the following. I suggest that you attempt, on your own, to respond to them all, but you need only write out the responses for the specific ones you'll be given. **NOTE:** Your group will be responsible for presenting the material to the rest of the class. You need to decide, together, how **best** to make the presentation in a short time. What ways work best for you in a learning situation? How can you make the teaching/learning situation good for your colleagues? Be creative, informative, collegial.

1. Look at lines 587 ff. Make a detailed list of the physical characteristics of the "commander." Note the similes and metaphors; select two and relate what you think are the reasons Milton chose to use those ways of describing Satan.

2. Look at 621–62. Satan, remember, is trying to revive, to convince, to sway his audience (you'll recall these tactics other works you've read). (a) What does he imply about his audience? (b) What does he imply about himself?

3. Lines 670–798 provide us with pandemonium—literally. (a)

What are the physical details of the building? (b) Look carefully at the preparation for the Great Council. To what other kinds of events can you compare the Council? (c) What is important about the epic simile in 768 ff?

4. Notice the word "infernal" in 793 (and elsewhere); look up this word in the *OED* and in a dictionary which provides etymologies—What are the associations M plays with when using this word?

5. Moving right into Book II: prepare a close reading of lines 5–10. These are important descriptions. What do they mean (in your own words)?

6. We begin the next passage with Satan's speech to the Council (10–42). (a) What is Satan's "political" stance here? That is, what will be his platform? (b) What are three major points of his argument in these lines?

MILTON—PARADISE LOST: ASSIGNMENT NUMBER 3

For the week of November 2–4: Books III and IV

In Books I and II we are introduced to Satan and his crew; in Book III we meet the Father and Onlybegottenson. We're going to have to move very quickly through this book. In preparation for this, do the following:

Group 1. Make a list of as many of the comparisons and contrasts you can find between The Son and Satan; be sure to list the line numbers.

Group 2. Make a list of as many of the comparisons and contrasts you can find between the Father and Satan, listing appropriate line numbers.

Group 3. Look at 540–742; in your book, mark all the references you can find to sight, seeing, perception, insight—vision. What do we learn about Satan in this section and because of these visual descriptions?

We'll go right on to Book IV, where Satan is "now in prospect of Eden."

Group 4. Look at IV. 32–130; this is Satan's first soliloquy on earth. Read it carefully and trace the development of the argument. (a) Find one "quotable quote" in this passage. (b) List three adjectives (not Milton's words, necessarily, but your own) that you feel *best* describe Satan's state of mind here. What important thing(s) does Satan know about himself that nobody else seems to know?

Group 5. Lines 131–201 depict Satan's early discoveries in Eden. To what animals is he compared—and why?

Everyone: The **geography of Eden** is important. How does Milton unfold it to us? What are the geographic, topographic, and "structural" elements? (For further consideration, how is the garden like Eve?)

Everyone: Describe Adam's relationship with Eve. How might this be compared with Satan's relationship with/to Sin? The Father's to/with The Son?

Group 6. Lines 775–end depict a number of things, among them further changes in Satan. Indicate as many of these as you can find, and explain their significance.

Everyone: Finally, in what ways might you connect Book IV with earlier works by Milton? Be creative!

MILTON—PARADISE LOST: ASSIGNMENT NUMBER 4

For the week of November 11–14: Books V–VI

Moving very quickly: Book V may be divided in the following way (one of several possibilities, and with categories of my own device):

1–135	A dream and its interpretation
136–208	The morning hymn/prayer
209–307	Raphael's mission
308–560	Garden hospitality
561–657	Enthronement of the Son
658–802	Conspiracy
803–907	Apostasy and Faith

1. Reread all of Books V and VI before November 11. You need not write out # 2–6, but we will discuss these in class:
2. Look at 1–135: what do we learn of Eve—and what of Adam—from these lines?

3. Look at 136–208; in a Bible, look at the book of Psalms and compare these lines with Psalm 148. What connections can you find?
4. Check out the "garden hospitality" scene: What is added to our info about Eve? about Adam? Note Raphael's greeting in 387ff.; of what does this remind you? What is the "meaning" of 470–505? Finally, what do we learn of angels?
5. In the Conspiracy section: Prepare to discuss everything you can that connects this section with what we've read earlier. Look at 673–94; to what in Book II might this be compared?
6. Book V ends with Abdiel (11. 803–end); what is significant about him and his actions?

Book VI. There is no break between V and VI, as the action moves toward the great epic battle. Prepare the following in writing:

(a) Prepare a general outline for Book VI. Do this on a separate sheet of paper (even if you also wish to do this in your book).
(b) Make a detailed list of the particular events of each of the "days" and events of the battle: specifically, what happens?
(c) Look finally at 825–912; read the lines very carefully, take some notes, and prepare to explicate them in detail.
(d) **Why** does the book end with the message in 893 ff.?

MILTON—*PARADISE LOST:* ASSIGNMENT NUMBER 5

For the week of November 18–20: Books VII–VIII

We will have to rush through Books VII and VIII on Tuesday and Thursday. You will need to do the following with the aid of a Bible. Bring the completed work **and your Bible** to class on the eighteenth. You will be working carefully with Genesis 1–3, short chapters but very, very important ones. If you can get a King James version, do so; that's the one Milton used.

1. Read Genesis 1–3 aloud, 2–3 times. Slow down; roll those words around, hear them, feel them. There are *countless* literary references to these chapters.

2. Book VII gives the days of creation (243–640).
   a. Prepare a simple outline, on a separate sheet of paper and in your book, of this section; indicate which lines are given to which days, and indicate what the major acts of creation are for those days.
   b. Indicate the corresponding verses in Genesis, and observe the . difference between the Genesis account and Milton's (you don't have to write this part out, but note, for discussion, the differences).
3. Book VIII gives us the creation of Adam and Eve.

Groups 1–3: On a sheet of paper, compare Milton's version here to what you find in the first chapters of Genesis, and compare this to the earlier accounts you've had of the creation in other parts of. PL (i.e., what other accounts do we have, where are they, what do they say that's different from what's here?).

Groups 4–6: Note the "philosophy of love" section (521–653): Why does Milton include it? Analyze the dialogue here between Adam and Raphael; what are its special points?

* Important (well, sort of) literary events:

- November 18: Robin Hood bled to death at the hands of a treacherous nun at Kirlees, in Yorkshire, 1247;
- November 18: Margaret Atwood b. 1939.
- November 20: Nadine Gordimer b. 1923.

MILTON—*PARADISE LOST:* ASSIGNMENT NUMBER 6

For Tuesday, November 25: Book IX

If there is one scene most central to *PL*, it is that which is depicted in **Book IX.** Pressures of the investigative paper should be over; give yourself time to read carefully and absorb deeply what Milton does here. We've been building up to Book IX, the primary action of which is the temptation and "man's first disobedience."

As you read you will find it useful, even informative, to read aloud using different voices: that of the narrator, of Satan, of Eve, of Adam. Go ahead; try! This will help you to hear as well as see the tension the narrator feels, the sly excitement Satan barely can control, the changing responses of Eve, and Adam's involvement in the pre- and post-fall (prelapsarian, *postlapsarian*) scene. As a good alternative, get together with some others and share the readings with them.

Here's a general outline of where the various topics are in this book.

Everyone: come up with "titles" for these sections, as I have done with the first one, and write these out:

Outline: 1–47   Narrator, on the subjects of epics
48–191
192–384
386–531
532–779
780–833
834–989
990–1045
1046–1189

Write out, **EVERYONE:** As you read this book, make a list of references to hands.

Everyone: Note the narrator's comments in 1–47. How do these relate back to Book I.1-26?

Now: In the small groups you'll discuss the following. Please prepare these ahead of time; be prepared to present your findings to the class, quickly and concisely. As we have much to cover in this one day, there will not be time for much group discussion of these; come prepared!

Groups 1 and 2: Note Satan's actions as he returns. How does he get into the Garden and where does he go once in? What time of day is it? Examine closely Satan's soliloquy in 99–178; what are the primary emotions he displays? If you were filming the action, what would be your camera directions? What time of day is it?

Groups 3 and 4: Note 192–384, the separation of Adam and Eve. Make a list of Eve's reasons for working alone (note that there are several). Make a similar list of Adam's reasons for their *not* working alone. Given our earlier study of methods of argumentation, how does he counter her arguments and how does she rebut his?

All: Note 385—hang on to that line; it's important.

Groups 5 and 6: Lines 385–531 show us the mutual approach of Eve and the Serpent. The temptation itself begins at 532 and extends to 779. Make a list of the major points of Satan's argument. What is the progress of Eve's considerations? That is to say, identify where she is, step by step, in her "buying" the argument. Recall our earlier reading of *Comus*; what similarities do you see between this seduction and the one presented there? At the same time, what's different here?

Groups 1 and 2: 780–833: Eve's transgression. Sin enters immediately after she eats. What sins can you spot here? Locate a list of the "seven deadly sins" and see which of these Milton includes. Note the order of their appearance, and be prepared to comment to the class on how these sins are linked with one another.

Groups 3 and 4: 834–989. The fall isn't complete without Adam. How is Eve different when she returns to him? What is his response to her new condition? How is his "sin" different from hers?

Groups 5 and 6: 990–1045. Immediately after Adam eats, what happens—and why?

All:

1. 1046–1189. What results of the fall are evident here in Adam? in Eve? in the two of them together?
2. In looking at Book IX as a key part of *PL*, which one line (or one sentence) here appears to you to be the most significant ("significant" for whatever reasons you are prepared to articulate)?
3. We've watched Satan since the start of the epic. Briefly (two to three sentences), what are your views of him at this point in the poem?
4. Not to be taken lightly: What responses do you have— intellectual, emotional, spiritual, whatever—to what occurs in this book? That is, how do you find yourself responding (head, heart, etc.) to what Milton accomplishes and describes in Book IX?

MILTON—*PARADISE LOST:* ASSIGNMENT NUMBER 7

For Tuesday, December 2

We *are* going to get through **Books X, XI, and XII.** The following pertains to X and XI:

After the Fall, Adam and Eve are rushed out of the garden—much as we are rushing to the end of this term. They *must* go, but not before they understand the consequences of what they have done—both immediate and long term—and not before God gives them some important messages.

We have much to cover in only two days. You can make it; we will do it. But I'm counting on your giving the work a final thrust of energy.

For Tuesday:

    (a) Prepare a typed list of as many consequences of the fall as you can find in **Book X;** merely list the item and the line number. Go for plenitude! It will be helpful to you if you also note these along the way in your book.
    (b) For **Book XI,** note especially Michael's message in 72–262. List the major things he tells them and point out which you believe to be the most important. Then skim the rest of XI.
    (c) **XII.** Look at 65–104; why does Milton include this? To what else you've read in Milton does it seem similar? Again look at Michael's speech in 285–465; basically, what does he say—and why? We'll go up to 464 this day and save the rest.

MILTON—*PARADISE LOST:* ASSIGNMENT NUMBER 8

Due Thursday, December 4

For our last class day you'll have two things to prepare; please write out the answers as directed:

1. Look at *PL* XII 65–104; why does Milton include this? To what else you've read in Milton does it seem similar? Again look at Michael's speech in 285–465; basically, what does he say—and why?
2. Reread, carefully, XII 465–end. Make a thorough list of the following:
   (a) What are the things Adam learns (as listed in these lines)?
   (b) What are the final warnings Michael gives?
   (c) Given that we think of Milton as such a great scholar, what does he say about the limits of knowledge?
   (d) What links can you make between the last passage (605–649) and earlier parts of the poem?

ENGLISH 409: LAST WRITTEN ASSIGNMENT

We've covered a considerable amount of material this term. You will pull much of this together as you prepare for the Final Opportunity—but let me also ask you to do the following.

Early in the term we discussed, and you were asked to consider, how the works we read pertained to you. To put that assignment in perspective, and to encourage your seriously doing this, please do the following:

Prepare a letter to John Milton (you may address it to "Dear John Milton," "Dear Mr. Milton," "Dear John"—if you feel that close!). In the letter, please let him know

   (a) which non-*PL* work had especial meaning for you—and why. Also,
   (b) let him know what was meaningful for you about *PL*—and why.

Then (and this is up to you), you may say whatever else you'd like to say to him, either positive or negative, praising or damning.

This letter should be no less than a typed page in length and will not be "graded" (but definitely will be read). Make sure your name is on it. You'll submit this at the time of the final opportunity.

PERITUS MILTONI

This is to certify that

Student's name

has argued with the Areopagitica, denied tenure to kings and magistrates, perused prolusions, debated divorce, calculated with Comus, expounded on education, noted the Nativity, lamented Lycidas, and—most especially—descended to the Burning Lake, ascended to the Celestial sites, sung with the Heav'nly Muse, tasted the Fruit of that Forbidden Tree, and left by Eden's East Gate, while pursuing things unattempted yet in Prose or Rhyme and going, from start to finish, through all of *Paradise Lost*, and is now generally accepted as a Peritus Miltoni—Milton expert.

Yea, verily.

Granted this 9th day of December
   in the year _____.

Appendix B: Interview One

Interview with Prof. J, Tuesday, August 12 (Prior To Class Observations)

> I do believe that God wanted a grand poem from that man and therefore blinded him that he might be able to write it. But He had trained him up to the point—given him thirty years in which he had not to provide the bread of a simple day, only to learn and think; then set him out to teach boys; then placed him at Cromwell's side, in the midst of the tumultuous movement of public affairs, into which the late student entered with all his heart and soul; and then last of all he cast the veil of a divine darkness over him, sent him into a chamber far more retired than that in which he laboured at Cambridge, and set him like the nightingale to sing darkling.
>
> —George MacDonald, *The Seaboard Parish* (Whitethorn, CA: Johannesen Press, 1995), 37–38.

K: Who would take your class?

J: Students in the Milton class are juniors, seniors, and grad students who don't want to take grad class for various reasons—people well along in their twenties and even thirties. Because all are at least juniors, few will be in [Perry's first] group of binary choice [right/wrong] ethical thinkers. [It is] more likely to find people further along in those stages.

K: Milton will present a very concrete and specific ethical system that will allow students to rub up against that ethical system and either accept or reject it, based upon where they are in their own ethical development. Do you agree?

J: Yes! (laughter). I don't know that I relish you seeing me in my 'undress' *all* the time. One of the things that's really fun about this [class] is that students are incredibly intimidated by taking Milton; this is a frightening prospect for them and they've put it off as long as possible—like eating vegetables. But what they find out—many, if not most, year after year—is that they'll say, "While I hated the thought of doing this, I really wound up liking it." And one of the things they get to like about it is that they encounter themselves. Because there is so much value identification, values in the way of the morality and ethics involved, they have somebody who is so identifiable as a touchstone, they can use where he is [Milton] to see where they are: their religion (or lack thereof), spirituality, their personal development, their struggles with idealism. Milton struggled, had a tremendous angst; he was alone, incredibly alone, in what he did; even when he linked up with people, that didn't last; nobody could hang in with him. It's great for students; they learn a lot about themselves. I'll tell them the first day there are two subjects in the course: the first is Milton, the second is themselves (himself or herself). They will learn about themselves *a lot* in this course.

K: As far as conduct of the course, I hope you will just do what you do?

J: I intend to; they'll see me climb up on the table, do a tap dance (laughter). After lo these many years, you have your own little . . . things just come to you; you may not have done them for fifteen years, but they just come to you—and it's the appropriate time to do it.

K: Why do you think there is so little research on teaching of college-level literature?

J: Do you suppose in part because literature is such a personal thing, and such a personal experience in so many ways? You and I can sit down and read a book that we both agree is terrific, and we can find things in it we both agree are terrific, yet what you're experiencing is quite different from what I'm experiencing. What I do in the classroom and what you do with the same material might be quite different.

K: I quite agree. It would be interesting to see if there's anything that you do . . . that you and I would consider intensely personal . . . that could be translatable to someone (English teachers) in training. For example, evaluating someone for tenure or post-tenure review; "I think X is a good teacher." And some hardnosed legislator says, "What makes you think so? What's your evidence?" Right now we have to rely either on anecdotal evidence or on our own personal ideas. But if we could identify specific moves—part science, part art—and say, Prof. J is an expert because he did—at *this* moment—this. And so the whole micro genetic method is much more descriptive, because I'm not that terribly interested in numbers per se—although I want to find things that are quantifiable—but in the *function* of a given move at a given moment, when I know the history of that student's mental process. You have an instinct that when a student is at this point of readiness, you'll do *this* and you just sort of know it. As an outsider, I want to find out what it is that you know at that moment, even though . . . it may be beyond description.

J: There are things I'm sure I won't be able to verbalize . . . because you just know them. That feeling, that sensitivity is an important part of teaching—that you're *feeling with* the student; that you have compassion.

K: [Being a good teacher] is rather like being a good therapist; part of what I'm doing now is writing about the way therapy relates to literary criticism. And like a therapist, you know that when someone does X, you do *this*. I'm reading a book [about Carl Whitaker] and he says, "until you prompted me, I never thought of that." So, as an outsider let me start off by asking you: In the very beginning, what do you hope to accomplish in the first two or three weeks of the semester as far as getting students *learning*?

J: Off the top of my head: Some of the things will be directly related to the literature and some not. To introduce them . . . to get to know Milton as a person, and not just as a writer who lived and died three hundred years ago and is considered very dull and dry; to get them to think about him as a human being, we'll start with early things (not *Paradise Lost*) . . . things he wrote when he was about their age. We'll begin with sonnets—'cause they're short—and I can show them how to read a sonnet.

K: Two interesting things you said: one, you want them to get to know Milton as a person; and two, you want them to know how to read a sonnet. Can you describe briefly the things that you are doing to get to each of those?

J: Yes. Milton as a person, they'll know that in two ways: one, I'll give them some information, stories about his growing up that they'll read about, and stories that I'll tell them. We'll use the literature to come back to Milton as a person; sometimes, I'll try to get back to question, "What does this [literature] mean to you [students]?" Projection: "You've just read a sonnet about Milton at twenty-one, when he thinks he's not getting anywhere." Well, they can identify with that. I try to build up a picture of Milton not being *that* dissimilar to them in some ways. He was just incredibly brilliant, but he loved, he hated, had passions, desires, and so forth just the way they have, too.

K: So, your first step—part of the first step—is to get students to identify with Milton at their age?

J: The Milton we think of—who wrote *Paradise Lost*, so ancient, so formidable—to start softening that picture. Secondly, they will *learn to read* in those first weeks; what to look for, how to read a poem or prose piece by him. I'll take them through *explication de texte*—that's why we do sonnets—they're short—and show them how to read.

K: Do you talk at all about sonnet-genre considerations?

J: A little, but they know that. We do a written assignment every day, and these lead to discussion in class, that leads to . . . the things we'll be talking about. So they will have to "Look up (say) the three to five things that make up a sonnet and write down where you found it." Then we share that information.

K: So, during those first two weeks you'll expect them to know or to familiarize themselves with the genre considerations of a sonnet?

J: First two days—we move quickly—I do the sonnets, because they're short and because Milton wrote some when he was young.

K: And while they're getting fairly technical information about sonnet, the actual dialogue in the classroom is more along the lines of, "Here's what Milton is doing when he wrote this sonnet." So you're doing two fronts simultaneously?

J: Yes. Actually, more than two fronts. First, use the sonnet to talk about Milton the person (as a young man); second, use the sonnet to try to have them identify with themselves what he is doing (Milton knows inside that there's something planned for him; they identify that with the struggles in their own lives); and third, technical expertise. Also, the bigger picture is that we're softening that hard, frightening view of the "Milton" they may have heard of.

K: Do you believe that your approach is typical of colleagues who also teach Milton? say, professors A, B, or C ?

J: This is not typical of A, B, or C.

K: May I asked how you evolved to a point where you're doing it [conducting the class] this way as opposed to the ways other professors do it? Since more typical English professor moves would be: (a) straight lecture; (b) maybe the polar opposite; or (c) Milton as he relates to your life?

J: I don't think (b) would be typical of an upper-level college English class.

K: So, beyond the lecture system, what other approaches have you seen? Look even at your own graduate training; you went to Iowa (late 1960s) when it was one of the top twenty graduate-training schools in English, one of the elite schools.

J: It's a good school.

K: Given your experience there, and your experience here at NIU with our colleagues, is there an alternative pattern to straight lecture that you have experienced yourself?

J: My experience as a student was primarily lecture. I don't know what professors A, B, and C do here at NIU. But Professor A is pretty much straight lecture still; others might encourage more discussion. When I started teaching, I did a lots and lots of lecture and my syllabus was very different. But, I tried . . . there's nothing wrong with lecturing; it depends on the situation. Times when I thought: "This calls for further explanation," I used little mini-lectures—but I really, *really* [emphasis] tried to encourage their participation in the process. Lecturing *gives* them information, and I want them to *do something with it*, ultimately.

K: Let's set another interview, later, with an agenda to talk about your evolution as a professor! But [returning to the original question], we have three fronts, . . . delivery of information via lecture and reading . . .

J: More than that, though! The delivery of information: part of the delivery includes [student preparation] . . . I am going to set up ahead of time written assignments that will . . . I am really guiding the way they're looking at this. They're going to have to come in with the information themselves. I give them a little, but they're going to be actively involved in finding the information and thinking about things themselves.

K: So you actually sort of prompt the students . . . ?

J: I do. The assignment they get . . . the work they do Tuesday night, for example, for Thursday morning will give them information to prompt them in the work we're going *to do* on Thursday.

K: So the pattern goes: you set up ahead of time—based on your experience and knowledge of Milton and of your students—a series of prompts, the answers to which allow the students to begin the thinking and feeling you want. You offer delivery of information to prompt them certain directions; you spend a good deal of time in your own conversation with students getting them to focus on their *feeling* level, their emotional life as it relates to the material.

J: We won't spend a *great* deal of time on it because they don't know one another and might be too uncomfortable.

K: What would you say you do then (I'm just trying to find out what you *do* ...)?

J: Right. Let's take the second day of class. . . . Those who have decided to stay . . . they will have had a written assignment from Tuesday on, say, the sonnet. I don't give them very much—it's all so good [the poetry] that it's hard to decide which to cut—and I'd rather have them understand a sonnet than read, say, five hundred lines of poetry. So, they'll have had the assignment, asking them for technical information on the sonnet and to find out what a word means—it is probably quite important; there could be two or three meanings that this word could mean, from the student looking at the sonnet. They have to *work with the sonnet* and keep thinking about it.

K: This question is a prompt you work out ahead of time?

J: Yes, and then they have to write it out. They have pages and pages of written work to do for this course.

K: This is the *Course Project Notebook!* It consists of the answers to these prompts?

J: Right. And I tell them that these responses don't have to be formal prose, polished, etc., but it does have to be written in full sentences and typed. I don't want someone doing it at five minutes of eight in the morning.

K: You require it to be typed ahead of time for discussion that day, and from time to time you walk around and check that it's done?

J: Right! At various times I ask that they submit this material to me [later called "Cards o'Doom!"]. They may add to it—it's not to be pristine appearing (indeed they're expected to, like adding to the margins of their book)—during, say, small group work. "It's expected that you're [students] going to get information from somebody else. These are your notes."
There will be levels to the questions. Part of it is strictly informational: elements of the sonnet; then, trace this pattern, word, image; what's an *image?* what does poem mean to you?

K: A colleague of ours—also from Iowa—uses a variation of that, called *Reading Notes.* Would you call yours [Course Project Notebook] a variation of that?

J: It's a variation. These are very detailed *prompted* reading notes.

K: What if a student comes up with a question of his or her own? Is it permissible to ask and answer that question in the Notebook?

J: Absolutely! It's wonderful. Because we'll have time in class to discuss the things I haven't thought of, particularly the variations . . .

K: Which would make sense, particularly when you're trying to get them to relate what they're learning about Milton to themselves.

J: I am very careful what I ask them to share [about themselves] in class—I want them to be comfortable about that. . . . I used to go in thinking, "Well, they're English majors; they know how to read poetry." Well, they don't. They're dealing with an intellectual system so far removed from where they are, with a heavy emphasis on the classics, tremendous dogmatism, and lots and lots of Christian theology; mixed with Milton, it's tremendous. Zealous patriotism, and all this stuff mixed in there, it's hard stuff. So my idea is to start small and show them what to look for. And later in the semester—I haven't always had time for this—I'm always hesitant to relate back until we get to *Comus,* for example, and I ask them "What two earlier poems remind you of what we're reading here?" The last day of class, we'll go back to two earlier poems, and I'll ask them to look at them and tell me "What in these poems reminds you of what we're reading here?" And when we've had time—the last day of class—I'll ask them to go back to it: "Does it mean anything to you now?" Same themes in Milton from the time he was a teenager until he's an old man.

K: From a cognitive point of view, at the end of the semester you ask them to circle back both to the early structure [students' mental structures] with which they came into the course *and* the content of Milton, his themes, etc.?

J: And I try to make sure I have time to do this.

K: Could you take me through the first two-to-four weeks—a typical week's worth of work? Not so much the content, but the structure of what you'll try to do?

J: What you'll probably observe will be different from what I'll tell you (laughter). Typically, I'll come in early (ten to fifteen minutes before 8:00am class begins) and chitchat, and I try to "work the crowd." If someone is going on a trip, or their dog caused trouble, etc., I joke about it; it's a funny thing to be in "Red-Eye Milton." It gets less a topic of conversation as the semester progresses, and I know that will happen. And it can be funny later, but not at first. They don't think they can do this, it's outrageous (class at 8:00 a.m.), and I tell them, "If you don't think you can do it, don't take this class. I'm rarin' to go by 8:00 (I get up at 5:00 a.m.), 'cause I've been up for hours." So before the class begins, there's a warm-up.

Then, typical class: "Take out your papers you were working on and let's look at them." [Then] either I might talk about something in preparation for work in their small group for five or ten minutes, or we might go directly into the small groups. I do some talking between small groups. I don't like them to spend too much time in small groups, even though they've got the papers in front of them [Course Project Notebook]. Then I'll ask them to look at Question number 3, let's say; I'll time them and then ask them, when done, to pull their information together. I don't tell them ahead of time who'll talk; who'll be the scribe.

K: How do you define a "small group"?

J: Usually four or five, depending on how many in the class. I've wrestled with this a number of times: *how* to divide them: arbitrarily, or let them choose? There are advantages and disadvantages to both ways.

K: Do you change the groups every class period?

J: No. I tried that, but there are times when I'd ask a group to do something outside of class; if they've built up some kind of recognition of one another, it works better I've found. But I know there are other ways of doing it . . .

K: Do you require in-office conferences for everybody, or just the groups you're working with?

J: Everybody. Individually, a couple of times a semester, especially about the time of the midterm. Sometimes, we'll set up a group project, and then a representative comes up to see me. When they're preparing to do the research papers— although not all do research papers—it's very, very carefully structured. They don't realize how structured "nonstructured" assignments are. Then I do get some feedback about the groups that way, too.

K: Small groups work for . . . time?

J: If there is something animated in the group, let it go; you play it by ear. I'll put something on the board or ask a student to be blackboard scribe. What we do in class will come out of work done outside of class. Once students start seeing patterns, we'll discuss it together *after* we've spent time in the small groups.

K: So, on Tuesday, small groups work anywhere from twenty to forty minutes, then whole group sharing, and that takes the period?

J: We might take some time reading the poem in class.

K: Then, on Thursday, what happens?

J: More of the same. Same pattern. I go through a great deal of minor poetry and some of the prose before we get to *Paradise Lost*. And threading themes together as we go. If students know that he's dealing with images of light and dark that he [Milton] really likes, or water, or he likes the dialectic (if this, then that) and this balance stuff—and we see this in four, five, six of the minor poems, then students know what to look for. They're learning to read Milton's poetry, too. And then as we move into the prose, Milton does the same thing there. Their assignments—they will have to use the *OED (Oxford English Dictionary)*—I'll tell them, this is what the *OED* is if they don't know where to find it; and then they look up specific things. Because they're going to use the *OED and bibliographies when they do Paradise Lost* assignments later. By the time they get to the research *per se* (or variations thereof), they know how to use research tools on Milton; they know how to look for metaphors, images, themes. . .

K: This is a fourth aspect, then. Summary: (1) the focus on delivery of information on a specific poem or prose; (2) the discussion of Milton as an emotional being just generally; (3) the relations between that and their own emotional life; and now (4) the use of the tools of our profession within these other assignments.

J: [I teach them] "How do you [students] do research in English?"

K: The Course Project Notebook: are some of the prompted assignments along the lines of, "Go to the OED and look up the meaning of word X in line 3," for example?

J: Right. And copy out three variations of that word and then do something with it. How are the variations of those words (looked up) going to impact on interpreting the meaning of the poetry? So you're always going back to the poetry.

K: Do you find resistance by students to writing out all this material?

J: Yes! This is work! You cannot pass my class—if you don't do the assignments, you can't participate in the group; if you don't work in the group, you have nothing to say in the whole-class discussion. But, these are English majors and this is an advanced Milton class and he's a major, major figure—a great thinker—a major force in Western thought. This demands a great deal of work, and I tell them that ahead of time. I tell them: "You've probably heard the scuttlebutt . . . and if you have, get in and drop right away because this is not a course where you can sit back and blow it off. I have an attendance policy—you're only allowed two absences.

K: I find all of this fascinating. Although most of this [types of teaching techniques] is known by our colleagues, what will be interesting is the implementation of it at a given moment with a given set of personalities.

J: You ask how students respond to these assignments? I'd say a majority of them accept that they have to do this to pass the class and some of them (*some* of them) will actually come to enjoy doing them, and for some the work will still be a chore, but they'll do it. Just got a letter from a student— the kind every teacher loves to get. I had him two semesters and I saw him go from a shy, mediocre type of fellow (notice, not *student*) to the star of the class—he ran the class discussions. And he learned not just to play me (give teacher what students thought the teacher wanted); he really, really came out from his shell. And then there were others, you know, students who just hated the whole thing, thought [the class] was terrible. There was one woman last semester—worked two jobs and never should have been in class anyway—and I bawled her out—(*not in class*, of course); I told her you have to do this. She didn't do well, got a D and didn't graduate. But it was her choice.

K: One of the drawbacks of this university (NIU) is that so many of our students are working and the working really eats into course time, and they [students] get resentful of just ordinary class work.

J: Right. And I feel sorry for such kids. I would do much more with group work outside [the classroom], but I know that some are commuters, and say, Sally, lives in Batavia (Il.), has a family, can only take one course a semester. However, I tell them that this [university life] is not a preparation for life—it *is* life. It's getting deeper into life. So do your best, and I'll help any way I can.

K: You ensure compliance by private jawboning?

J: Yes I do.

K: Do you grade the Course Notebook at all?

J: No. I read it; it is assessed, not even in a critical way. A couple of times a semester, I'll gather them and write a half-page or a page on what I see. I spend a huge amount of time on this course. The assignments?—I'll spend five, six, seven hours writing up [a single] assignment, and they have twenty-four assignments.

K: Is the primary focus in the seven hours of preparation for these assignments on the students' intellectual structures or knowledge, i.e., how much they know at a given moment? Two ways of looking at this: (1) you have an abstract sense (not negative-abstract) in your experience, a given class should know X about Milton in this point in the semester, and so the assignments track your sense of where their Miltonic expertise is at a given stage; or (2) where that particular class (personalities) is in the, say, third week. Are your decisions largely (or mostly) influenced by what they actually know about Milton, or what you think they should know?

J: The answer is a balancing act. I know that not every class is where last semester's class was, on, say, March 21. But because I know where I want them to go in terms of reading Milton, there are things they *are* going need to read *Paradise Lost*, which we will have to start on a particular date in order to finish. Hence, I *do* push them, and make some adjustments based on the fact that this group is not, say, working the way the last one did. The work in their Course Notebooks is very individualized; students need not be embarrassed by listing things in their notebook. There may be several themes in a poem, and I don't care which, say, two or three they choose. By the time we do whole group work, they may collectively come up with eight—and that's great, because they're learning from one another. Adjustments are made because they are able to do this, unable to do that—as long as they make an honest try.

K: So you make a single assignment . . .

J: That has multiple parts . . .

K: But you organize assignments in such a way that students can individualize—by asking, instead of what are the three themes in a poem, what are three major themes [Nystrand's Quasi-Authentic Questions]. You assume that the grounding they do on their own will get enhanced by small-group or whole-group discussion. That new information they can write on their Course Notebook; you assume there'll be lots of scribbles . . .

J: Right. Don't have to retype; I'm not reading CNs looking for a formal essay, because you've got a great deal of material to get through. Course game-plan is adjusted somewhat because we do have *Paradise Lost* to get through (start on a certain date), and I'll make adjustments to make sure they have the technical experience; they know what to look at. Lots of flexibility.

K: What percentage of time would you say you do "stand-up" to deliver information, tell jokes, etc.(contrasted to student-centered work)?

J: I am tempted to say 15 to 20 percent, but it's a lot more than that. In actuality, I would guess its 30 to 40 percent; there are days when there'll be a lot—75 percent—and days when it'll be quite a bit less. I haven't micro-designed the classes, but I have macro-designed them, so that there's a lot of flexibility for me, too.

K: Anything important in first two-to-three weeks that I haven't asked?

J: Good Question: (1) I try to make an effort to learn their names, to get to know them; (2) to warm them up to not be afraid—no joking at someone's expense; (3) that there's no such thing as a bad answer. We can't know it all—*I* don't know it all. These are efforts to make students comfortable—although it doesn't work for all. I also (5) try to put Milton in a time context; who else was writing at this time; when did he live? What was it like living in 1620, 1630, in England? What was going on? There's historical information that's *very* important, because Milton was involved (more than most of his contemporaries) in the politics of his time, which is incredibly involved with his religion.
But most [students] don't know the Puritans; they don't know Puritans, James I, or Charles I, or what the Restoration was . . . and there are wonderful stories, and so I try to fill them in. In many, many courses I've asked them to read a short history book—I have that assigned for this semester, but it's difficult because most history books are filled with facts. So I try to take some of those and talk around them; when they describe that Milton's father was a wealthy *scrivener* (for exam, *Paradise Lost*), what does that mean? Did they have servants, etc.? So I try to do that [tell them little stories about historical info], and to bring in the biography, because we know more about Milton than many others (he saved everything). Which is just fascinating because the ego was just tremendous; Milton knew he would be great. He knew that what he would be doing was of earth-shaking consequence, that he would help prepare for the second coming of Christ—he'd help prepare the way. So there was this tremendous obligation to do it right, and to save everything to be sure that all these messages would be available (over and over, just in different form).

K: So your training as a teacher of Milton includes ongoing reading of his biographical material?

J: Yes. It's huge, a massive amount for *Paradise Lost*. I'm interested in ancient history and what's going on in art, music . . .

K: Do you bring in art, music into this class?

J: Not in this class. There isn't enough time. In the seventeenth century [Renaissance] and in the Shakespeare class, I'll talk about art, music, the history of science . . . It was important to Milton, but we just don't have time to do it in this class. In *Paradise Lost*, he talks about the war in heaven and makes up all these great battles, and he is really drawing on seventeenth-century warfare patterns. If you know how battles were set up, you'd know what those devils were doing.

Appendix C: Interview Two

Second Interview with Prof. J, October 29th

K: [How would you] define scholarship and its relationship to teaching?

J: I'll explain how the Milton convention in Atlanta, Georgia (1997) is connected to teaching Milton:
It's about a student whose paper was on *Comus*, third week of class; the class discussion surrounding his topic gave me an idea. I then began revising my own paper on the relationship between the Lady (in the play) and Comus, and the kinds of language he uses. The student was joking about his younger brothers and their sleazy language, which led me to making changes. I worked on my paper in the summer (on "Magic and Music"), rethinking what the student had said. The scholarship I also read led into the teaching, and my teaching, in turn, led into the scholarship; I don't know how many students caught it.
I am a student at the same time as [I am] a teacher, but my audience is larger than who is in the room; not just students and teacher. That was the path of rediscovery from our class.

K: Was there a certain question or response that was said in class that caused these changes to come about?

J: Changes came about at the time when the class was focused on *Comus* (I attempt to say, these passages); we focused upon the same passages that are in the paper. Responses of the students were taken into account in writing my own paper, each feeding upon the other.

K: In what ways do you see the students in this class developing their own abilities to argue interpretive points in *Paradise Lost?*

J: Undergraduates are quite different from a graduate class, who are reading at a different level with a different background. But there are good students here in this [undergraduate] class; they give wonderful answers and share with the class; these helped with my insights. As for the students, their group work and peer discussions influence their experiences with the text. You would not find it [the same reactions] when thoughts sink in after the class; the fresh responses thus changed the paper. Some undergraduates view Milton as an "unknown," and fear one must go into it being a expert.

K: In your mind, what are the most important modes and means of developing literary arguments from the tasks you assign?

J: The most important thing is to be prepared for class. This is an assumption which underlies being a teacher, but some students may believe reading along with the class is better because of how little they feel they know beforehand. But homework is affected, and completely unknown material cannot be discussed, so the end effect is not worth it. And my questions require that they know the material. I think they keep going back to the text [in whole- and small-group work] all the time. You would just have one hour and fifteen minutes of references to something you haven't read. Although this is the case with some of the students.

K: Well, there is a strand of scholarship that talks about *knowledge transfers:* Types of learning are transferred to any domain; others think that knowledge is domain-specific. Learning Milton is different from learning, say, a math problem. Your inclination is that the kinds of demands you make on your students are the demands that Milton specifically makes or that his texts make?

J: No. It's a good try. I'm not familiar with the "domains." I don't know what I'm doing a lot of the time, I just go and do it. But that's what you're looking at. I would like to think two things are going on. One—the kinds of things I have them do can be transferred to other types of English classes. They've had lots of different ways into the texts. They've learned, because I know some of them haven't done that before and it surprises me. The approaches that they've learned, hopefully, can be used in reading or history, not just literary classes. In addition, (and I hope I'm not sounding arrogant), but I think an important part of the process is the teacher, acting as a catalyst. For positive or negative reasons, or both. It's what we do in the class with it; we've got the elements in the class and now we're the catalyst.

K: Moving to a question which bears directly on what you've said: There's some scholarship on conversations, pros and cons on IRE [Interrogation, Response, Evaluation]. Your view seems to be that this is a very important part for the teacher, being a director; are there a limitations in this? Do you feel that the benefits decrease? In your mind, do the benefits outweigh the drawbacks of that pattern?

J: I'm not familiar with the research on this particular subject, but I've done the same course in other ways.

K: What, where it's been more student-directed?

J: No. More teacher-directed, less student response. Where I've really been more involved in giving the information and not so much in interrogation, not even calling upon them. I see advantages in doing it the way we're doing it now. I can see limitations in it, too. I'd be very happy if questions came out of that . . . well, we started out yesterday with questions I wasn't anticipating, and *that was fun.* I wish there were lot and lots more time. We'll never get through *Paradise Lost* now, and I do want to get through it. Not just to "get through it," but because it's a great work and there's lots for them to learn and have fun with. So I do understand the time constraints and can see limitations of the process. This seems to be a workable way, with this course, at this point in my life.

K: So do you see any changes in this pattern between now and the end of the semester, or does what we've been doing for the past month or so is that going to continue through the end?

J: I think that because time is short, I think there will be more of me taking us through the text faster. So there's less time for me to keep asking them to respond to things. When this is all over, when you can talk to me about all this, I would really be interested in your responses and comments and how things are with that. I'm aware of limitations that are occurring, but I just don't know how to do that. I would really be happy if they would be creating some of the situations instead of my creating them and setting them up. But we have so much to do. I don't know how to open up and free the time. I would like to go in, and some day and say, "I'm not going to tell you anything at all. You have the questions." There would be a few who would ask questions, but a lot wouldn't.

K: Back to an earlier question: What do you see is the most important function of small-group work in your class?

J: Well, it allows the student, who doesn't feel able to speak out in class, to be able to have a much smaller, more intimate arena to be able to express herself or himself. Although there are people in the small groups who still aren't responding, I know who they are and you know who they are, and they know that I know who they are. But there's that. And it allows for a personalization and a place for people to say "This was the stupidest assignment I've ever done," or "I couldn't get anything." But it also allows them to learn from each other, in all sorts of ways. Some people just copy down the answers, but in some of those papers there have been people who have done a lot of work on their own, and you can see where they've added a lot from what the others have said. To me that would be a valuable experience, where there's been an exchange of information from peers. There are a good number of people who have done that.

K: In your mind, are there any controls that you've instituted to keep the same people from being "vampire-ish" in small groups?

J: I haven't, and I know in the groups who the vampire people are. As I walk around to some of the groups I purposefully say, "What can you add to this?" So I have put them on the spot in the little group, which is a safer place to put them on the spot than in front of the whole class. And still some people have said, "Well, I don't know." Then again, they'll never know. They've missed the point of being an English major. I don't have controls on that.

K: What do you hope is accomplished by the use of the "Words du jour"? I like that a lot.

J: I really want them to see that the words, in Milton—it's not just throwing in a word to fit the meter or because it fits the gap. Every word is packed with meaning; that is one part of it. The other part is—and again I know that some are responding this way—I want them to see there is a joy in playing with the language. We're in English because we love the language and here's where the word comes from and words are fun. Milton is playing elaborate games with this.

Notes

INTRODUCTION

1. Ken Bain, *What the Best College Teachers Do* (Cambridge: Harvard University Press, 2004), 137.

2. See Shari Stenberg and Amy Lee, "Developing Pedagogies: Learning the Teaching of English," *College English* 64.3 (2002): 326–47.

3. See Bain, *What the Best College Teachers Do*; Gerald Graff, *Professing Literature: An Institutional History* (Chicago: University of Chicago Press, 1987), 79; Stenberg and Lee, "Developing Pedagogies."

4. See Franklin E. Court, *Institutionalizing English Literature: The Culture and Politics of Literary Study, 1750–1900* (Stanford: Stanford University Press, 1992); Graff, *Professing Literature*, 77–78.

5. Mike Rose, *Lives on the Boundary* (New York: Penguin, 1990), 26, 28.

6. Ibid., 32.

7. Ibid., 35 (emphasis added).

8. Ibid., 37.

9. Wendy Luttrell, "'The Teachers, They All had their Pets': Concepts of Gender, Knowledge, and Power," *Second Signs Reader, Feminist Scholarship, 1983–1996*, ed. Ruth Ellen B. Joeres and Barbara Laslett (Chicago: University of Chicago Press, 1996), 391.

10. Rita Kramer, *Ed School Follies: The Miseducation of America's Teachers* (New York: Free Press, 1991).

11. Larry Cuban, *How Scholars Trumped Teachers: Change without Reform in University Curriculum, Teaching and Research, 1890–1990* (New York: Teachers College Press, 1999), 33, 53–54; Stenberg and Lee, "Developing Pedagogies," 327.

12. Bain, *What the Best College Teachers Do*, 169.

13. See Court, *Institutionalizing English Literature*; Kathleen McCormick, *The Culture of Reading and the Teaching of English* (Manchester, UK: Manchester University Press, 1994), 4–5.

14. Cuban, *How Scholars Trumped Teachers*, 25.

15. James D. Marshall and Janet Smith, "Teaching as We're Taught: The University's Role in Education of English Teachers," *English Education* 29.4 (1997): 258–60.

16. Peter Smagorinsky and Melissa E. Whiting, *How English Teachers Get Taught: Methods of Teaching the Methods Class* (Urbana: NCTE, 1995), 88–90; McCormick, *The Culture of Reading*, 13–67.

17. René Wellek and Austin Warren, *Theory of Literature* (New Haven: Yale University Press, 1949).

18. Arthur N. Applebee, *The Teaching of Literature in Programs with Reputations for Excellence in English* (Albany: State University of New York Press, 1989), 37; John V. Knapp, "Wandering Between Two Worlds: The MLA and English Department Follies," *Style* 34 (2000): 644; Peter J. Rabinowitz and Michael W. Smith, *Authorizing Readers: Resistance and Respect in the Teaching of Literature* (New York: Teachers College Press, 1998), 97.

19. Smagorinksy and Whiting, *How English Teachers Get Taught*, 88; cf. Robert E. Probst, "Five kinds of Literary Knowing," *Literature Instruction: A Focus on Student Response*, ed. Judith Langer (Albany: NCTE, 1992), 54–77.

20. Neal Learner, "The Teacher-Student Writing Conference and the Desire for Intimacy," *College English* 68.2 (2005): 205.

21. Louise Rosenblatt, *Literature as Exploration* (1938; repr., New York: Barnes and Noble, 1976).

22. Smagorinsky and Whiting, *How English Teachers Get Taught*, 89; McCormick, *The Culture of Reading*, 30 ff.

23. Norman Holland, *5 Readers Reading* (New Haven: Yale University Press, 1975); Judith Langer, *Envisioning Literature: Literary Understanding and Literature Instruction* (New York: Teachers College Press, 1995); Louise Rosenblatt, *Literature as Exploration* (1938/76) and *The Reader, The Text, The Poem* (Carbondale: Southern Illinois University Press, 1978).

24. Stanley Fish, *Is There a Text in this Class?* (Cambridge: Harvard University Press, 1980).

25. Ann Gere, C. Fairbanks, A. Howes, L. Roop, and David Shaafsma, *Language and Reflection: An Integrated Approach to Teaching English* (New York: Macmillan, 1992); Smagorinsky and Whiting.

26. Smagorinsky and Whiting, *How English Teachers Get Taught*, 89.

27. Gere et al., *Language and Reflection*, 126–29.

28. Peter J. Rabinowitz and Michael W. Smith, *Authorizing Readers: Resistance and Respect in the Teaching of Literature* (New York: Teachers College Press, 1998); Joseph F. Trimmer, *Narration as Knowledge: Tales of the Teaching Life* (Portsmouth, NH: Boynton-Cook, 1997).

29. Michael Foucault, "What is an Author?" *Textual Strategies*, ed. Jose V. Harari (Ithaca: Cornell University Press, 1979), 141–60.

30. Rabinowitz and Smith, *Authorizing Readers*, 112.

31. Ibid., 116, 128.

32. Bain, *What the Best College Teachers Do*, 189.

33. Cleanth Brooks, *The Well-Wrought Urn* (New York: Harvest, 1947), 8.

34. Rosenblatt, *Literature as Exploration*, 49–51.

35. Paul Fussell, *Poetic Meter and Poetic Form* (1965, reprint New York: Random House, 1979), 18; Eleanor Berry, "The Free Verse Spectrum," *College English* 59.8 (1997): 873–97.

36. Gaea Leinhardt and Kathleen McCarthy Young, "Two Texts, Three Readers: Distance and Expertise in Reading History," *Cognition and Instruction* 14.4 (1996): 441–86.

37. Rabinowitz and Smith, *Authorizing Readers*, 71; Thomas C. Foster, *How to Read Literature Like a Professor* (New York: Harper-Quill, 2003), 226–32.

38. Carl Bereiter and Marlene Scardamalia, *Surpassing Ourselves: An In-*

quiry into the Nature and Implications of Expertise (Chicago: Open Court, 1993).

39. James Phelan, *Reading People, Reading Plots: Character, Progression, and the Interpretation of Narrative* (Chicago: University of Chicago Press, 1989), 7–12.

40. Rabinowitz and Smith, *Authorizing Readers*, 88–93.

41. Ibid., 100.

42. Leinhardt and Young, "Two Texts, Three Readers."

43. Paul Kameen, *Writing/Teaching: Essays Toward a Rhetoric of Pedagogy* (Pittsburgh: University of Pittsburgh Press, 2000), 157.

44. Alan C. Purves, Theresa Rodgers, and Anna O. Soter, *How Porcupines Make Love II* (New York: Longman, 1990), 60. Purves states: "The classic is the work—not the author."

45. Rabinowitz and Smith, *Authorizing Readers*, 21–22; Michael W. Smith, *Understanding Unreliable Narrators* (Urbana: NCTE, 1991).

46. Jean Lave, *Cognition in Practice* (New York: Cambridge University Press, 1988); Jean Lave and Etienne Wenger, *Situated Learning: Legitimate Peripheral Participation* (Cambridge: Cambridge University Press, 1991); John Seely Brown, Allan Collins, and Paul Duguid, "Situated Cognition and the Culture of Learning," *Educational Researcher* 18.1 (1989): 32–42; Barbara Rogoff, *Apprenticeship in Thinking: Cognitive Development in Social Context* (New York: Oxford University Press, 1990).

47. Jean Lave, *Cognition in Practice*, 14.

48. Brown et al., "Situated Cognition," 32.

49. Ibid., 33.

50. Ibid.

51. Aristotle. *Poetics*, translated by Samuel H. Butcher (New York: Courier Dover Publications, 1951).

52. Raymond Williams, *Modern Tragedy* (Stanford: Stanford University Press, 1966), xiii.

53. Thomas C. Foster, *How to Read Literature Like a Professor* (New York: Harper-Quill, 2003).

54. Rabinowitz and Smith, *Authorizing Readers*, 102, 115.

55. Brown et al., "Situated Cognition," 33.

56. Ibid., 33, 37.

CHAPTER 1. CURRENT CONSERVATIONS

1. Ruth-Ellen Boetcher-Joeres, "Elusive Theory and Illusive Practice? Editing *Signs*," *PMLA* 118 (2003): 319.

2. Larry Cuban, *How Scholars Trumped Teachers*, 76; Paul Kameen, *Writing/Teaching*, 168–70.

3. Cary Nelson and Stephen Watt, *Academic Keywords: A Devil's Dictionary for Higher Education* (New York: Routledge, 1999), 285.

4. George Levine, Foreword to *Teaching Literature: A Companion*, ed. Tanya Agathocleous and Ann C. Dean (New York: Palgrave-Macmillan, 2003), xii; Jerome McGann et al., "Reading Fiction/Teaching Fiction: A Pedagogical

Experiment," *Pedagogy* 1.1(2001): 157; Elaine Showalter, *Teaching Literature* (Malden, MA: Blackwell, 2003), 39.

5. John Guillory, "The Very Idea of Pedagogy," *Profession 2002* (New York: MLA, 2002), 164–71; Jerome McGann et al., "Reading Fiction/Teaching Fiction; Robert Scholes, *The Crafty Reader* (New Haven: Yale University Press, 2001); Elaine Showalter, *Teaching Literature.*

6. Charles W. Anderson, *Prescribing the Life of the Mind* (Madison: University of Wisconsin Press, 1993), 86; Victor Nell, *Lost in a Book: The Psychology of Reading for Pleasure* (New Haven: Yale University Press, 1988).

7. Rabinowitz and Smith, *Authorizing Readers.*

8. David Downing, Patricia Harkin, and James Sosnoski, "Configurations of Lore: The Changing Relations of Theory, Research, and Pedagogy," *Changing Classroom Practices,* ed. David Downing (Urbana: NCTE, 1994), 6.

9. See also Diane F. Sadoff and William E. Cain, eds., *Teaching Contemporary Theory to Undergraduates* (New York: MLA, 1994).

10. Carl Bereiter and Marlene Scardamalia, *Surpassing Ourselves;* Tony Noice and Helga Noice, *The Nature of Expertise in Professional Acting* (Mahwah, NJ: Erlbaum, 1997).

11. Michelle Chi, Robert Glaser, and M. J. Farr, eds., *The Nature of Expertise* (Hillsdale, NJ: Erlbaum, 1988); Barbara Graves, "The Study of Literary Expertise as a Research Strategy," *Poetics* 23 (1996): 385–403; Barbara Graves and Carl H. Frederiksen, "A Cognitive Study of Expertise," *Empirical Approaches to Literature and Aesthetics* 52, ed. Roger J. Kreuz, and Mary Sue MacNealy (Norwood, NJ: Ablex, 1996), 397–416; Graves and Frederiksen, "Literary Expertise in the Description of Fictional Narrative," *Poetics* 20 (1991): 1–26; John V. Knapp, "Situated Learning: Red-Eye Milton and the Loom of Learning: English Professor Expertise," *Tomorrow's Professor Listserv* number 236, July 6, 2000.

12. See also Stenberg and Lee, "Developing Pedagogies," 334.

13. George Levine, "The Two Nations," *Pedagogy* 1 (2001): 8.

14. Tanya Agathocleous and Ann C. Dean, eds., *Teaching Literature: A Companion* (New York: Palgrave-Macmillan, 2003) 2; Kramer, *Ed School Follies.*

15. Graves and Frederiksen, "Cognitive," "Literary Expertise" [see note 11]; Larry Johannessen and Thomas M. McCann, *In Case You Teach English: An Interactive Casebook for Prospective and Practicing Teachers* (Upper Saddle River, NJ: Merrill–Prentice Hall, 2002); Rogoff, *Apprenticeship* 39–41, *Cultural* 293 ff.

16. Peter Smagorinsky, *Teaching English Through Principled Practice* (Columbus, OH: Merrill-Prentice Hall, 2002).

17. Johathan Culpeper, *Language and Characterization: People in Plays and Other Texts* (Harlow, UK: Longman-Pearson Education, 2001); Richard J. Gerrig, "Participatory Effects of Narrative Understanding," *Empirical Approaches to Literature and Aesthetics* 52, ed. Roger J. Kreuz and Mary Sue MacNealy (Norwood, NJ: Ablex, 1996), 127–42; Norman Holland, "The Brain and the Book," Seminar syllabus, online.

18. R. C. Anderson and P. D. Pearson, "A Schema-Theoretic View of Basic Processes in Reading Comprehension," *Handbook of Reading Research,* ed.

P. D. Pearson (New York: Longman, 1984), 255–91; Walter Kintsch and Teun van Dijk, "Toward a Model of Text Comprehension and Production," *Psychological Review* 85 (1978): 363–94, and *Strategies of Discourse Comprehension,* (New York: Academic Press, 1983); Jean Mandler and N. S. Johnson, "Remembrance of Things Parsed: Story Structure and Recall," *Cognitive Psychology* 9 (1977): 111–51; Dietrich Meutsch, "Mental Models in Literary Discourse," *Poetics* 15 (1986): 307–31.

19. Knapp, "Situated"; Foster, *How to Read Literature,* xvii; Lave, *Cognition;* Lave and Wenger, *Situated Learning;* Rogoff, *Apprenticeship, Cultural.*

20. Gerald Graff, *Clueless in Academe* (New Haven: Yale University Press, 2003); Guillory, "The Very Idea of Pedagogy," 165; George Hillocks Jr., *The Testing Trap: How State Writing Assessments Control Learning* (New York: Teachers College-Columbia University Press, 2002) 6; Kameen, *Writing/Teaching* 206–7; Gary Tate et al., *A Guide to Composition Pedagogies* (Oxford: Oxford University Press, 2000), 8–16.

21. See *PMLA* 112.1 (January 1997), and more recently *Pedagogy* 1.1 (Winter 2001) and 2.3 (Fall 2002).

22. See also Brenda Jo Brueggemann and Debra A. Moddelmog, "Coming-Out Pedagogy: Risking Identity in Language and Literature Classrooms," *Pedagogy* 2.3 (Fall 2002): 320–21.

23. Avrom Fleishman, *The Condition of English: Literary Studies in a Changing Culture* (Westport, CT: Greenwood Press, 1998); Holland, *Brain;* John V. Knapp, "Wandering Between Two Worlds: The MLA and English Department Follies," *Style* 34 (2000): 650–51.

24. Miriam Gamoran Sherin, "When Teaching Becomes Learning," *Cognition and Instruction* 20 (2002): 119.

25. Ann C. Dean, "The River and the Chestnut Tree: When Students Already Know the Answers," *Teaching Literature: A Companion,* ed. Tanya Agathocleous and Ann C. Dean (New York: Palgrave-Macmillan, 2003), 139–48; Larry Johannessen, *Illumination Rounds: Teaching the Literature of the Vietnam War* (Urbana: NCTE, 1992); Johannessen and McCann, *In Case You Teach English;* Robert C. Scholes, *Crafty,* "The Transition to College Reading" *Pedagogy* 2 (2002): 170; Anna O. Soter, *Young Adult Literature and the New Literary Theories* (New York: Teachers College Press, 1999), 13; Dennis J. Sumara, *Why Reading Literature in School Still Matters: Imagination, Interpretation, Insight* (Mahwah, NJ: Erlbaum, 2002).

26. Graff, *Clueless* 185.

27. Arthur N. Applebee, *Literature in the Secondary School: Studies of Curriculum and Instruction in the United States,* NCTE Research Report number 25 (Urbana, IL: NCTE, 1993).

28. Knapp, "Wandering," 635.

29. John V. Knapp, "Teaching Poetry via HEI (Hypothesis-Experiment-Instruction)," *Journal of Adolescent and Adult Literacy* 45 (2002): 718–29; Court, *Institutionalizing English Literature;* Gerald Graff, *Professing Literature: An Institutional History* (Chicago: University of Chicago Press, 1987).

30. Cuban, *How Scholars Trumped Teachers.*

31. Pamela L. Grossman, *The Making of a Teacher: Teacher Knowledge and Teacher Education* (New York: Teachers College Press, 1990), 87–95;

Diane Holt-Reynolds, "Good Readers, Good Teachers? Subject Matter Expertise as a Challenge to Learning to Teach," *Harvard Educational Review* 69.1 (1999): 29–50; Kathleen McCormick, "Reading Lessons and Then Some," *Critical Theory and the Teaching of Literature: Politics, Curriculum, Pedagogy*, ed. James F. Slevin and Art Young (Urbana: NCTE, 1996), 292–315; Rabinowitz and Smith, *Authorizing Readers*.

32. Kameen, *Writing/Teaching*, 174.

33. Christopher L. Schroeder, *Re-Inventing the University: Literacies and Legitimacy in the Postmodern Academy* (Logan: Utah State University Press, 2001), 90.

34. Holland, *Brain*; Culpeper, *Language and Characterization*.

35. Joseph Carroll, ed. *On The Origin of Species by Charles Darwin*. Ontario: Broadview Press, 2003; Robert Storey, *Mimesis and the Human Animal: On the Biogenetic Foundations of Literary Representations* (Evanston, IL: Northwestern University Press, 1996).

36. John V. Knapp, "Creative Reasoning in the Interactive Classroom: Experiential Exercises for Teaching George Orwell's *Animal Farm*," *College Literature* 23 (1996): 143–56; Knapp, "Family Systems Psychotherapy, Literary Character, and Literature: An Introduction," *Style* 31 (1997): 223–54; John V. Knapp and Kenneth Womack, eds. *Reading the Family Dance: Family Systems Therapy and Literary Studies* (Cranbury, NJ: University of Delaware Press, 2003).

37. William E. Cain, "Contemporary Theory, The Academy, and Pedagogy," *Teaching Contemporary Theory to Undergraduates*, ed. Dianne F. Sadoff, and William E. Cain (New York: MLA, 1994), 9.

38. Ibid., 16–17.

39. Dan McIntyre, "Using Foregrounding Theory as a Teaching Methodology in a Stylistics Course," *Style* 37 (Spring 2003): 1–13; Lesley Jeffries, "Analogy and Multi-Modal Exploration in the Teaching of Language Theory," *Style* 37 (2003): 67–85.

40. P. Brody, C. DeMilo, and Alan C. Purves, *The Current State of Assessment in Literature* Report Series 2.1 (Albany, NY: Center for Learning and Teaching of Literature, 1989); Michael J. Bugeja, "Why We Stopped Reading Poetry," *English Journal* 81 (1992): 32–42; Kathleen McCormick, *The Culture of Reading and the Teaching of English* (Manchester, UK: Manchester University Press, 1994); Robert E. Probst, "Five kinds of Literary Knowing," *Literature Instruction: A Focus on Student Response*, ed. Judith Langer (Albany, NY: NCTE, 1992), 54–77; Alan C. Purves, Theresa Rodgers, and Anna O. Soter, *How Porcupines Make Love II and III* (New York: Longman, 1990); Michael Sprinker, "The War Against Theory," *Minnesota Review* ns no. 39 (1992–93): 103–21; René Wellek and Austin Warren, *Theory of Literature* (New Haven: Yale University Press, 1949).

41. Arthur N. Applebee, *The Teaching of Literature in Programs with Reputations for Excellence in English* (Albany: State University of New York Press, 1989), 37; Todd Davis and Kenneth Womack, *Formalist Criticism and Reader-Response Theory* (New York: Palgrave-St. Martins Press, 2002), 14; Probst, "Five"; Rabinowitz and Smith, *Authorizing Readers*, 97.

42. Walter Jackson Bate, ed. *Criticism: The Major Texts* (New York: Harcourt, Brace, Jovanovich, 1963), 275.

43. See also James Phelan, *Reading People, Reading Plots: Character, Progression, and the Interpretation of Narrative* (Chicago: University of Chicago Press, 1989), 47.

44. See also David Bartholomae and Anthony Petrosky, *Facts, Artifacts, and Counterfacts: Theory and Method for a Reading and Writing Course* (Portsmouth, NH: Heinemann, 1986).

45. Scholes, *Crafty*, 54–55.

46. See also Stanley Aronowitz, *The Knowledge Factory: Dismantling the Corporate University and Creating True Higher Learning* (Boston: Beacon Press, 2000), 128–29.

47. T. S. Eliot, *The Sacred Wood: Essays on Poetry and Criticism* (London: Metheun, 1920).

48. Alice Glarden Brand and Richard L. Graves, eds. *Presence of Mind: Writing and the Domain Beyond the Cognitive* (Portsmouth, NH: Boynton-Cook, 1994); Deborah P. Britzman, "Structures of Feeling in Curriculum and Teaching," *Theory into Practice* 31 (1992): 252–58.

49. Levin, qtd. in Phelan, *Reading People*, 47.

50. Ibid.

51. Frederick Crews, *PostModern Pooh* (New York: North Point Press, 2001).

52. McCormick, "Reading," 297; see also Isabel Beck and Margaret McKeown, "Application of Theories of Reading to Instruction," *Literacy in American Schools: Learning to Read and Write*, ed. Nancy Stein (Chicago: University of Chicago Press, 1986), 61–81.

53. Phelan, *Reading People*, 12–13.

54. Davis and Womack, *Formalist Criticism*, 14.

55. See also I. A. Richards, *Practical Criticism* (New York: Harvest Books, 1929).

56. Showalter, *Teaching Literature*, 49 (original emphasis).

57. Ibid., 52 (emphasis added).

58. Graff, *Clueless*, 179.

59. Showalter, *Teaching Literature*, 53.

60. Ibid., 55.

61. Ibid., 78.

62. Ibid., 67, 77.

63. Scholes, *Crafty*, 170; Graff, *Clueless*, 180–81; Stenberg and Lee, *Developing Pedagogies*, 333.

64. Graves, *Literary Expertise*; Graves and Frederiksen, "Cognitive."

65. Aronowitz, *The Knowledge Factory*, 61; Crews, *Postmodern*, 37; Schroeder, *Re-Inventing the University*, 99–102.

66. H. M. Collins, *Artificial Experts: Social Knowledge and Intelligent Machines* (Cambridge: MIT Press, 1990); Lave and Wenger, *Situated Learning*; Neil Mercer, *The Guided Construction of Knowledge: Talk Amongst Teachers and Learners* (Clevedon, UK: Multilingual Matters, 2000), 74; Nelson and Watt, *Academic Keywords*, 282; Rogoff, *Cultural*.

67. Schroeder, 91, 102.

68. Stanley Fish, "What Makes an Interpretation Acceptable?" in *Is There a Text in This Class?* (1980), 338–55, 390; Norman Holland, *5 Readers Read-*

ing. (New Haven: Yale University Press, 1975); McCormick, "Reading," 299; Wolfgang Iser, *The Act of Reading* (Baltimore: Johns Hopkins University Press, 1978); Hans Robert Jauss, *Aesthetic Experience and Literary Hermeneutics,* trans. Michael Shaw (Minneapolis: University of Minnesota Press, 1982); David S. Miall, "Empowering the Reader: Literary Response and Classroom Learning," *Empirical Approaches to Literature and Aesthetics,* 52, ed. Roger J. Kreuz, and Mary Sue MacNealy (Norwood, NJ: Ablex, 1996), 463–78; Louise Rosenblatt, *Literature as Exploration* (1938), and *The Reader, The Text, The Poem* (1978).

69. Terence R.Wright, "Reader-Response Under Review: Art, Game, or Science?" *Style* 29.4 (1995): 529.

70. Norman Holland, "Note to Ellen Moody: Reader-Response." *Psyart,* June 13, 2001.

71. Ibid.

72. Rabinowitz and Smith, *Authorizing Readers,* 134.

73. David Bleich, *Subjective Criticism* (Baltimore: Johns Hopkins University Press, 1978).

74. Louise Rosenblatt, *The Reader,* xiii, 4.

75. Rosenblatt, 75.

76. Cf. Jyl Lynn Felman, *Never a Dull Moment: Teaching and the Art of Performance* (New York: Routledge, 2001), 40–45.

77. Judith Langer, ed. *Literature Instruction: A Focus on Student Response* (Albany, NY: NCTE, 1992); Judith Langer, *Envisioning Literature: Literary Understanding and Literature Instruction* (New York: Teachers College Press, 1995); Probst, "Five."

78. Fish, "What?" 353.

79. M. Dressman and J. P. Webster, "Retracing Rosenblatt: A Textual Archaeology," *Research in the Teaching of English* 36 (2001): 110–45.

80. Ibid., 133.

81. Ibid., 129.

82. Ibid., 136–37.

83. Graff, *Clueless,* 109.

84. Carol D. Lee, *Signifying as a Scaffold for Literary Interpretation: The Pedagogical Implications of an African-American Discourse Genre* (NCTE Research Report number 26. Urbana: NCTE, 1993).

85. Deborah Appleman, "'I Understood the Grief': Theory-Based Introduction to *Ordinary People.*" *Reader-Response in Secondary and College Classrooms,* 2nd ed., ed. N. J. Karolides (Mahwah, NJ: Erlbaum, 2000), 126–27.

86. Felman, *Never a Dull Moment,* 94–95; cf. Arthur N. Applebee, *Curriculum as Conversation: Transforming the Traditions of Teaching and Learning* (Chicago: University of Chicago Press, 1996), 45; Knapp, "Wandering," 647.

87. David Bleich, *Readings and Feelings: An Introduction to Subjective Criticism* (Urbana: NCTE, 1975); Wayne C. Booth, *The Rhetoric of Fiction* (Chicago: University of Chicago Press, 1961); Holland, *5 Readers;* Nicholas J. Karolides, ed., *Reader-Response in the Classroom* (New York: Longman, 1992); Langer, *Envisioning;* Langer, *Literature Instruction;* Purves et al., *Porcupines;* Rosenblatt, *Literature, Reader.*

88. Britzman, "Who Has the Floor? Curriculum, Teaching, and the English Student Teacher's Struggle for Voice," *Curriculum Inquiry* 19 (1989): 143–62.

89. Cf. George Hillocks, Jr., "Literary Texts in Classrooms," *From Socrates to Software: The Teacher as Text and the Text as Teacher*, ed. Phillip W. Jackson and Sophie Haroutunian-Gordon, Eighty-eighth Yearbook of the National Society for the Study of Education (Chicago: University of Chicago Press, 1989), 135–58; Judith Langer and Arthur N. Applebee, *How Writing Shapes Thinking: A Study of Teaching and Learning* (Urbana: NCTE, 1987); Robert E. Probst, *Response and Analysis: Teaching Literature in Junior and Senior High School* (Portsmouth, NH: Heinemann, 1988); Peter Smagorinsky and Steven Gevinson, *Fostering the Reader's Response* (Palo Alto, CA: Dale Seymour, 1989).

90. Rabinowitz and Smith, 31.

91. Holland, *5 Readers.*

92. Cf. simulations of these in Johannessen and McCann, *In Case You Teach.*

93. Mercer, *Guided Instruction;* Martin Nystrand and Adam Gamoran "Instructional Discourse, Student Engagement, and Literature Achievement," *Research in the Teaching of English* 25.3 (1991): 261–90; Nystrand et al.; Gordon Wells, *Dialogic Inquiry: Toward a Sociocultural Practice and Theory of Education* (Cambridge: Cambridge University Press, 1999), 119.

94. Rabinowitz and Smith, 26; cf. Peter J. Rabinowitz, *Before Reading: Narrative Conventions and the Politics of Interpretation* (Ithaca: Cornell University Press, 1987), 194–95.

95. Holt-Reynolds, "Good Readers," 35.

96. Ibid., 40.

97. Langer, *Envisioning*, 93.

98. Applebee, *Curriculum*, 36.

99. Sumara, *Why Reading Literature*, 95.

100. McCormick, *Culture*, 36.

101. Langer, *Envisioning;* James D. Marshall, Peter Smagorinsky, and Michael W. Smith, *The Language of Interpretation: Patterns of Discourse in Discussions of Literature* (NCTE Report no. 27. Urbana: NCTE, 1995); McCormick, "Reading"; Probst, "Five"; John Willinsky, *The New Literacy: Redefining Reading and Writing in the Schools* (New York: Routledge, 1990), 117–33.

102. Fish, "What?"; McCormick, "Reading."

103. Barnes and Barnes, qtd. in McCormick, "Reading," 303.

104. See Bartholomae and Petrosky, *Facts.*

105. Marshall et al., *Language*, 29; cf. Francine Prose, "I Know Why the Caged Bird Cannot Read," *Harpers*, September 1999, 76–84, here cited from 78.

106. Mercer, *Guided Construction*, 31, 61; Wells, *Dialogic Inquiry*, 241.

107. Langer, *Envisioning*, 10.

108. Langer, "Discussion," 13.

109. Cf. Mercer, 29–32, Wells, 242–43.

110. Cf. Wells, 76.

111. Douglas Bush, "Literary History and Literary Criticism," *Criticism: The Major Texts*, ed. Walter Jackson Bate (New York: Harcourt, Brace, Jovanovich, 1963), 704.

112. Rabinowitz and Smith, 11.

113. Dietrich Meutsch and Sigfried Schmidt, "On the Role of Conventions in Understanding Literary Texts," *Poetics* 14 (1985): 551–74.

114. Davis and Womack, *Formalist Criticism*, 58.

115. Martin Montgomery et al., *Ways of Reading: Advanced Reading Skills for Students of English Literature* (NY: Routledge, 1992); Raman Selden, *Practicing Theory and Reading Literature* (Lexington: University Press of Kentucky, 1989), 107.

116. Nick Peim, *Critical Theory and the English Teacher* (New York: Routledge, 1993), 55.

117. Roland Barthes, *S/Z: An Essay*, trans. Richard Miller (New York: Hill and Wang, 1974), 16.

118. John Ellis, *Against Deconstruction* (Princeton: Princeton University Press, 1989); Holt-Reynolds, "Good Readers"; Bruce K. Martin, "Teaching Literature as Experience," *College English* 51.4 (1989): 377–85; Thomas K. Rudel and Judith M. Gerson, "Postmodernism, Institutional Change, and Academic Workers: A Sociology of Knowledge," *Social Science Quarterly* 80.2 (1999): 213–28.

119. Henry A. Giroux and Peter McLaren, eds., *Between Borders: Pedagogy and the Politics of Cultural Studies* (New York: Routledge, 1994).

120. Ava Collins, "Intellectuals, Power, and Quality Television," ed. Giroux and McLaren, 60 (emphasis added).

121. Graff, *Clueless*, 109.

122. Cf. Bill Martin, "Response to Poetry: Making Use of Differences," *English Record* 42.2 (1992): 23–26.

123. Arthur N. Applebee et al., "Creating Continuity and Coherence in High School Literature Curricula." *Research in the Teaching of English* 34.3 (2000): 396–429), 398; cf. Applebee, *Curriculum*, 30; Graff, *Clueless*, 181–89.

124. Cynthia L. Greenleaf et al., "Apprenticing Adolescent Readers to Academic Literacy," (*Harvard Educational Review* 71 (2001): 79–127; Lave, *Cognition*; Lave and Wenger, *Situated Learning*; Rogoff, *Apprenticeship, Cultural.*

125. See also Knapp, "Situated."

126. Knapp, "Creative."

127. Stanley Fish, *Professional Correctness: Literary Studies and Political Change* (Cambridge: Harvard University Press, 1995), 15.

128. Mark Edmundson, "On the Uses of a Liberal Education," *Harpers*, September 1997, 39–49, here cited from 49.

129. Langer, "Discussion," "Literary"; Gaea Leinhardt et al., eds., *Teaching and Learning in History* (Hillsdale, NJ: Erlbaum, 1994); Gaea Leinhardt and Kathleen McCarthy Young, "Two Texts, Three Readers: Distance and Expertise in Reading History," *Cognition and Instruction* 14.4 (1996): 441–86; Leona Schauble and Robert Glaser, eds., *Innovations in Learning: New Environments for Education* (Mahwah, NJ: Erlbaum, 1996).

130. Wendy Bishop, "Attitudes and Expectations: How Theory in the Graduate Student (Teacher) Complicates the English Curriculum," *Critical Theory and the Teaching of Literature: Politics, Curriculum, Pedagogy*, ed. James F. Slevin and Art Young (Urbana: NCTE, 1996), 207–22; Walter Doyle and Kathy Carter, "Educational Psychology and the Education of Teachers: A Reaction,"

Educational Psychologist 31 (1996): 23–28; Donald Freeman, "To Take Them at Their Word: Language Data in the Study of Teacher's Knowledge," *Harvard Education Review* 66 (1996): 732–61; David Galloway et al., "Maladaptive Motivational Style: The Role of Domain Specific Task Demand in English and Mathematics," *British Journal of Educational Psychology* 66 (1996): 197–207; Graff, *Clueless*; Holland, *Brain*; Langer, "Literary," *Envisioning*; McCormick, *Culture*, "Reading"; George E. Newell, "Reader-Based and Teacher-Centered Instructional Tasks: Writing and Learning about a Short Story in Middle-Track Classrooms," *Journal of Literacy Research* 28.2 (1996): 147–72; Joan Peskin, "Constructing Meaning when Reading Poetry: An Expert-Novice Study," *Cognition and Instruction* 16.3 (1998): 235–63; Rabinowitz and Smith; Jeffrey D. Wilhelm and Brian Edmiston, *Imagining to Learn: Inquiry, Ethics, and Integration Through Drama* (Portsmouth, NH: Heinemann, 1998), 17.

131. Leinhardt and Young.

132. Barak Rosenshine et al., "Teaching Students to Generate Questions: A Review of Intervention Studies," *Review of Educational Research* 66.2 (1996): 181–221, here cited from 182.

133. Langer, *Envisioning*, 7.

134. Applebee, *Curriculum*, 26.

135. Roger C. Schank, *Tell Me a Story: A New Look at Real and Artificial Memory.* (New York: Scribner's, 1990).

136. Rosenshine et al., 182; Jim Minstrell and Virginia Stimpson, "A Classroom Environment for Learning: Guiding Students' Reconstruction of Understanding and Reasoning," *Innovations in Learning: New Environments for Education*, ed. Leona Schauble and Robert Glaser (NJ: Erlbaum, 1996), 175–202.

137. Leinhardt and Young; Samuel S. Weinberg, "The Cognitive Representation of Historical Texts," *Teaching and Learning in History*, ed. Gaea Leinhardt, Isabel L. Beck, and Catherine Stainton (Hillsdale, NJ: Erlbaum, 1994), 89–99. Mandler and Johnson; Van Dijk and Kintsch, *Strategies*.

138. Ernst Mayr, *The Growth of Biological Thought* (Cambridge: Harvard University Press, 1982), 341.

139. Ibid., 65; see also Douglas Hofstadter, *Gödel, Escher, Bach: An Eternal Golden Braid* (New York: Vintage, 1979), 709–10.

140. Mayr, 65.

141. Cf. R. Keith Sawyer, *Social Emergence: Societies as Complex Systems* (New York: Cambridge University Press, 2005), 29.

142. Walter Kintsch and Teun van Dijk, *Strategies of Discourse Comprehension* (New York: Academic Press, 1983).

143. Rabinowitz and Smith, *Authorizing Readers*, 94–95. Italics in original.

144. Knapp, "Situated."

145. Kintsch and van Dijk, *Strategies*.

146. H. Munby, "Metaphor in the Thinking of Teachers: An Exploratory Study," *Journal of Curriculum Studies* 18 (1986): 197–209.

147. Freema Elbaz, *Teacher Thinking: A Study of Practical Knowledge* (New York: Nichols, 1983).

148. Donald Polkinghorne, *Methodology for the Human Sciences: Systems of Inquiry* (Albany: State University of New York Press, 1983), *Narrative*

Knowing and the Human Sciences (1988); Mark Turner, *Reading Minds: The Study of English in the Age of Cognitive Science* (Princeton: Princeton University Press, 1991).

149. Rosenshine, "Teaching Students," 182.

150. Courtney Cazden, *Classroom Discourse: The Language of Teaching and Learning* (Portsmouth, NH: Heinemann, 1988); John V. Knapp, "Classy Questions: Raising Student Achievement through Authentic Discourse," *Illinois English Bulletin* 78 (1991): 42–55; Marshall et al., *Language of Interpretation*; Hugh Mehan, *Learning Lessons* (Cambridge: Harvard University Press, 1979); Nystrand and Gamoran, "Instructional Discourse"; Nystrand et al.

151. Rosenshine, 183.

152. Annemarie Sullivan Palincsar and A. L. Brown, "Reciprocal Teaching of Comprehension-Fostering and Comprehension-Monitoring Activities," *Cognition and Instruction* 2 (1984): 117–75; D. J. Wood et al., "The Role of Tutoring in Problem Solving," *Journal of Child Psychology and Psychiatry* 17 (1976): 89–100.

153. Rosenshine, 186–87, 190–91.

154. Rosenshine, 210.

155. Cf. Anderson, *Prescribing*; Kameen, *Writing/Teaching*.

156. Hillocks, *Testing*, 21–29; Ellen Lagemann, *An Elusive Science: The Troubling History of Education Research* (Chicago: University of Chicago Press, 2000), 222.

157. Cynthia L. Greenleaf et al., "Apprenticing Adolescent Readers to Academic Literacy," *Harvard Educational Review* 71 (2001): 79–127, here cited from 85.

158. Ibid., 88.

159. Ibid., 99.

160. Ibid., 101.

161. Tony Noice and Helga Noice, *The Nature of Expertise in Professional Acting* (Mahwah, NJ: Erlbaum, 1997), 43–44.

162. *Authorizing Readers*, 90–102.

163. Noice and Noice, 48.

164. Ibid., 44–46; cf. Greenleaf et al., 108.

165. Peskin, *Constructing Meaning*, 255.

166. Ibid., 256.

167. Michael S. Meloth and Paul D. Deering, "Task Talk and Task Awareness Under Different Cooperative Learning Conditions," *American Education Research Journal* 31 (1994): 138–65, here cited from 139.

168. Rabinowitz and Smith, 81–82.

169. Elise Ann Earthman, "Creating the Virtual Work: Reader's Processes in Understanding Literary Texts," *Research in the Teaching of English* 26 (1992): 351–84, here cited from 356.

170. qtd. in Earthman, 357.

171. Earthman, 366.

172. Cf. David Hammer, "Discovery Learning and Discovery Teaching," *Cognition and Instruction* 15 (1997): 485–529; Foster, *How to Read Literature*.

173. Ola Hallden, "On the Paradox of Understanding History in an Educational Setting," *Teaching and Learning in History*, ed. Gaea Leinhardt et al. (Hillsdale, NJ: Erlbaum, 1994), 34.

174. Phelan, *Reading People*, 18.

175. Rabinowitz and Smith, 92.

176. M. Anne Britt et al., "Learning from History Texts: From Causal Analysis to Argument Models," *Teaching and Learning in History*, ed. Gaea Leinhardt et al. (Hillsdale, NJ: Erlbaum, 1994), 70.

177. Noice and Noice, 67.

178. Samuel S. Wineberg, "The Cognitive Representation of Historical Texts," *Teaching and Learning in History*, ed. Leinhardt et al. (Hillsdale, NJ: Erlbaum, 1994), 92; cf. Graff, *Clueless*, 228 ff.

179. Wineberg, 92.

180. Leinhardt, "Math Lessons," 73.

181. Knapp, "Teaching"; Yoshikazu Kobayashi, "Conceptual Acquisition and Change Through Social Interaction," *Human Development* 37 (1994): 233–41.

182. Peskin, "Constructing Meaning," 253.

183. Patt Dodds, "Cognitive and Behavioral Components of Expertise in Teaching Physical Education," *Quest* 46 (1994): 153–63.

184. Elbaz, *Teaching Thinking*; Nystrand and Gamoran, "Instructional Discourse."

185. Leinhardt, "Development," "Math Lessons."

186. Britt et al., Hallden.

187. Peskin, 236.

188. Colin Martindale and Audrey Dailey, "I. A. Richards Revisited: Do People Agree on Their Interpretations of Literature?" *Poetics* 23 (1995): 300.

189. Peskin, 237.

190. Ibid., 238.

191. Peskin, 238; see also Rabinowitz's "authorial audience" in *Before Reading: Narrative Conventions and the Politics of Interpretation* (Ithaca: Cornell University Press, 1987).

192. Peskin , 245.

193. Ibid., 238.

194. Cf. Knapp, "Classy," and question types nos. 3, 4, 5: "generalization," "analysis," and "speculation"; Nystrand and Gamoran.

195. Peskin, 238.

196. Cf. Paul Fussell and "meter-making meaning."

197. Peskin, 239.

198. Ibid., 241

199. Ibid.

200. Ibid.

201. Peskin, 234.

202. Peskin, 243.

203. Peskin 244; Prose, "Caged Bird," 78.

204. Peskin, 250.

205. Ibid., 251.

206. Ibid., 253.

207. Mark Bauerlein, "A Very Long Disengagement," *The Chronicle of Higher Education*, January 6, 2006, B7.

208. Edmundson, "Liberal Education," 41.

209. Ibid.

210. Bauerlein, B6.

211. Martin Nystrand et al., "Questions in Time: Investigating the Structure and Dynamics of Unfolding Classroom Discourse," *Discourse Processes* 35.2 (2003): 135–98.

212. Ibid., 136.

213. Ibid., 183–84.

214. Ibid., 188.

215. Ibid.

216. Seung lee Do and Diane Lemonnier Shallert, "Emotion and Classroom Talk: Toward a Model of the Role of Affect in Student Experiences of Classroom Discussions," *Journal of Educational Psychology* 96.4 (2004): 631.

217. Ibid., 632.

218. Ibid.

219. Ibid.

220. Ibid.

221. Do and Shallert, 633.

CHAPTER 2. SCANT BEGINNINGS

1. Plato, "The Republic," *Great Dialogues of Plato,* trans. W. H. D. Rouse (New York: Mentor, 1956), 173–74; 375a376e.

2. See Second Interview, appendix C.

3. John T. Bruer, *Schools for Thought: A Science of Learning in the Classroom* (Cambridge, MA: MIT Press, 1993), 194.

4. Franklin E. Court, *Institutionalizing English Literature,* 186; Graff, *Professing Literature,* 41.

5. Galbraith M. Crump, *Approaches to Teaching Milton's Paradise Lost* (New York: MLA, 1986); Colin Burrow, *Epic Romance: Homer to Milton* (Oxford: Clarendon Press, 1993); John T. Shawcross, "Milton and Epic Revisionism," *Epic and Epoch: Essays on the Interpretation of a Genre.,* ed. Steven M. Oberhelman, Van Kelley, and Richard J. Golsan (Lubbock: Texas Tech University Press, 1994).

6. Bonnie Melchior, "Teaching *Paradise Lost:* The Unfortunate Fall," *College Literature* 14.1 (1987): 84.

7. Melchior, 76.

8. Janice Almasi, Margaret McKeown, and Isabel L. Beck, "The Nature of Engaged Reading in Classroom Discussions of Literature," *Journal of Literacy Research* 28.1 (1996): 107–46.

9. Stanley Fish, "Being Interdisciplinary Is So Very Hard to Do," *Profession* 89 (1989a), 141.

10. G. Hantano and K. Inagaki, "Sharing Cognition through Collective Comprehension Activity," *Perspectives on Socially Shared Cognition,* ed. L.B. Resnick, J. M. Levine, and S.D. Teasley (Washington, D.C.: American Psychological Association, 1991: 331–48.

11. Peter Elbow, "Reflections on Academic Discourse: How it Relates to Freshman and Colleagues," *College English* 53.2 (1991): 135–55; Yoshikazu

Kobayashi, "Conceptual Acquisition and Change Through Social Interaction," *Human Development* 37 (1994): 233–41; Timothy J. Lensmire, "The Teacher as Dostoevskian Novelist," *Research in the Teaching of English* 31 (1997): 367–92; Neal Norrick, "Involvement and Joking in Conversation," *Journal of Pragmatics* 22 (1994): 409–30.

12. Mark W. Aulls, "Contributions of Classroom Discourse to What Content Students Learn During Curriculum Enactment," *Journal of Educational Psychology* 90.1 (1998): 65.

13. Mary Sue Garay and Stephen A. Bernhardt, eds., *Expanding Literacies: English Teaching and the New Workplace* (Albany: State University of New York Press, 1998).

14. Victor Nell, *Lost in a Book: The Psychology of Reading for Pleasure.* (New Haven: Yale University Press, 1988).

15. Carl Bereiter and Marlene Scardamalia, *Surpassing Ourselves: An Inquiry into the Nature and Implications of Expertise* (Chicago: Open Court, 1993), 9–16; Brian White, "Assuming Nothing: A Pre-Methods Diagnostic in the Teaching of Literature," *English Education* 27.4 (1995): 34.

16. Avrom Fleishman, *The Condition of English: Literary Studies in a Changing Culture* (Westport, CT: Greenwood Press, 1998), 115; cf. Graff, *Clueless,* 177.

17. Albert C. Baugh, *A History of the English Language,* 2nd ed. (New York: Appleton-Century-Crofts, 1957).

18. John V. Knapp, "Teaching Poetry via HEI (Hypothesis-Experiment-Instruction)," *Journal of Adolescent and Adult Literacy* 45 (2002): 718–29.

19. Following Basil Bernstein's *The Structuring of Pedagogic Discourse,* vol. 4: *Class, Codes, and Control,* 2nd ed. (London: Routledge, 1975), 106ff.

20. Gerald Graff, *Clueless,* 59.

21. Langer, *Envisioning,* 129.

22. Interview, B-2.

23. Ibid.

24. Interview, B-3.

25. Donald Lemen Clark, *John Milton at St. Paul's School: A Study of Ancient Rhetoric in English Renaissance Education* (New York: Archon Books, 1964).

26. William G. Perry Jr., *Forms of Intellectual and Ethical Development in the College Years* (New York: Holt, Rinehart and Winston, 1970).

27. See Beiriter and Scardemalia, *Surpassing Ourselves.*

28. Barbara Graves, "The Study of Literary Expertise as a Research Strategy," *Poetics* 23 (1996): 397.

29. Richard S. Prawat, "Dewey, Peirce, and the Learning Paradox," *AERJ* 36.1 (1999b): 59–60.

30. Ibid., 60.

31. See Interview, appendix B.

32. See Neal Norrick, "Involvement and Joking in Conversation," *Journal of Pragmatics* 22 (1994): 429.

CHAPTER 3. MILTON'S SONNETS

1. Theodore R. Sizer, *Horace's Hope: What Works for the American High School* (New York: Houghton Mifflin, 1996).

2. Cf. Ann E. Berthoff, "Reclaiming the Active Mind," *College English* 61.6 (1999): 673.

3. Graff, *Clueless*, 242–43; cf. 234–37.

4. Cf. Paul Fussell, *Poetic Meter*; Hollander, *Rhyme's Reason*.

5. Charles W. Anderson, *Prescribing the Life of the Mind* (Madison: University of Wisconsin Press, 1993).

6. Michael R. G. Spiller, *Development of the Sonnet: An Introduction* (New York: Routledge, 1992), 1–2.

7. Ibid., 3–4.

8. Ibid., 3.

9. Alastair Fowler, *Kinds of Literature* (Oxford: Oxford University Press, 1982), 31.

10. Joan Peskin, "Constructing Meaning."

11. Fussell, *Poetic Meter*.

12. Cf. I. A. Richards, *Practical Criticism* (New York: Harvest Books, 1929).

13. Jane Agee, "Negotiating Different Conceptions about Reading and Teaching Literature in a Preservice Literature Class," *Research in the Teaching of English* 33 (1998): 96.

14. Ibid., 96, 115.

15. Jane Tompkins, *A Life in School: What the Teacher Learned* (Reading, MA: Addison-Wesley, 1996), 137.

16. Merritt Y. Hughes, *John Milton: Complete Poems and Major Prose* (New York: Odyssey Press, 1957), 76.

17. John V. Knapp, "Classy Questions"; Nystrand et al., *Opening Dialogue*; Nystrand and Gamoran, "Instructional Discourse."

18. Nystrand's "report-type questions."

CHAPTER 4. LONGER POEMS

1. See Assignment no. 2.

2. David Bartholomae and Anthony Petrosky, *Facts, Artifacts, and Counterfacts*.

3. R. F. Thompson, *The Brain: A Neuroscience Primer*, 338; cf. Greenleaf et al., "Apprenticing Adolescent Readers to Academic Literacy, 88; William Hirst, "The Psychology of Attention," 129.

4. See chapter 4 summary, note 4.

5. Jane Hirshfield, *Nine Gates: Entering the Mind of Poetry* (New York: Harper-Perennial, 1998), 11.

6. Merritt Y. Hughes, *John Milton: Complete Poems and Major Prose*, 43.

7. René Wellek and Austin Warren, *Theory of Literature* (New Haven: Yale University Press, 1949), 45–46.

8. From Claus Otto Scharmer's "Conversation with Robert Kegan," *Dialog on Leadership*.

9. Dona M. Kagan, *Laura and Jim and What They Taught Me about the Gap between Educational Theory and Practice* (Albany: State University of New York Press, 1993), 129.

10. Peter Rabinowitz thinks that recognizing "the ways in which authors,

as well as readers, are subject to social constraints can help students learn to be patient with older texts" (Rabinowitz and Smith, *Authorizing Readers*, 71). Although he didn't say it, the same may be said about professors teaching students about those "social constraints."

11. Hughes, 73.

12. Carol D. Lee, *Signifying as a Scaffold for Literary Interpretation: The Pedagogical Implications of an African-American Discourse Genre* (NCTE Research Report no. 26, Urbana: NCTE, 1993), 35–36.

13. Kagan, 134–38.

CHAPTER 5. DRAMA AND NONFICTIONAL PROSE

1. Cf. Nystrand and Gamoran, "Instructional Discourse"; Knapp, "Classy Questions."

2. Rabinowitz (1977), 124.

3. See also Class no. 8, Part Three.

4. James Phelan, *Reading People, Reading Plots.*

5. Helen Vendler, *The Art of Shakespeare's Sonnets* (Cambridge: Harvard University Press, 1997), 11–12.

6. Hall, 45.

7. W. Van Peer, "Paraphrase as Paradox in Literary Education," *Poetics* 21 (1993): 449.

8. Ibid., 447.

9. Harvey Daniels, *Literature Circles: Voice and Choice in the Student-Centered Classroom* (York, ME: Stenhouse, 1994), 10.

10. Graff, *Clueless*, 268.

11. Cf. Rabinowitz and Smith, *Authorizing Readers*, 13.

CHAPTER 6. MILTON'S *PARADISE LOST*

1. Cf. John Hollander, *Rhyme's Reason* (New Haven: Yale University Press, 1999).

2. Joan Peskin, "Constructing Meaning," 247.

3. Cf. Rabinowitz and Smith, *Authorizing Readers*, 63ff.

4. Peskin, 241 (italics mine).

5. David Hammer, "Discovery Learning and Discovery Teaching," *Cognition and Instruction* 15 (1997): 491.

6. Cleanth Brooks and Robert Penn Warren, *Understanding Fiction* (New York: Appleton-Century-Crofts, 1943).

7. Arthur N. Applebee, *Curriculum as Conversation: Transforming the Traditions of Teaching and Learning* (Chicago: University of Chicago Press, 1996), 106.

8. Arthur N. Applebee, *Curriculum as Conversation*, 123.

9. Martin Nystrand, Adam Gamoran, and Mary Jo Heck, "Using Small Groups for Response to and Thinking about Literature," *English Journal* 82.1 (1993): 15.

Chapter 7. Completion of *Paradise Lost*

1. Cf. Hughes, *John Milton*, 306.
2. Jane Hirshfield, *Nine Gates: Entering the Mind of Poetry* (New York: Harper-Perennial, 1998), 11.
3. Seung lee Do and Diane Lemonnier Shallert, "Emotion and Classroom Talk: Toward a Model of the Role of Affect in Student Experiences of Classroom Discussions," *Journal of Educational Psychology* 96.4 (2004): 631.

Chapter 8. Study Discussion

1. Jean Lave, *Cognition in Practice.*
2. James Phelan, *Reading People, Reading Plots.*
3. Alan C. Purves et al., *How Porcupines Make Love II, III.*
4. Harvey Daniels, *Literature Circles: Voice and Choice in the Student-Centered Classroom* (York, ME: Stenhouse, 1994), 23.
5. Albert C. Baugh, *A History of the English Language.*
6. Alice Glarden Brand and Richard L. Graves, eds., *Presence of Mind*, 3.
7. Carl Bereiter and Marlene Scardamalia, *Surpassing Ourselves.*
8. Nystrand and Gamoran, "Instructional Discourse; Knapp, "Classy Questions."
9. Theodore R. Sizer, *Horace's Hope: What Works for the American High School* (New York: Houghton-Mifflin, 1996), 91–95.
10. First Interview, B-3.
11. Donald Lemen Clark, *John Milton at St. Paul's School.*
12. David Bartholomae and Anthony Petrosky, *Facts, Artifacts, and Counterfacts.*
13. Barbara Graves, "The Study of Literary Expertise," 397.
14. Knapp, "Family Systems."

Bibliography

Agathocleous, Tanya, and Ann C. Dean, eds. *Teaching Literature: A Companion.* New York: Palgrave-Macmillan, 2003.

Agee, Jane. "Negotiating Different Conceptions about Reading and Teaching Literature in a Preservice Literature Class." *Research in the Teaching of English* 33 (1998): 85–124.

Almasi, Janice, Margaret McKeown, and Isabel L. Beck. "The Nature of Engaged Reading in Classroom Discussions of Literature." *Journal of Literacy Research* 28.1 (1996): 107–46.

Ambert, Anne-Marie, Patricia A. Adler, Peter Adler, and Daniel F. Detzner. "Understanding and Evaluating Qualitative Research." *Journal of Marriage and the Family* 57 (1995): 879–93.

Anderson, Charles W. *Prescribing the Life of the Mind.* Madison: University of Wisconsin Press, 1993.

Anderson, Debra J., Robert L. Major, and Richard R. Mitchell. *Teacher Supervision that Works: A Guide for University Supervisors.* Westport, CT: Praeger, 1992.

Anderson, John R., Lynne M. Reder, and Herbert Simon. "Situated Learning and Education." *Educational Researcher* 25.4 (1996): 5–11.

Anderson, L. M., et al. "Educational Psychology for Teachers: Reforming our Courses; Rethinking our Roles." *Educational Psychologist* 30 (1995): 143–57.

Anderson, R. C., and P. D. Pearson. "A Schema-Theoretic View of Basic Processes in Reading Comprehension." *Handbook of Reading Research.* Edited by P. D. Pearson. New York: Longman, 1984. 255–91.

Antczak, Frederick J. *Thought and Character: The Rhetoric of Democratic Education.* Ames: Iowa State University Press, 1985.

Applebee, Arthur N. *Curriculum as Conversation: Transforming the Traditions of Teaching and Learning.* Chicago: University of Chicago Press, 1996.

———. *Literature in the Secondary School: Studies of Curriculum and Instruction in the United States.* NCTE Research Report number 25. Urbana, IL: NCTE, 1993.

———. *The Teaching of Literature in Programs with Reputations for Excellence in English.* Albany: State University of New York Press, 1989.

Applebee, Arthur N., Robert Burroughs, and Anita Stevens. "Creating Continuity and Coherence in High School Literature Curricula." *Research in the Teaching of English* 34.3 (2000): 396–429.

Appleman, Deborah. "'I Understood the Grief': Theory-Based Introduction to *Ordinary People.*" In *Reader-Response in Secondary and College Classrooms,* 2nd ed., edited by N. J. Karolides, 123–34. Mahwah, NJ: Erlbaum, 2000.

Appleyard, J. A. *Becoming a Reader: The Experience of Fiction from Adolescence to Adulthood.* New York: Cambridge University Press, 1990.

Arac, Jonathan. "An Introductory Texts and Theory Course." In *Teaching Contemporary Theory to Undergraduates,* edited by D. F. Sadoff and W. E. Cain, 169–78. New York: MLA, 1994.

Argyris, Chris, and Donald A. Schon. *Organizational Learning II.* New York: Addison-Wesley, 1996.

Aronowitz, Stanley. *The Knowledge Factory: Dismantling the Corporate University and Creating True Higher Learning.* Boston: Beacon Press, 2000.

Arreola, Raoul A. "Evaluating the Dimensions of Teaching." *Instructional Evaluation* 8 (1986): 4–12.

Attili, Grazia. "Successful and Disconfirmed Children in the Peer Group: Indices of Social Competence within an Evolutionary Perspective." *Human Development* 33 (1990): 238–49.

Aulls, Mark W. "Contributions of Classroom Discourse to What Content Students Learn During Curriculum Enactment." *Journal of Educational Psychology* 90.1 (1998): 56–69.

Bain, Ken. *What the Best College Teachers Do.* Cambridge: Harvard University Press, 2004.

Baker, Eva L. "Learning-based Assessments of History Understanding." *Educational Psychologist* 29.2 (1994): 97–106.

Bal, Mieke. "The Narrating and the Focalizing: A Theory of the Agents in Narrative." *Style* 17 (1983): 234–69.

Barnes, Douglas, and Dorthy Barnes. "Reading and Writing as a Social Activity." In *Developing Discourse Practices in Adolescence and Adulthood,* edited by Richard Beach and Susan Hynds, 34–64. Norwood, NJ: Ablex, 1990.

Barrone, T. "On the Demise of Subjectivity in Educational Inquiry." *Curriculum Inquiry* 22.1 (1992): 25–37.

Barthes, Roland. *S/Z: An Essay.* Translated by Richard Miller. New York: Hill and Wang, 1974.

Bartholomae, David, and Anthony Petrosky. *Facts, Artifacts, and Counterfacts: Theory and Method for a Reading and Writing Course.* Portsmouth, NH: Heinemann, 1986.

Bate, Walter Jackson, ed. *Criticism: The Major Texts.* New York: Harcourt, Brace, Jovanovich, 1963.

Bauerlein, Mark. "A Very Long Disengagement." *The Chronicle of Higher Education,* January 6, 2006, B6–8.

Baugh, Albert C. *A History of the English Language,* 2nd ed. New York: Appleton-Century-Crofts, 1957.

Beach, Richard. *A Teacher's Introduction to Reader-Response Theories.* Urbana: NCTE, 1993.

Beach, Richard, Judith Greene, Michael L. Kamil, and Timothy Shanahan, eds. *Multidisciplinary Perspectives on Literary Research.* Urbana: NCTE, 1992.

Beck, Isabel, and Margaret McKeown. "Application of Theories of Reading to Instruction." In *Literacy in American Schools: Learning to Read and Write,* edited by Nancy Stein, 61–81. Chicago: University of Chicago Press, 1986.

Bereiter, Carl, and Marlene Bird. "Use of Think-Aloud in Identification and Teaching of Reading Comprehension Strategies." *Cognition and Instruction* 2 (1985): 131–56.

Bereiter, Carl, and Marlene Scardamalia. *Surpassing Ourselves: An Inquiry into the Nature and Implications of Expertise.* Chicago: Open Court Press, 1993.

Bernstein, Basil B. *The Structuring of Pedagogic Discourse.* Vol. 4, *Class, Codes, and Control,* 2nd ed. London: Routledge, 1990.

Berry, Eleanor. "The Free Verse Spectrum." *College English* 59.8 (1997): 873–97.

Berthoff, Ann E. "Reclaiming the Active Mind." *College English* 61.6 (1999): 671–80.

Berube, Michael. *The Employment of English: Theory, Jobs, and the Future of Literary Studies.* New York: New York University Press, 1998.

———. *Public Access: Literary Theory and American Cultural Politics.* New York: Verso, 1994.

Billig, Michael. *Arguing and Thinking.* Cambridge: Cambridge University Press, 1987.

Bishop, Wendy. "Attitudes and Expectations: How Theory in the Graduate Student (Teacher) Complicates the English Curriculum." In *Critical Theory and the Teaching of Literature: Politics, Curriculum, Pedagogy,* edited by James F. Slevin and Art Young, 207–22. Urbana: NCTE, 1996.

Black, John, and Robert Wilensky. "An Evaluation of Story Grammars." *Cognitive Science* 3 (1979): 213–30.

Blake, Robert W. "Using the Personal Response to Become a Learning Community: A Model for Secondary Students to Learn to Read Short Fiction." *English Record* 41.2 (1991): 22–30.

Bleich, David. *Readings and Feelings: An Introduction to Subjective Criticism.* Urbana: NCTE, 1975.

———. *Subjective Criticism.* Baltimore: Johns Hopkins University Press, 1978.

Boetcher-Joeres, Ruth-Ellen. "Elusive Theory and Illusive Practice? Editing *Signs.*" *PMLA* 118 (2003): 318–20.

Bogdan, Deanne. *Re-Educating the Imagination: Toward a Poetics, Politics, and Pedagogy of Literary Engagement.* Portsmouth, NH: Boynton-Cook, 1992.

Booth, Wayne C. *The Rhetoric of Fiction.* Chicago: University of Chicago Press, 1961.

Bordo Susan. *Unbearable Weight: Feminism, Western Culture, and the Body.* Berkeley: University of California Press, 1993.

Boyatzis, Chris J. "Let the Caged Birds Sing: Using Literature to Teach Developmental Psychology." *Teaching of Psychology* 19.4 (1992): 221–22.

Brand, Alice Glarden, and Richard L. Graves, eds. *Presence of Mind: Writing and the Domain Beyond the Cognitive.* Portsmouth, NH: Boynton-Cook, 1994.

———. (1994b). "Defining Our Emotional Life: The Cool End (Plus Motivation)." In *Presence of Mind,* edited by Alice Glarden Brand and Richard L. Graves, 167–78.

———. (1994c). "Defining Our Emotional Life: The Valuative System—A Continuum Theory." In *Presence of Mind,* edited by Alice Glarden Brand and Richard L. Graves, 155–65.

Bresnick, Adam. "They've Been Cheated." Review of *The Rise and Fall of English,* by Robert Scholes. *Times Literary Supplement* 4993, December 11, 1998, 11.

Britt, M. Anne, Jean François Rouet, Mara C. Georgi, and Charles A. Perfetti. "Learning from History Texts: From Causal Analysis to Argument Models." In *Teaching and Learning in History,* edited by Gaea Leinhardt, Isabel L. Beck, and Catherine Stainton, 47–84. Hillsdale, NJ: Erlbaum, 1994.

Britzman, Deborah P. "Structures of Feeling in Curriculum and Teaching." *Theory into Practice* 31 (1992): 252–58.

———. "Who Has the Floor? Curriculum, Teaching, and the English Student Teacher's Struggle for Voice." *Curriculum Inquiry* 19 (1989): 143–62.

Brody, P., C. DeMilo, and Alan C. Purves. *The Current State of Assessment in Literature.* Report Series 2.1. Albany, NY: Center for Learning and Teaching of Literature, 1989.

Brooks, Cleanth. *The Well-Wrought Urn.* New York: Harvest, 1947.

Brooks, Cleanth, and Robert Penn Warren. *Understanding Fiction.* New York: Appleton-Century-Crofts, 1943.

Brown, B. Bradford. "The Role of Peer Groups in Adolescent's Adjustment to Secondary School." In *Peer Relationships in Child Development,* edited by Thomas J. Berndt and Gary W. Ladd, 188–215. New York: John Wiley, 1989.

Brown, John Seely, Allan Collins, and Paul Duguid. "Situated Cognition and the Culture of Learning." *Educational Researcher* 18.1 (1989): 32–42.

Brueggemann, Brenda Jo, and Debra A. Moddelmog. "Coming-Out Pedagogy: Risking Identity in Language and Literature Classrooms." *Pedagogy* 2.3 (Fall 2002): 311–35.

Bruer, John T. *Schools for Thought: A Science of Learning in the Classroom.* Cambridge, MA: MIT Press, 1993.

Bruffee, Kenneth A. *Collaborative Learning: Higher Education, Interdependence, and the Authority of Knowledge.* Baltimore: Johns Hopkins University Press, 1993.

Bruner, Jerome. *Acts of Meaning.* Cambridge: Harvard University Press, 1990.

———. *The Culture of Education.* Cambridge: Harvard University Press, 1996.

Bugeja, Michael J. "Why We Stopped Reading Poetry." *English Journal* 81 (1992): 32–42.

Burrow, Colin. *Epic Romance: Homer to Milton.* Oxford: Clarendon Press, 1993.

Bush, John B., and Susan R. Goldman. "Expertise Differences in the Analysis of Poetry." Unpublished manuscript, Vanderbilt University, Nashville, 1998.

Bush, Douglas. "Literary History and Literary Criticism." In *Criticism: The Major Texts,* edited by Walter Jackson Bate, 699–706. New York: Harcourt, Brace, Jovanovich, 1963.

Byrnes, J. P. "Domain-Specificity and the Logic of using General Ability as an Independent Variable or Covariate." *Merrill-Palmer Quarterly* 41 (1995): 1–24.

Cain, William, E. "Contemporary Theory, The Academy, and Pedagogy." In *Teaching Contemporary Theory to Undergraduates,* edited by Dianne F. Sadoff and William E. Cain, 3–14. New York: MLA, 1994.

Calkins, Lucy M. *Living Between the Lines.* Portsmouth, NH: Heinemann, 1991.

Carroll, Joseph, ed. *On The Origin of Species by Charles Darwin.* Ontario: Broadview Press, 2003.

Carter, Kathy. "The Place of Story in the Study of Teaching and Teacher Education." *Educational Researcher* 22.1 (1993): 5–12.

———. "Teachers' Knowledge and Learning to Teach." In *Handbook of Research on Teacher Education,* edited by W. R. Houston, 291–310. New York: Macmillan, 1990.

Carter, Kathy, and Luz Gonzales. "Beginning Teacher's Knowledge of Classroom Events." *Journal of Teacher Education* 44.3 (1993): 223–32.

Cazden, Courtney. *Classroom Discourse: The Language of Teaching and Learning.* Portsmouth, NH: Heinemann, 1988.

Chambers, Ross. *Story and Situation: Narrative Seduction and the Power of Fiction.* Minneapolis: University of Minnesota Press, 1984.

Chandler, Susanne. "Displaying our Lives: An Argument against Displaying our Theories." *Theory into Practice* 31.2 (1992): 126–31.

Chi, Michelle, Robert Glaser, and M. J. Farr, eds. *The Nature of Expertise.* Hillsdale, NJ: Erlbaum, 1988.

Chrisler, Joan C. "Novels as Case-Study Materials for Psychology Students." *Teaching of Psychology* 17 (1990): 55–57.

Clark, Donald Lemen. *John Milton at St. Paul's School: A Study of Ancient Rhetoric in English Renaissance Education.* New York: Archon Books, 1964.

Cobb, Paul and Janet Bowers. "Cognitive and Situated Learning: Perspectives in Theory and Practice." *Educational Researcher* 28.2 (1999): 4–15.

Cocking, Rodney R., and K. Ann Renninger, eds. *The Meaning and Development of Psychological Distance.* Hillsdale, NJ: Erlbaum, 1993.

Cohen-Shalev, Amir and Tamar Rapport. "Developmental Assumptions in Literary Criticism and their Implications for Conceptions of Continuity and Change in Literary Creativity." *Psychology and Aging* 5.1 (1990): 79–85.

Collins, Alan, John S. Brown, and Susan E. Newman. "Cognitive Apprenticeship: Teaching the Craft of Reading, Writing, and Mathematics." In *Knowing,*

Learning and Instruction: Essays in Honor of Robert Glaser, edited by L. B. Resnick, 453–94. Hillsdale, NJ: Erlbaum, 1989.

Collins, Alan, and William Ferguson. "Epistemic Forms and Epistemic Games: Structures and Strategies to Guide Inquiry." *Educational Psychologist* 28.1 (1993): 25–42.

Collins, Ava. "Intellectuals, Power, and Quality Television." In *Between Borders: Pedagogy and the Politics of Cultural Studies,* edited by Giroux and McLaren, 56–63. New York: Routledge, 1994.

Collins, H. M. *Artificial Experts: Social Knowledge and Intelligent Machines.* Cambridge: MIT Press, 1990.

Comeaux, M. A. "The Reflective Teacher: Fact or Fiction? A Study of the Reflective Processes of Twelve High School English Teachers" (Dissertation, University of Wisconsin-Madison) 1989.

Conle, Carola. "Resonance in Preservice Teacher Inquiry." *AERA* 33.2 (1996): 279–325.

Connelly, M., and J. Clandinin. "Stories of Experience and Narrative Inquiry." *Educational Researcher* 19.5 (1990): 2–14.

Cooper, J., ed. *Classroom Teaching Skills.* Lexington, MA: D. C. Heath, 1990.

Cooper, James L., Pamela Robinson, and Molly McKinney. "Cooperative Learning in the Classroom." In *Changing College Classrooms,* edited by Diane Halpern, 74–92. San Francisco: Jossey-Bass, 1994.

Court, Franklin E. *Institutionalizing English Literature: The Culture and Politics of Literary Study, 1750–1900.* Stanford: Stanford University Press, 1992.

Craig, Madge T., Robin M. Bright, and Susan A. Smith. "Preservice Teachers' Reactions to an Interactive Constructive Approach to English Language Arts Coursework." *Journal of Teacher Education* 45.2 (1994): 96–103.

Crews, Frederick. *PostModern Pooh.* New York: North Point Press, 2001.

Cronin, Frank C. "Textuality, Reader-Response Theory, and the English Classroom." *The English Record* 40.1 (1989): 29–31.

Crump, Galbraith M. *Approaches to Teaching Milton's Paradise Lost.* New York: MLA, 1986.

Crutcher, Robert J. "Telling Us What We Know: The Use of Verbal Report Methodologies in Psychological Research." *Psychological Science* 5.5 (1994): 241–44.

Csikszentmihalyi, M., and R. Larson. *Being Adolescent: Conflict and Growth in the Teenage Years.* New York: Basic Books, 1984.

Cuban, Larry. *How Scholars Trumped Teachers: Change without Reform in University Curriculum, Teaching and Research, 1890–1990.* New York: Teacher's College Press, 1999.

Culler, Jonathan. "Poststructuralist Criticism." *Style* 21.2 (1987): 167–80.

———. *Structuralist Poetics: Structuralism, Linguistics, and the Study of Literature.* Ithaca: Cornell University Press, 1975.

Culpeper, Jonathan. *Language and Characterization: People in Plays and Other Texts.* Harlow, UK: Longman-Pearson Education, 2001.

Damon, William. "Commentary." *Human Development* 37 (1994): 140–42.

———. "Strategic Uses of Peer Learning in Children's Education." In *Peer Relationships in Child Development*, edited by Thomas J. Berndt and Gary W. Ladd, 135–57. New York: John Wiley, (1989b).

Damon, William, and Erin Phelps. "Critical Distinctions among Three Approaches to Peer Education." *International Journal of Educational Research* 13 (1989a): 9–19.

Daniels, Harvey. *Literature Circles: Voice and Choice in the Student-Centered Classroom*. York, ME: Stenhouse, 1994.

Dante. *The Divine Comedy of Dante Alighieri; Inferno*. Translated by Allen Mandlebaum. New York: Bantam, 1982.

Dasenbrock, Reed Way. "Why Read Multicultural Literature? An Arnodlian Perspective." *College English* 61.6 (1999): 691–701.

Davis, Todd, and Kenneth Womack. *Formalist Criticism and Reader-Response Theory*. New York: Palgrave–St. Martin's Press, 2002.

Dean Ann C. "The River and the Chestnut Tree: When Students Already Know the Answers." In *Teaching Literature: A Companion*, edited by Tanya Agathocleous and Ann C. Dean, 139–48. New York: Palgrave-Macmillan, 2003.

Delandshere, Ginette, and Anthony R. Petrosky. "Capturing Teachers' Knowledge: Performance Assessment." *Educational Researcher* 23.5 (1994): 11–18.

Dias, Patricia X. "Literary Reading and Classroom Constraints: Aligning Practice with Theory." In *Literature Instruction: A Focus on Student Response*, edited by Judith A. Langer, 131–62. Urbana: NCTE, 1992.

Dilthey, Wilhelm. "The Constitution of the Historical World in the Human Sciences." In *Selected Writings (W. Dilthey, 1900–1976)*, 213–310. Translated by H. P. Rickman. Cambridge: Cambridge University Press, 1976.

DiPardo, Anne. *A Kind of Passport: A Basic Writing Program and the Challenge of Student Diversity*. Research Report No. 24. Urbana: NCTE, 1993.

Do, Seung lee, and Diane Lemonnier Shallert. "Emotion and Classroom Talk: Toward a Model of the Role of Affect in Student Experiences of Classroom Discussions." *Journal of Educational Psychology* 96.4 (2004): 619–34.

Dodds, Patt. "Cognitive and Behavioral Components of Expertise in Teaching Physical Education." *Quest* 46 (1994): 153–63.

Downing, David, Patricia Harkin, and James Sosnoski. "Configurations of Lore: The Changing Relations of Theory, Research, and Pedagogy." In *Changing Classroom Practices*, edited by David Downing, 3–34. Urbana: NCTE, 1994.

Doyle, Walter. "Academic Work." *Review of Educational Research* 53 (1983): 159–99.

———. "Classroom Knowledge as a Foundation for Teaching." *Teachers College Record* 91 (1990): 347–60.

Doyle, Walter, and Kathy Carter. "Educational Psychology and the Education of Teachers: A Reaction." *Educational Psychologist* 31 (1996): 23–28.

Dressman, M., and J. P. Webster. "Retracing Rosenblatt: A Textual Archaeology." *Research in the Teaching of English* 36 (2001): 110–45.

Earthman, Elise Ann. "The Lonely, Quiet Concert: Readers Creating Meaning from Literary Texts." *DAI* (Stanford University, 50, 06A 1583), 1989.

——. "Creating the Virtual Work: Reader's Processes in Understanding Literary Texts." *Research in the Teaching of English* 26 (1992): 351–84.

Eaves, L. J., Hans Eysenck, and N. G. Martin. *Genes, Culture, and Personality.* London: Academic Press, 1989.

Edmundson, Mark. "On the Uses of a Liberal Education." *Harpers,* September 1997, 39–49.

Egan, Kieran. *Romantic Understanding: The Development of Rationality and Imagination, Ages 8–15.* London: Routledge, 1990.

Eisner, Elliot W. "The New Frontier in Qualitative Research Methodology." *Qualitative Inquiry* 3.3 (1997): 259–73.

——. "On the Differences between Scientific and Artistic Approaches to Qualitative Research." *Educational Researcher* 10 (1981): 5–9.

——. "The Primacy of Experience and the Politics of Method." *Educational Researcher* 17.5 (1988): 15–20.

Elbaz, Freema. *Teacher Thinking: A Study of Practical Knowledge.* New York: Nichols, 1983.

Elbow, Peter. "Reflections on Academic Discourse: How it Relates to Freshman and Colleagues." *College English* 53.2 (1991): 135–55.

Eliot, T. S. *The Sacred Wood: Essays on Poetry and Criticism.* London: Methuen, 1920.

Ellis, John. *Against Deconstruction.* Princeton: Princeton University Press, 1989.

Ennis, Catherine D. "Knowledge and Beliefs Underlying Curricular Expertise." *Quest* 46 (1994): 164–75.

Ennis, Robert H. "The Extent to Which Critical Thinking is Subject-Specific: Further Clarification." *Educational Researcher* 19.4 (1990): 13–16.

Epstein, E. L. *Language and Style.* London: Methuen, 1978.

Ericsson, K. A., and N. Charness. "Expert Performance: Its Structure and Acquisition." *American Psychologist* 49.8 (1994): 725–47.

Feinman, Saul, ed. *Social Referencing and the Social Construction of Reality in Infancy.* New York: Plenum Press, 1992.

Felman, Jyl Lynn. *Never a Dull Moment: Teaching and the Art of Performance.* New York: Routledge, 2001.

Finn, Chester, Diane Ravitch, and Robert T. Fancher, eds. *Against Mediocrity: The Humanities in America's High Schools.* New York: Holmes and Meier, 1984.

Fisch, Harold. "Character as Linguistic Sign." *New Literary History* 21 (1990): 593–606.

Fish, Stanley. "Aim Low." *Chronicle of Higher Education,* May 16, 2003, C7.

——. "Being Interdisciplinary is So Very Hard to Do." *Profession* 89 (1989a): 15–22.

——. *Doing What Comes Naturally: Change, Rhetoric, and the Practice of*

Theory in Literary and Legal Studies. Durham, NC: Duke University Press, 1989b.

———. *Is There a Text in this Class?* Cambridge: Harvard University Press, 1980.

———. "What Makes an Interpretation Acceptable?" In *Is There a Text in This Class?* (1980), 338–55, 390.

———. *Professional Correctness: Literary Studies and Political Change.* Cambridge: Harvard University Press, 1995.

Fleckenstein, Kristie S. "Mental Imagery, Text Engagement, and Underprepared Writers." In *Presence of Mind: Writing and the Domain Beyond the Cognitive,* edited by Alice Glarden Brand and Richard L. Graves, 125–32. Portsmouth, NH: Boynton-Cook, 1994.

Fleishman, Avrom. *The Condition of English: Literary Studies in a Changing Culture.* Westport, CT: Greenwood Press, 1998.

Foster, Thomas C. *How to Read Literature Like a Professor.* New York: Harper-Quill, 2003.

Fotos, Sandra S. "Integrating Grammar Instruction and Communicative Language Use Through Grammar Consciousness-Raising Tasks." *TESOL Quarterly* 28.2 (1994): 323–51.

Foucault, Michel. "What is an Author?" In *Textual Strategies,* edited by Jose V. Harari, 141–60. Ithaca, NY: Cornell University Press, 1979.

Fowler, Alistair. *Kinds of Literature.* Oxford: Oxford University Press, 1982.

Franklin, Phyllis, David Laurence, and Elizabeth B. Wells, eds. *Preparing a Nation's Teachers: Models for English and Foreign Language Programs.* New York: MLA, 1999.

Freeman, Donald. "To Take Them at Their Word: Language Data in the Study of Teacher's Knowledge." *Harvard Education Review* 66 (1996): 732–61.

Frye, Northrop. *Anatomy of Criticism.* New York: Atheneum, 1966.

Fussell, Paul. *Poetic Meter and Poetic Form.* 1965. New York: Random House, 1979.

Galloway, David, Elizabeth L. Leo, Colin Rogers, and Derrick Armstrong. "Maladaptive Motivational Style: The Role of Domain Specific Task Demand in English and Mathematics." *British Journal of Educational Psychology* 66 (1996): 197–207.

Garay, Mary Sue, and Stephen A. Bernhardt, eds. *Expanding Literacies: English Teaching and the New Workplace.* Albany: State University of New York Press, 1998.

Gardner, Howard. *Frames of Mind: The Theory of Multiple Intelligences.* 1983. New York: Basic Books, 1985.

———. *Multiple Intelligences: The Theory in Practice.* New York: Basic Books, 1993.

Genette, Gérard. *Narrative Discourse: An Essay in Method.* Translated by Jane E. Lewin. Ithaca: Cornell University Press, 1980.

Gere, Ann, C. Fairbanks, A. Howes, L. Roop, and David Shaafsma. *Language and Reflection: An Integrated Approach to Teaching English.* New York: Macmillan, 1992.

Gergan, Kenneth. "Textual Considerations in the Scientific Construction of Human Character." In *Literary Character*, edited by John V. Knapp, 17–31. Lanham, MD: University Press of America, 1993.

Gerrig, Richard J. "Participatory Effects of Narrative Understanding." In *Empirical Approaches to Literature and Aesthetics.* Vol. 52, edited by Roger J. Kreuz and Mary Sue MacNealy, 127–42. Norwood, NJ: Ablex, 1996.

———. *Experiencing Narrative Worlds: On the Psychological Activities of Reading.* Boulder, CO: Westview Press, 1998. First published 1993 by Yale University Press.

Ginsburg, M. B. *Contradictions in Teacher Education and Society.* Philadelphia, PA: Falmer Press, 1988.

Giroux, Henry A., and Peter McLaren, eds. *Between Borders: Pedagogy and the Politics of Cultural Studies.* New York: Routledge, 1994.

Glaser, Robert. "Learning Theory and Instruction." *XXV International Congress of Psychology.* Brussels, Belgium, 1992. (Unpublished.)

———. "Application and Theory: Learning Theory and the Design of Learning Environments." Keynote Address: *23rd International Congress of Applied Psychology.* Madrid, Spain, 1994.

Gould, Christopher. "Assessing Teaching Effectiveness in English: Procedures, Issues, Strategies." *ADE Bulletin* 102 (1992): 44–52.

Graff, Gerald. *Clueless in Academe.* New Haven: Yale University Press, 2003.

———. *Professing Literature: An Institutional History.* Chicago: University of Chicago Press, 1987.

Graves, Barbara. "Literary Expertise in the Description of a Fictional Narrative." *Poetics* 20 (1991): 1–26.

———. "The Study of Literary Expertise as a Research Strategy." *Poetics* 23 (1996): 385–403.

Graves, Barbara, and Carl H. Frederiksen. "A Cognitive Study of Expertise." In *Empirical Approaches to Literature and Aesthetics* Vol. 52, edited by Roger J. Kreuz and Mary Sue MacNealy, 397–416. Norwood, NJ: Ablex, 1996.

Greenblatt, Stephen. "Resonance and Wonder." *Literary Theory Today.* Edited by Peter Collier and Helga Geyer-Ryan. New York: Cornell University Press, 1990.

Greenblatt, Stephen, and Giles Gunn, eds. *Redrawing the Boundaries: The Transformation of English and American Literary Studies.* New York: MLA, 1992.

Greenfield, Patricia Marks. "Representational Competence in Shared Symbol Systems: Electronic Media from Radio to Video Games." In *The Development and Meaning of Psychological Distance*, edited by Rodney R. Cocking and K. Ann Renninger, 161–84. Hillsdale, NJ: Erlbaum, 1993.

Greenleaf, Cynthia L., Ruth Schoenbach, Christine Cziko, and Faye L. Mueller. "Apprenticing Adolescent Readers to Academic Literacy." *Harvard Educational Review* 71 (2001): 79–127.

Gross, Alan G. *The Rhetoric of Science.* Cambridge: Harvard University Press, 1990.

Grossman, Pamela L. *The Making of a Teacher: Teacher Knowledge and Teacher Education.* New York: Teachers College Press, 1990.

Gudmundsdottir, S. "Story-Maker, Story-Teller: Narrative Structures in Curriculum." *Journal of Curriculum Studies* 23 (1991): 207–18.

Guillory, John. "The Very Idea of Pedagogy." *Profession 2002.* New York: MLA, 2002. 164–71.

Hall, Peter. *Exposed by the Mask: Form and Language in Drama.* London: Oberon Books, 2000.

Hallden, Ola. "On the Paradox of Understanding History in an Educational Setting." In *Teaching and Learning in History,* edited by Gaea Leinhardt, Isabel L. Beck, and Catherine Stainton, 27–46. Hillsdale, NJ: Erlbaum, 1994.

Halpern, Diane F. *Changing College Classrooms.* San Francisco: Jossey Bass, 1994.

Hammer, David. "Discovery Learning and Discovery Teaching." *Cognition and Instruction* 15 (1997): 485–529.

Hansen, C. Bobbi. "Questioning Techniques for the Active Classroom." In *Changing College Classrooms,* edited by Diane F. Halpern, 96–106. San Francisco: Jossey-Bass, 1994.

Hansson, Gunnar. "Readers Responding—and Then?" *Research in the Teaching of English* 26.2 (1992): 135–48.

Hantano, G., and K. Inagaki. "Sharing Cognition through Collective Comprehension Activity." In *Perspectives on Socially Shared Cognition,* edited by L. B. Resnick, J. M. Levine, and S. D. Teasley, 331–48. Washington, DC: American Psychological Association, 1991.

Hardy, Donald, ed. *The Pedagogy of Style and Stylistics,* Special issue, *Style* 37.1 (Spring 2003): 1–118.

Hari-Smith, Tori. "The Importance of Theory in the Training of Teaching Assistants." *ADE Bulletin* 82 (1985): 33–39.

Harris, David M. "Some Questions about Fiction." *Journal of Social and Evolutionary Sciences* 20.2 (1999): 107–15.

Haste, Helen. "The Thinker as Arguer: An Interview with Michael Billig." *New Ideas in Psychology* 12.2 (1994): 169–81.

Hatch, Jill A., Charles A. Hill, and John R. Hayes. "When the Messenger is the Message." *Written Communication* 10.4 (October 1993): 569–98.

Hawkey, Kate. "Image and the Pressure to Conform in Learning to Teach." *Teaching and Teacher Education* 12.1 (1996): 99–108.

Henly, Carolyn P. "Reader-Response Theory as Antidote to Controversy: Teaching *The Bluest Eye.*" *English Journal* 82.3 (March 1993): 14–19.

Henry, Marvin A., and W. Wayne Beasley. *Supervising Student Teachers: The Professional Way.* Terre Haute: Sycamore Press, 1996.

Hidi, Suzanne, and William Baird. "Interestingness—A Neglected Variable in Discourse Processing." *Cognitive Science* 10 (1986): 179–94.

Hill, Christopher. *Liberty Against the Law: Some Seventeenth-century Controversies.* London: Allen Lane-Penguin, 1996.

Hillocks, George, Jr. "Literary Texts in Classrooms." In *From Socrates to Software: The Teacher as Text and the Text as Teacher,* edited by Phillip W. Jackson and Sophie Haroutunian-Gordon, 135–58. *Eighty-eighth Yearbook of the National Society for the Study of Education.* Chicago: University of Chicago Press, 1989.

———. *The Testing Trap: How State Writing Assessments Control Learning.* New York: Teachers College–Columbia University Press, 2002.

Hillocks, George, Jr., and Larry H. Ludlow. "A Taxonomy of Skills in Reading and Interpreting Fiction." *American Educational Research Journal* 21.1 (1984): 7–24.

Hirsch, E. D. *The Schools We Need: And Why We Don't Have Them.* New York: Doubleday, 1996.

———. *Validity in Interpretation.* New Haven: Yale University Press, 1967; 1976.

Hirshfield, Jane. *Nine Gates: Entering the Mind of Poetry.* New York: Harper-Perennial, 1998.

Hirst, William. "The Psychology of Attention." In *Mind and Brain: Dialogues in Cognitive Neuroscience,* edited by Joseph E. LeDoux and William Hirst, 105–41. Cambridge: Cambridge University Press, 1990.

Hofstadter, Douglas. *Godel, Escher, Bach: An Eternal Golden Braid.* New York: Vintage, 1979.

Holland, Norman. *5 Readers Reading.* New Haven: Yale University Press, 1975.

———. "The Brain and the Book." Seminar syllabus, online. http://www.clas.ufl.edu/users/nnh/seminar/memo-s02.htm

———. "Note to Ellen Moody: Reader-Response." *Psyart,* June 13, 2001. psyart@lists.ufl.edu

Hollander, John. *Rhyme's Reason.* New Haven: Yale University Press, 1999.

Holt-Reynolds, Diane. "Good Readers, Good Teachers? Subject Matter Expertise as a Challenge to Learning to Teach." *Harvard Educational Review* 69.1 (1999): 29–50.

Hourigan, Maureen M. *Literacy as Social Exchange: Intersections of Class, Gender, and Culture.* Foreword by Gary A. Olsen. Albany: State University of New York Press, 1994.

Howard, G. S. "Culture Tales: Excursions into a Narrative Approach to Thinking, Cross-Cultural Psychology and Psychotherapy." *American Psychologist* 46 (1991): 187–97.

Hoy, Wayne K., and Anita E. Woolfolk. "Socialization of Student Teachers." *AERA* 27.2 (1990): 279–300.

Hughes, Merritt Y. *John Milton: Complete Poems and Major Prose.* New York: Odyssey Press, 1957.

Isen, A. M., K. A. Daubman, and J. M. Gorgoglione. "The Influence of Positive Affect on Cognitive Organization: Implications for Education." In *Aptitude,*

Learning, and Instruction: Conative and Affective Process Analysis. Vol. 3, edited by R. E. Snow and M. J. Farr, 143–64. Hillsdale, NJ: Erlbaum, 1987.

Iser, Wolfgang. *The Act of Reading.* Baltimore: Johns Hopkins University Press, 1978.

Itakura, Katsutaka. "Instruction and Learning of the Concept, 'Force,' in Static Based on *Kasetsu-Jikken-Jigyo (hypothesis-experiment-instruction)*: A New Method of Science Teaching." *Bulletin of National Institute for Educational Research* 52 (1967): 1–121 [in Japanese].

Jackson, Phillip W., and Sophie Haroutunian-Gordon, eds. *From Socrates to Software: The Teacher as Text and the Text as Teacher. Eighty-eighth Yearbook of the National Society for the Study of Education.* Chicago: University of Chicago Press, 1989.

James, W. B. and M. W. Galbraith. "Perceptual Learning Styles: Implications and Techniques for the Practitioner." *Lifelong Learning* 8 (1985): 20–23.

Janssen, Tanja, and Gert Rijaarsdam. "Approaches to the Teaching of Literature: A National Survey of Literary Education in Dutch Secondary Schools." In *Empirical Approaches to Literature and Aesthetics.* Vol. 52, edited by Roger J. Kreuz and Mary Sue MacNealy, 513–35. Norwood, NJ: Ablex, 1996.

Jauss, Hans Robert. *Aesthetic Experience and Literary Hermeneutics.* Translated by Michael Shaw. Minneapolis: University of Minnesota Press, 1982.

Jeffries, Lesley. "Analogy and Multi-Modal Exploration in the Teaching of Language Theory." *Style* 37 (2003): 67–85.

Jipson, Janice A., and Nicholas Paley. "Is There a Base to Today's Literature-Based Reading Programs?" *English Education* 24.2 (1992): 77–90.

Joeres, Ruth Ellen B., and Barbara Laslett, eds. *Second Signs Reader: Feminist Scholarship, 1983–1996.* Chicago: University of Chicago Press, 1996.

Johannessen, Larry. *Illumination Rounds: Teaching the Literature of the Vietnam War.* Urbana: NCTE, 1992.

Johannessen, Larry, and Thomas M. McCann. *In Case You Teach English: An Interactive Casebook for Prospective and Practicing Teachers.* Upper Saddle River, NJ: Merrill-Prentice Hall, 2002.

Johnson, Scott. "Structural Elements in Franz Kafka's *The Metamorphosis.*" *Journal of Marital and Family Therapy* 19.2 (1993): 149–57.

Johnson, David W., and Roger T. Johnson. *Cooperation and Competition: Theory and Research.* Edina, MN: Interaction Books, 1989.

———. "Instructional Goal: Cooperative, Competitive, or Individualistic." *Review of Educational Research* 44 (1974): 213–40.

Jordon, J. Scott, ed. *Systems Theories and A Priori Aspects of Perception.* Advances in Psychology, 126. New York: Elsevier, 1998.

Juel, Connie. "Learning to Learn from Effective Tutors." *Innovations in Learning: New Environments for Education.* Edited by Leona Schauble and Robert Glaser. Mahwah, NJ: Erlbaum, 1996.

Kagan, Dona M. *Laura and Jim and What They Taught Me about the Gap between Educational Theory and Practice.* Albany: State University of New York Press, 1993.

Kagan, Jerome. *Galen's Prophecy.* In collaboration with Nancy Snidman, Doreen Arcus, and J. Steven Reznick. NY: Basic Books, 1994.

Kameen, Paul. *Writing/Teaching: Essays Toward a Rhetoric of Pedagogy.* Pittsburgh: University of Pittsburgh Press, 2000.

Karolides, Nicholas J., ed. *Reader-Response in the Classroom.* New York: Longman, 1992.

Kegan, Robert. *In Over our Heads: The Mental Demands of Modern Life.* Cambridge: Harvard University Press, 1994.

———. *The Evolving Self: Problem and Process in Human Development.* Cambridge: Harvard University Press, 1982.

Kennedy, Mary M. *Learning to Teach Writing: Does Teacher Education Make a Difference?* New York: Teachers College Press, 1998.

Kintsch, Walter, and Teun van Dijk. "Toward a Model of Text Comprehension and Production." *Psychological Review* 85 (1978): 363–94.

———. *Strategies of Discourse Comprehension.* New York: Academic Press, 1983.

Knapp, John V. "Classy Questions: Raising Student Achievement through Authentic Discourse." *Illinois English Bulletin* 78 (1991): 42–55.

———. "Creative Reasoning in the Interactive Classroom: Experiential Exercises for Teaching George Orwell's *Animal Farm.*" *College Literature* 23 (1996): 143–56.

———, ed. *Literary Character.* Lanham, MD: University Press of America, 1993.

———. "Family Systems Psychotherapy, Literary Character, and Literature: An Introduction." *Style* 31 (1997): 223–54.

———. "Situated Learning: Red-Eye Milton and the Loom of Learning: English Professor Expertise." *Tomorrow's Professor Listserv,* 236, July 6, 2000. tomorrows-professor@lists.stanford.edu

———. *Striking at the Joints: Contemporary Psychology and Literary Criticism.* Lanham, MD: University Press of America, 1996.

———. "Teaching Poetry via HEI (Hypothesis-Experiment-Instruction)." *Journal of Adolescent and Adult Literacy* 45 (2002): 718–29.

———. "Wandering Between Two Worlds: The MLA and English Department Follies." *Style* 34 (2000): 635–69.

Knapp, John V., and Kenneth Womack, eds. *Reading the Family Dance: Family Systems Therapy and Literary Studies.* Cranbury, NJ: University of Delaware Press, 2003.

Kobayashi, Yoshikazu. "Conceptual Acquisition and Change Through Social Interaction." *Human Development* 37 (1994): 233–41.

Kohl, Herbert. *Growing Minds: On Becoming a Teacher.* New York: Harper and Row, 1984.

Kopff, E. Christian. The *Devil Knows Latin: Why America Needs the Classical Tradition.* Wilmington, DE: Isi Books, 2001.

Kosslyn, Stephen M. *Image and Mind.* Cambridge: Harvard University Press, 1980.

Kourilsky, Marilyn, Mahtash Esfandiari, and Merlin Wittrock. "Generative Teaching and Personality Characteristics of Student Teachers." *Teaching and Teacher Education* 12.4 (1996): 355–63.

Kozulin, Alex. "Literature as a Psychological Tool." *Educational Psychologist* 28 (1993): 253–64.

Kramer, Rita. *Ed School Follies: The Miseducation of America's Teachers.* New York: Free Press, 1991.

Kranidas, Thomas. "Milton on Teachers and Teaching." *Milton Quarterly* 20.1 (1986): 26–29.

Kreuz Roger J., and Mary Sue MacNealy, eds. *Empirical Approaches to Literature and Aesthetics.* Vol. 52. Norwood, NJ: Ablex, 1996. 397–416.

Kutz, Eleanor, and Hephzibah Roskelly. *An Unquiet Pedagogy: Transforming Practice in the English Classroom.* Portsmouth, NH: Boynton-Cook, 1991.

LaBoskey, Vicki Kubler. *Development of Reflective Practice: A Study of Pre-Service Teachers.* New York: Teacher's College Press, 1994.

Lagemann, Ellen. *An Elusive Science: The Troubling History of Education Research.* Chicago: University of Chicago Press, 2000.

Langer, Judith. "Discussion as Exploration: Literature and the Horizon of Possibilities." Report Series 6.3. Albany, NY: National Research Center on Literature, Teaching, and Learning, 1991.

———. *Envisioning Literature: Literary Understanding and Literature Instruction.* New York: Teachers College Press, 1995.

———. "Literary Understanding and Literature Instruction." Report Series 2.11. Albany, NY: Center for the Learning and Teaching of Literature, 1991.

———, ed. *Literature Instruction: A Focus on Student Response.* Albany, NY: NCTE, 1992.

———. (1992a). "Rethinking Literature Instruction" in Langer, ed., *Literature Instruction.*

Langer, Judith, and Arthur N. Applebee. *How Writing Shapes Thinking: A Study of Teaching and Learning.* Urbana: NCTE, 1987.

Larson, James R., Jr., and Caryn Christensen. "Groups as Problem-Solving Units: Toward a New Meaning of Social Cognition." *British Journal of Social Psychology* 32 (1993): 5–30.

Lave, Jean. *Cognition in Practice.* New York: Cambridge University Press, 1988.

Lave, Jean, and Etienne Wenger. *Situated Learning: Legitimate Peripheral Participation.* Cambridge: Cambridge University Press, 1991.

Learner, Neal. "The Teacher-Student Writing Conference and the Desire for Intimacy." *College English* 68.2 (2005): 186–208.

LeDoux, Joseph E., and William Hirst, eds. *Mind and brain: Dialogues in Cognitive Neuroscience.* Cambridge: Cambridge University Press, 1990.

Lee, Carol D. *Signifying as a Scaffold for Literary Interpretation: The Pedagogical Implications of an African-American Discourse Genre.* NCTE Research Report number 26. Urbana: NCTE, 1993.

Lehr, Susan S. *The Child's Developing Sense of Theme: Responses to Literature.* New York: Teachers College, Columbia University, 1991.

Leinhardt, Gaea. "Capturing Craft Knowledge in Teaching." *Educational Researcher* 19.2 (1990): 18–25.

———. "Development of an Expert Explanation: An Analysis of a Sequence of Subtraction Lessons." *Cognition and Instruction* 4 (1987): 225–82.

———. "Math Lessons: A Contrast of Novice and Expert Competence." *Journal for Research in Mathematics Education* 20.1 (1989): 52–75.

Leinhardt, Gaea, Catherine Stainton, and Salim M. Virji. "A Sense of History." *Educational Psychologist* 29.2 (1994): 79–88.

Leinhardt, Gaea, Isabel L. Beck, and Catherine Stainton, eds. *Teaching and Learning in History.* Hillsdale, NJ: Erlbaum, 1994.

Leinhardt, Gaea, and Stallan Ohlsson. "Tutorials on the Structure of Tutoring from Teachers." *Journal of Artificial Intelligence in Education* 2.1 (1990): 21–46.

Leinhardt, Gaea, and Kathleen McCarthy Young. "Two Texts, Three Readers: Distance and Expertise in Reading History." *Cognition and Instruction* 14.4 (1996): 441–86.

Leitch, Vincent B. *Deconstructive Criticism: An Advanced Introduction.* New York: Columbia University Press, 1983.

Lensmire, Timothy J. "The Teacher as Dostoevskian Novelist." *Research in the Teaching of English* 31 (1997): 367–92.

Levin, Richard. *New Readings versus Old Plays.* Chicago: University of Chicago Press, 1979.

Levine, George. "The Two Nations." *Pedagogy* 1 (2001): 7–19.

———. Foreword. *Teaching Literature: A Companion,* edited by Tanya Agathocleous and Ann C. Dean, vii–xii. New York: Palgrave-Macmillan, 2003.

Lightfoot, Judy. "A Short Course of Independent Study for Teachers of Modern Poetry." *English Journal* 81.1 (1992): 54–59.

Lim, Richard. *Public Disputation, Power, and Social Order in Late Antiquity.* Berkeley: University of California Press, 1995.

Lindauer, Martin S. *The Psychological Study of Literature.* Chicago: Nelson-Hall, 1974.

Livingston, Paisley. "Intentionalism in Aesthetics." *New Literary History* 29.4 (1998): 831–46.

Luttrell, Wendy. " 'The Teachers, They All had their Pets': Concepts of Gender, Knowledge, and Power." In *Second Signs Reader, Feminist Scholarship, 1983—1996,* edited by Ruth Ellen B. Joeres and Barbara Laslett, 357–98. Chicago: University of Chicago Press, 1996.

Lykken, D. T., M. McGue, A. Tellegen, and T. J. Bouchard Jr. "Emergenesis: Genetic Traits that May Not Run in Families." *American Psychologist* 47 (1992): 1565–77.

Mackenzie, Jim. "The English Literature Curriculum: Some Changes." *Educational Theory and Practice* 19.1 (1997): 57–67.

Mandl, Heinz, Nancy Stein, Tom Trabasso, eds. *Learning and Comprehension of Text.* Hillsdale, NJ: Erlbaum, 1984.

Mandler, Jean M. "On the Psychological Reality of Story Structures." *Discourse Processes* 10 (1987): 1–29.

Mandler, Jean, and N. S. Johnson. "Remembrance of Things Parsed: Story Structure and Recall." *Cognitive Psychology* 9 (1977): 111–51.

Marshall, James D., Peter Smagorinsky, and Michael W. Smith. *The Language of Interpretation: Patterns of Discourse in Discussions of Literature.* NCTE Report number 27. Urbana: NCTE, 1995.

Marshall, James D., and Janet Smith. "Teaching as We're Taught: The University's Role in Education of English Teachers." *English Education* 29.4 (1997): 246–68.

Martin, Bill. "Response to Poetry: Making Use of Differences." *English Record* 42.2 (1992): 23–26.

Martin, Bruce K. "Teaching Literature as Experience." *College English* 51.4 (1989): 377–85.

Martindale, Colin, and Audrey Dailey. "I. A. Richards Revisited: Do People Agree on Their Interpretations of Literature?" *Poetics* 23 (1995): 299–314.

Maxwell, Rhoda J., and Mary Jordan Meiser. *Teaching English in Middle and Secondary Schools.* 2nd ed. Columbus, Ohio: Merrill-Prentice Hall, 1997.

Mayr, Ernst. *The Growth of Biological Thought.* Cambridge: Harvard University Press, 1982.

McCormick, Kathleen. *The Culture of Reading and the Teaching of English.* Manchester, UK: Manchester University Press, 1994.

———. "Reading Lessons and Then Some." In *Critical Theory and the Teaching of Literature: Politics, Curriculum, Pedagogy,* edited by James F. Slevin and Art Young, 292–315. Urbana: NCTE, 1996.

McGann, Jerome. "Reading Fiction/Teaching Fiction: A Pedagogical Experiment.." In collaboration with John Griffith, Jennifer Kremer, Rebecca L. Kroeger, Brooks Moriarty, Jason Pikler, Bennett Simpson, and Kate Stephensonin. *Pedagogy* 1.1 (2001): 143–66.

McGee, Tim. "The Adolescent Novel in AP English: A Response to Patricia Spencer." *English Journal* 81.4 (1992): 57–58.

McIntyre, Dan. "Using Foregrounding Theory as a Teaching Methodology in a Stylistics Course." *Style* 37 (Spring 2003): 1–13.

McKeough, Anne, and Alex Sanderson. "Teaching Storytelling: A Microgenetic Analysis of Developing Narrative Competency." *Journal of Narrative and Life History* 6.2 (1996): 157–92.

McKeown, Margaret G., and Isebel L. Beck. "Making Sense of Accounts of History: Why Young Students Don't and How They Might." *Teaching and Learning in History.* Edited by Gaea Leinhardt, Isabel L. Beck, and Catherine Stainton. Hillsdale, NJ: Erlbaum, 1994.

McLaughlin, Terence H. "Mentoring and the Demands of Reflection." In *Collaboration and Transition in Initial Teacher Training,* edited by Margaret Wilkin and Derek Sankey, 151–60. London: Kogan Page, 1994.

McLean, Monica, and Richard Blackwell. "Opportunity Knocks? Professionalism and Excellence in University Teaching." *Teachers and Teaching: Theory and Practice* 3.1 (1997): 85–99.

McPeck, John E. "Critical Thinking and Subject Specificity: A Reply to Ennis." *Educational Researcher* 19.4 (1990): 10–12.

Mehan, Hugh. *Learning Lessons.* Cambridge: Harvard University Press, 1979.

Meier, Scott T. *The Chronic Crisis in Psychological Measurement and Assessment: A Historical Survey.* New York: Academic Press, 1994.

Melchior, Bonnie. "Teaching *Paradise Lost:* The Unfortunate Fall." *College Literature* 14.1 (1987): 76–84.

Meloth, Michael S., and Paul D. Deering. "Task Talk and Task Awareness Under Different Cooperative Learning Conditions." *American Education Research Journal* 31 (1994): 138–65.

Mercer, Neil. *The Guided Construction of Knowledge: Talk Amongst Teachers and Learners.* Clevedon, UK: Multilingual Matters, 2000.

Meutsch, Dietrich. "Mental Models in Literary Discourse." *Poetics* 15 (1986): 307–31.

Meutsch, Dietrich, and Sigfried Schmidt. "On the Role of Conventions in Understanding Literary Texts." *Poetics* 14 (1985): 551–74.

Miall, David S. "Empowering the Reader: Literary Response and Classroom Learning." *Empirical Approaches to Literature and Aesthetics.* Vol. 52, edited by Roger J. Kreuz and Mary Sue MacNealy, 463–78. Norwood, NJ: Ablex, 1996.

Miller, Suzanne M., and Sharon Legge. "Supporting Possible Worlds: Transforming Literature Teaching and Learning through Conversations in the Narrative Mode." *Research in the Teaching of English* 34.1 (August 1999): 10–64.

Minstrell, Jim, and Virginia Stimpson. "A Classroom Environment for Learning: Guiding Students' Reconstruction of Understanding and Reasoning." In *Innovations in Learning: New Environments for Education,* edited by Leona Schauble and Robert Glaser, 175–202. Hillsdale, NJ: Erlbaum, 1996.

Morgan, Dan. "Connecting Literature to Students' Lives." *College English.* 55.5 (1993): 491–500.

Morgan, Edmund S. "Bewitched." Review of *The Crucible,* directed by Nicholas Hytner. *New York Review of Books,* January 9, 1997, 4–6.

Montgomery, Martin, Alan Durant, Nigel Fabb, Tom Furniss, and Sara Mills. *Ways of Reading: Advanced Reading Skills for Students of English Literature.* New York: Routledge, 1992.

Montgomery, Paula Kay. *Approaches to Literature through Literary Form.* Phoenix: Oryx Press, 1995.

Moreland, Richard L., and Michael A. Hogg. "Theoretical Perspectives on Social Processes in Small Groups." *British Journal of Social Psychology* 32 (1993): 1–4.

Morris, Vivian, Satomi Taylor, Janie Knight, and Rebecca Wasson. "Preparing

Teachers to Reach out to Families and Communities." *Action in Teacher Education* 18.1 (1996): 10–22.

Mosenthal, James. "Situated Learning and Methods Coursework in the Teaching of Literacy." *Journal of Literacy Research* 28.3 (1996): 379–403.

Morson, Gary Saul. "Prosaics: An Approach to the Humanities." *American Scholar* 57 (1988): 515–28.

Mumford, Michael, Garnet S. Stokes, and William A. Owens. *Patterns of Life History: The Ecology of Human Individuality.* Hillsdale, NJ: Erlbaum, 1990.

Munby, H. "Metaphor in the Thinking of Teachers: An Exploratory Study." *Journal of Curriculum Studies* 18 (1986): 197–209.

Nell, Victor. *Lost in a Book: The Psychology of Reading for Pleasure.* New Haven: Yale University Press, 1988.

Nelson, Cary, and Stephen Watt. *Academic Keywords: A Devil's Dictionary for Higher Education.* New York: Routledge, 1999.

Newell, George E. "Reader-Based and Teacher-Centered Instructional Tasks: Writing and Learning about a Short Story in Middle-Track Classrooms." *Journal of Literacy Research* 28.2 (1996): 147–72.

Noice, Tony, and Helga Noice. *The Nature of Expertise in Professional Acting.* Mahwah, NJ: Erlbaum, 1997.

Norrick, Neal. "Involvement and Joking in Conversation." *Journal of Pragmatics* 22 (1994): 409–30.

Norris, S. P., and L. Phillips. "Explanations of Reading Comprehension: Schema Theory and Critical Thinking Theory." *Teachers College Record* 89.2 (1987): 281–306.

Nystrand, Martin, and Adam Gamoran. "Instructional Discourse, Student Engagement, and Literature Achievement." *Research in the Teaching of English* 25.3 (1991): 261–90.

———, and Mary Jo Heck. "Using Small Groups for Response to and Thinking about Literature." *English Journal* 82.1 (1993): 14–22.

———, Robert Kachur, and Catherine Prendergast. *Opening Dialogue: Understanding the Dynamics of Language and Learning in the English Classroom.* New York: Teachers College Press, 1997.

Nystrand, Martin, and Jeffery Wiemelt. "When is a Text Explicit? Formalist and Dialogical Conceptions." *Text* 11.1 (1991): 25–41.

Nystrand, Martin, Lawrence Wu, and Adam Gamoran, et al. "Questions in Time: Investigating the Structure and Dynamics of Unfolding Classroom Discourse." *Discourse Processes* 35.2 (2003): 135–98.

Olson, David R. "Mining the Human Sciences: Some Relations Between Hermeneutics and Epistemology." *Interchange* 17 (1986): 159–71.

Olson, David R., and Janet Wilde Astington. "Thinking About Thinking: Learning How to Take Statements and Hold Beliefs." *Educational Psychologist* 28.1 (1993): 7–23.

Ohmann, Richard. *English in America: A Radical View of the Profession.* Hanover, NH: Wesleyan University Press, 1996.

Palincsar, Annemarie Sullivan. "Less Charted Waters." In "Responses to

Brown, Collins, and Duguid's 'Situated Cognition and the Culture of Learning.'" *Educational Researcher* 18.4 (May 1989): 5–7.

Palincsar, Annemarie Sullivan, and A. L. Brown. "Reciprocal Teaching of Comprehension-Fostering and Comprehension-Monitoring Activities." *Cognition and Instruction* 2 (1984): 117–75.

Parini, Jay. *The Art of Teaching.* New York, Oxford University Press, 2005.

Pascual-Leone, Juan. "Learning and Development as Dialectical Factors in Cognitive Growth." *Human Development* 38 (1995): 338–48.

Patai, Daphne, and Will H. Corral, eds. *Theory's Empire: An Anthology of Dissent.* New York: Columbia University Press, 2005.

Payne, John W. "Thinking Aloud: Insights into Information Processing." *Psychological Science* 5.5 (1994): 241, 245–48.

Pearcy, Lee T., *The Grammar of Our Civility: Classical Education in America.* Waco, TX: Baylor University Press, 2005.

Peim, Nick. *Critical Theory and the English Teacher.* New York: Routledge, 1993.

Perkins, David N., and Gavriel Salomon. "Are Cognitive Skills Context-Bound?" *Educational Researcher* 18.1 (1989): 16–25.

Perrone-Moises, Leyla. "Lecon: Testament and Prophecy." *The Yale Journal of Criticism* 14.2 (Fall 2001): 463–68.

Perry, William G., Jr. *Forms of Intellectual and Ethical Development in the College Years.* New York: Holt, Rinehart and Winston, 1970.

Peskin, Joan. "Constructing Meaning when Reading Poetry: An Expert-Novice Study." *Cognition and Instruction* 16.3 (1998): 235–63.

Peterson, Bill E., and Abigail J. Stewart. "Using Personal and Fictional Documents to Assess Psychosocial Development: A Case Study of Vera Brittain's Generativity." *Psychology and Aging* 5 (1990): 400–411.

Petrosky, Anthony. "To Teach (Literature)?" In *Literature Instruction: A Focus on Student Response,* edited by Judith Langer, 163–205. Albany, NY: NCTE, 1992.

Phelan, James. *Reading People, Reading Plots: Character, Progression, and the Interpretation of Narrative.* Chicago: University of Chicago Press, 1989.

Phillips, D. C. "Telling It Straight: Issues in Assessing Narrative Research." *Educational Psychologist* 29.1 (1994): 13–21.

Pirie, Bruce. *Reshaping High School English.* Urbana: NCTE, 1997.

Plato. "The Republic." In *Great Dialogues of Plato,* translated by W. H. D. Rouse, 118–422. New York: Mentor, 1956.

Polkinghorne, Donald. *Methodology for the Human Sciences: Systems of Inquiry.* Albany: State University of New York Press, 1983.

———. *Narrative Knowing and the Human Sciences.* Albany: State University of New York Press, 1988.

Pope, Carol. "Reflection and Refraction: A Reflexive Look at an Evolving Model for Methods Instruction." *English Education* 31.3 (1999): 177–204.

Posner, George J. *Field Experience: A Guide to Reflective Teaching.* 3rd ed. New York: Longman, 1993.

Prawat, Richard S. "Cognitive Theory at the Crossroads: Head Fitting, Head Splitting, or Somewhere in Between?" *Human Development* 42 (1999a): 59–77.

———. "Dewey, Peirce, and the Learning Paradox." *AERJ* 36.1 (1999b): 47–76.

Probst, Robert E. "Dialogue with a Text." *Teaching Secondary English* (1988/Report 1993): 59–68.

———. "Five Kinds of Literary Knowing." *Literature Instruction: A Focus on Student Response*. Edited by Judith Langer. Albany, NY: NCTE, 1992. 54–77.

———. *Response and Analysis: Teaching Literature in Junior and Senior High School*. Portsmouth, NH: Heinemann, 1988.

Proctor, Anne. "Supervision Strategies and their Application in the School Context." In *Collaboration and Transition in Initial Teacher Training*, edited by Margaret Wilkin and Derek Sankey, 136–50. London: Kogan Page, 1994.

Prose, Francine. "I Know Why the Caged Bird Cannot Read." *Harpers*, September 1999, 76–84.

Purves, Alan C. *How Porcupines Make Love*. New York: Longman, 1972.

Purves, Alan C., Theresa Rodgers, and Anna O. Soter. *How Porcupines Make Love II*. New York: Longman, 1990.

———. *How Porcupines Make Love III*. New York: Longman, 1995.

Rabinowitz, Peter J. *Before Reading: Narrative Conventions and the Politics of Interpretation*. Ithaca: Cornell University Press, 1987.

Rabinowitz, Peter J., and Michael W. Smith. *Authorizing Readers: Resistance and Respect in the Teaching of Literature*. New York: Teachers College Press, 1998.

Reiser, Brian J., John B. Black, and Wendy Lehnert. "Thematic Knowledge Structures in the Understanding and Generation of Narratives." *Discourse Processes* 8 (1985): 357–89.

Resnick, Lauren, ed. *Knowing, Learning, and Instruction: Essays in Honor of Robert Glaser*. Hillsdale, NJ: Erlbaum, 1989.

Reynolds, Michael. *Groupwork in Education and Training*. London: Kogan Page, 1994.

———, ed. "Knowledge Base for the Beginning Teacher." New York: Pergamon Press, 1989.

Richards, I. A. *Practical Criticism*. New York: Harvest Books, 1929; see also in *Criticism: The Major Texts*, edited by Walter Jackson Bate, 573–87. New York: Harcourt, Brace, Jovanovich, 1963.

Rogoff, Barbara. *Apprenticeship in Thinking: Cognitive Development in Social Context*. New York: Oxford University Press, 1990.

———. *The Cultural Nature of Human Development*. New York: Oxford University Press, 2003.

———. "Three Ways to Relate Person and Culture: Thoughts Sparked by Valsiner's Review of *Apprenticeship in Thinking*." *Human Development* 35 (1992): 316–20.

Rose, Mike. *Lives on the Boundary.* New York: Penguin, 1990.

Rosenblatt, Louise. *Literature as Exploration.* 1938. New York: Barnes and Noble, 1976.

———. *The Reader, The Text, The Poem.* Carbondale: Southern Illinois University Press, 1978.

Rosenshine, Barak, Carla Meister, and Saul Chapman. "Teaching Students to Generate Questions: A Review of Intervention Studies." *Review of Educational Research* 66.2 (1996): 181–221.

Roth, Jeffery, and Sandra Bowman Damico. "Continuing the Bifurcation of Affect and Cognition." Review of *Student Engagement in American Secondary Schools,* edited by Fred Newmann. *Curriculum Inquiry* 26.1 (Spring 1996): 89–99.

Rouet, Jean-François, Monica Favart, M. Anne Britt, and Charles A. Perfetti. "Studying and Using Documents in History: Effects of Discipline Expertise." *Cognition and Instruction* 15.1 (1997): 85–106.

Rudel, Thomas K., and Judith M. Gerson. "Postmodernism, Institutional Change, and Academic Workers: A Sociology of Knowledge." *Social Science Quarterly* 80.2 (1999): 213–28.

Ryder, Randall J., and Richard D. Western. "Teaching Literature in High School: Comments on a National Survey." *Wisconsin English Journal* 32.1 (1989): 3–11.

Sadoff, Dianne F., and William E. Cain, eds. *Teaching Contemporary Theory to Undergraduates.* New York: MLA, 1994.

Sadoff, Dianne F. "Frameworks, Materials, and the Teaching of Theory." In Sadoff and Cain, 15–27.

Sancilio, Leonard, Jr. "Two versus One: The Effects of Pairing Friends on Cognition during Collaborative Learning with Logo. Ph.D. dissertation, University of Wisconsin-Madison, 1992.

Sarbin, Theodore R., ed. *Narrating Psychology: The Storied Nature of Human Conduct.* New York: Praeger, 1986.

Sato, K. "Processes of Knowledge Acquisition in School Learning." *Journal of Hokkaido University of Education.* Section IC, *Education* 37 (1987): 101–15 [in Japanese].

Sawyer, R. Keith. *Social Emergence: Societies as Complex systems.* New York: University of Cambridge Press, 2005.

Schank, Roger C. *Tell Me a Story: A New Look at Real and Artificial Memory.* New York: Scribner's, 1990.

Scharmer, Claus Otto. "Conversation with Robert Kegan." *Dialog on Leadership,* March 23, 2000, www.dialogonleadership.org/kegan~1999.html

Schauble, Leona, and Robert Glaser, eds. *Innovations in Learning: New Environments for Education.* Mahwah, NJ: Erlbaum, 1996.

Schmidt, Sigfried J. *Foundation of the Empirical Study of Literature.* Hamburg: Buske, 1982.

Scholes, Robert. *The Crafty Reader.* New Haven: Yale University Press, 2001.

———. *The Rise and Fall of English: Reconstructing English as a Discipline.* New Haven: Yale University Press, 1998.

———. *Textual Power: Literary Theory and the Teaching of English.* New Haven: Yale University Press, 1985.

———. "The Transition to College Reading." *Pedagogy* 2 (2002): 165–72.

Schon, Donald A. "Coaching Reflective Teaching." In *Reflection in Teacher Education,* edited by Peter P. Grimmett and Gaalen L. Erickson, 19–29. New York: Teachers College Press, 1988.

———. *Educating the Reflective Practitioner: How Professionals Think and Act.* New York: Basic Books, 1987.

Schroeder, Christopher L. *Re-Inventing the University: Literacies and Legitimacy in the Postmodern Academy.* Logan: Utah State University Press, 2001.

Selden, Raman. *Practicing Theory and Reading Literature.* Lexington: University Press of Kentucky, 1989.

Sexias, Peter. "When Psychologists Discuss Historical Thinking: A Historian's Perspective." *Educational Psychologist* 29.2 (1994): 107–9.

Sharan, Shlomo, ed. *Cooperative Learning: Theory and Research.* New York: Praeger, 1990.

Shawcross, John T. "Milton and Epic Revisionism." *Epic and Epoch: Essays on the Interpretation of a Genre.* Edited by Steven M. Oberhelman, Van Kelley, and Richard J. Golsan. Lubbock: Texas Tech University Press, 1994.

Sheridan, Daniel, ed. *Teaching Secondary English: Readings and Applications.* New York: Longman, 1993.

Sherin, Miriam Gamoran. "When Teaching Becomes Learning." *Cognition and Instruction* 20 (2002): 119–50.

Showalter, Elaine. *Teaching Literature.* Malden, MA: Blackwell, 2003.

Shuell, Thomas J. "The Role of Educational Psychology in the Preparation of Teachers." *Educational Psychologist* 31.1 (1996): 5–14.

Shulman, L. S. "Those who Understand: Knowledge Growth in Teaching." *Educational Researcher* 15.2 (1986): 4–14.

Siegler, Robert S., and Kevin Crowley. "The Microgenetic Method: A Direct Means of Studying Cognitive Development." *American Psychologist.* 46 (1991): 606–20.

Siegler, Robert S., and Eric Jenkins. *How Children Discover New Strategies.* Hillsdale, NJ: Erlbaum, 1989.

Sizer, Theodore R. *Horace's Hope: What Works for the American High School.* New York: Houghton Mifflin, 1996.

Slavin, Robert E. "Comprehensive Cooperative Learning Models: Embedded Cooperative Learning in the Curriculum and the School." In *Cooperative Learning: Theory and Practice,* edited by Shlomo Sharan, 261–83. New York: Praeger, 1990.

Slavin, Robert E. "When Does Cooperative Learning Increase Student Achievement?" *Psychological Bulletin* 94.3 (1983): 429–45.

Slevin, James F., and Art Young, eds. *Critical Theory and the Teaching of Literature: Politics, Curriculum, Pedagogy.* Urbana: NCTE, 1996. 292–315.

Slick, Gloria Appelt, ed. *The Field Experience: Creating Successful Programs for New Teachers.* Thousand Oaks, CA: Corwin Press, 1995.

Smagorinsky, Peter. *Teaching English Through Principled Practice.* Columbus, OH: Merrill–Prentice Hall, 2002.

Smagorinsky, Peter, and Steven Gevinson. *Fostering the Reader's Response.* Palo Alto, CA: Dale Seymour, 1989.

Smagorinsky, Peter, and Michael W. Smith. "Nature of Knowledge in Composition and Literary Understanding: The Question of Specificity." *Review of Educational Research* 62.3 (Fall 1992): 279–305.

Smagorinsky, Peter, and Melissa E. Whiting. *How English Teachers Get Taught: Methods of Teaching the Methods Class.* Urbana: NCTE, 1995.

Smeby, Jens-Christian. "Disciplinary Differences in University Teaching." *Studies in Higher Education* 21.1 (1996): 69–79.

Smith, Michael W. "A Declaration of Independence: On Teaching Interpretive Strategies." *Wisconsin English Journal* 32.1 (1989): 12–17.

———.*Understanding Unreliable Narrators.* Urbana: NCTE, 1991.

———,and George Hillocks. "Sensible Sequencing: Developing Knowledge about Literature Text by Text." *English Journal* 96.2 (1988): 44–49.

Smorti, A. "The Narrative Approach to Reality in Relation to Children's Cooperative Interaction." *Journal of Social and Personal Relationships* 12.2 (1995): 229–41.

Sorenson, R. C., and J. P. Linde. "Self Ratings of Students Engaged in Collaborative Learning." *NACTA Journal.* 37 (1993): 23–24.

Soter, Anna O. *Young Adult Literature and the New Literary Theories.* New York: Teachers College Press, 1999.

Spiller, Michael R. G. *Development of the Sonnet: An Introduction.* New York: Routledge, 1992.

Spoehr, Kathryn T., and Luther Spoehr. "Learning to Think Historically." *Educational Psychologist* 29.2 (1994): 71–77.

Sprinker, Michael. "The War Against Theory." *Minnesota Review* ns 39 (1992–93): 103–21.

Staats, A. W. "Paradigmatic Behavior, Unified Theory, Unified Theory Construction, and the Zeitgeist of Separatism." *American Psychologist* 36 (1981): 239–56.

Stables, Andrew. "Speaking and Listening at Key Stage 3: Some Problems of Teacher Assessment." *Educational Research* 34.2 (1992): 107–15.

Stanovich, Keith E., Richard F. West, and Michele R. Harrison. "Knowledge Growth and Maintenance across the Life Span: The Role of Print Exposure." *Developmental Psychology* 31.5 (1995): 811–26.

Stein, Nancy, ed. *Literacy in American Schools: Learning to Read and Write.* Chicago: University of Chicago Press, 1986.

———. "What's the Point?" *Behavioral and Brain Sciences* 6 (1983): 611–12.

———,and C. G. Glenn. "An Analysis of Story Comprehension in Elementary school Children." *New Directions in Discourse Processing.* New York: Ablex, 1979.

———, and Margaret Policastro. "The Concept of a Story: A Comparison between Children's and Teacher's Viewpoints." *Learning and Comprehension of Text.* Edited by Heinz Mandl, Nancy Stein, and Tom Trabasso. Hillsdale, NJ: Erlbaum, 1984.

Stenberg, Shari, and Amy Lee. "Developing Pedagogies: Learning the Teaching of English." *College English* 64.3 (2002): 326–47.

Sternberg, Robert J., and Joseph A. Horvath. "A Prototype View of Expert Teaching." *Educational Researcher* 24.6 (1995): 9–17.

Stillinger, Jack. "Poets who Revise, Poets who Don't, and Critics who Should." *Journal of Aesthetic Education* 30.2 (1996): 119–33.

Stoddart, Rebecca M., and Ann Kimble Loux. "And, Not But: Moving from Monologue to Dialogue in Introductory Psychology/English Writing Courses." *Teaching of Psychology* 19.3 (1992): 145–59.

Storey, Robert. *Mimesis and the Human Animal: On the Biogenetic Foundations of Literary Representations.* Evanston, IL: Northwestern University Press, 1996.

Strauss, Sidney. "Confessions of a Born-again Constructivist." *Educational Psychologist* 31.1 (1996): 15–21.

Straw, Stanley, and Deanne Bogdan, eds. *Constructive Reading: Teaching Beyond Communication.* Portsmouth, NH: Boynton-Cook, 1993.

Strelau, Jan, and Hans J. Eysenck, eds. *Personality Dimensions and Arousal.* New York: Plenum Press, 1987.

Style 37.1 (Spring 2003). "The Pedagogy of Style and Stylistics." Edited by Donald Hardy, 1–118.

Sumara, Dennis J. *Why Reading Literature in School Still Matters: Imagination, Interpretation, Insight.* Mahwah, NJ: Erlbaum, 2002.

Tate, Gary, Amy Rupiper, and Kurt Sclick. *A Guide to Composition Pedagogies.* Oxford: Oxford University Press, 2000.

Thompson, Charles P., John J. Skowronski, Steen F. Larsen, and Andrew L. Betz. *Autobiographical Memory: Remembering What and Remembering When.* Mahwah, NJ: Erlbaum, 1996.

Thompson, R. F. *The Brain: A Neuroscience Primer.* New York: W. H. Freeman, 1993.

Thorndyke, P. W. "Cognitive Structures in Comprehension and Memory of Narrative Discourse." *Cognitive Psychology* 9 (1977): 77–110.

Tompkins, Jane. *A Life in School: What the Teacher Learned.* Reading, MA: Addison-Wesley, 1996.

———, ed. *Reader-Response Criticism: From Formalism to Post-Structuralism.* Baltimore, MD: Johns Hopkins University Press, 1980.

Travers, John F., Stephen N. Elliot, and Thomas R. Kratochwill. *Educational Psychology: Effective Teaching, Effective Learning.* Madison, WI: Brown and Benchmark, 1993.

Travers, Molly. "The Poetry Teacher: Behaviour and Attitudes." *Research in the Teaching of English* 18.4 (1984): 367–84.

Trimmer, Joseph F. *Narration as Knowledge: Tales of the Teaching Life.* Portsmouth, NH: Boynton-Cook, 1997.

Turner, Mark. *Reading Minds: The Study of English in the Age of Cognitive Science.* Princeton, NJ: Princeton University Press, 1991.

Ulichny, Polly, and Wendy Schoener. "Teacher-Researcher Collaboration From Two Perspectives." *Harvard Educational Review* 66.3 (1996): 496–524.

Van Dijk, Teun, and Walter Kintsch. *Strategies of Discourse Comprehension.* New York: Academic Press, 1983.

Van Peer, W. "Paraphrase as Paradox in Literary Education." *Poetics* 21 (1993): 443–59.

Vendler, Helen. The Art of Shakespeare's Sonnets. Cambridge: Harvard University Press, 1997.

Verba, Mina. "The Beginnings of Collaboration in Peer Interaction." *Human Development* 37 (1994): 125–39.

Vipond, D., R. A. Hunt, and L. C. Wheeler. "Social Reading and Literary Engagement." *Reading Research and Instruction* 26.3 (1987): 151–61.

Vitz, Paul C. "The Use of Stories in Moral Development: New Psychological Reasons for an Old Education Method." *American Psychologist* 45 (1990): 709–20.

Vonk, Roos, and Ad van Knippenberg. "Processing Attitude Statements from In-group and Out-Group Members: Effects of Within-group and Within-person Inconsistencies on Reading Times." *Journal of Personality and Social Psychology* 68.2 (1995): 215–27.

Voss, James F., and Laurie Ney Silfies. "Learning from a History Text: The Interaction of Knowledge and Comprehension Skill with Text Structure." *Cognition and Instruction* 14.1 (1996): 45–68.

Vygotsky, Lev. *Thought and Language.* Cambridge, MA: MIT Press, 1986.

Warren, Beth, and Ann S. Rosebery. "This Question is Just Too Easy! Students Perspectives on Accountability in Science." In *Innovations in Learning: New Environments for Education,* edited by Leona Schauble and Robert Glaser, 97–125. Mahwah, NJ: Erlbaum, 1996.

Webb, N. "Peer Interaction and Learning in Small Groups." *International Journal of Educational Research* 13 (1989): 21–40.

Weinberg, Samuel S. "The Cognitive Representation of Historical Texts." In *Teaching and Learning in History.* Edited by Gaea Leinhardt, Isabel L. Beck, and Catherine Stainton, 89–99. Hillsdale, NJ: Erlbaum, 1994.

Welch, Nancy. "Resisting the Faith" *College English* 55.4 (1993): 387–401.

Wellek, René, and Austin Warren. *Theory of Literature.* New Haven: Yale University Press, 1949.

Wells, Gordon. *Dialogic Inquiry: Toward a Sociocultural Practice and Theory of Education.* Cambridge: Cambridge University Press, 1999.

White, Brian. "Assuming Nothing: A Pre-Methods Diagnostic in the Teaching of Literature." *English Education* 27.4 (1995): 1–39.

Wilensky, Robert. "Story Grammars vs. Story Points." *Behavioral and Brain Sciences* 6 (1983): 579–623.

Wilhelm, Jeffery D., and Brian Edmiston. *Imagining to Learn: Inquiry, Ethics, and Integration Through Drama.* Portsmouth, NH: Heinemann, 1998.

Wilkin, Margaret, and Derek Stanley. *Collaboration and Transition in Initial Teacher Training.* London: Kogan Page, 1994.

Williams, Raymond. *Modern Tragedy.* Stanford, CA: Stanford University Press, 1966.

Willinsky, John. *The New Literacy: Redefining Reading and Writing in the Schools.* New York: Routledge, 1990. 117–33.

Wineberg, Samuel S. "The Cognitive Representation of Historical Texts." In *Teaching and Learning in History,* edited by Gaea Leinhardt, Isabel L. Beck, and Catherine Stainton, 81–135. Hillsdale, NJ: Erlbaum, 1994.

Wislock, Robert F. "What are Perceptual Modalities and How Do They Contribute to Learning? In *Applying Cognitive Learning Theory to Adult Learning* number 59, edited by Daniele D. Flannery, 5–13. San Francisco: Jossey-Bass, 1993.

Wolf, Shelby Anne. "Learning to Act/Acting to Learn: Children as Actors, Critics, and Characters in Classroom Theatre." *Research in the Teaching of English* 28.1 (1994): 7–44.

Wong, Chau-Ming T., Jeanne D. Day, Scott E. Maxwell, and Naomi M. Meara. "A Multitrait-Multimethod Study of Academic and Social Intelligence in College Students." *Journal of Educational Psychology* 87.1 (1995): 117–33.

Wood, D. J., Jerome Bruner, and G. Ross. "The Role of Tutoring in Problem Solving." *Journal of Child Psychology and Psychiatry* 17 (1976): 89–100.

Woods, Tim. *Beginning Postmodernism.* New York: Manchester University Press-St. Martin's, 1999.

Wright, Terence R. "Reader-Response Under Review: Art, Game, or Science?" *Style* 29.4 (1995): 529–48.

Zeichner, Kenneth M. "The Ecology of Field Experience: Toward an Understanding of the Role of Field Experiences in Teacher Development." In *Advances in Teacher Education,* vol. 3, edited by M. Haberman and J. M. Backus, 94–117. Norwood, NJ: Ablex, 1987.

———, Daniel Liston, Marc Mahlios, and Mary Gomez. "The Structure and Goals of a Student Teaching Program and the Character and Quality of Supervisory Discourse." *Teaching and Teacher Education* 4.4 (1988): 349–62.

———, Susan Melnick, and Mary Louise Gomez. *Currents of Reform in Preservice Teacher Education.* New York: Teachers College Press, 1996.

Zeitz, Colleen Mary. "Expert-Novice Differences in Memory and Analysis of Literary and Non-Literary Texts." DAI, Brown University, 1990.

Zigmond, Naomi, and Gaea Linhardt. "The Effects of Self-Questioning and Story Structure Training on the Reading Comprehension of Poor Readers." *Learning Disabilities Research* 4.1 (1988): 45–51.

Zuber, Johannes A., Helmut W. Croft, and Joachim Werner. "Choice Shift and Group Polarization: An Analysis of the Status of Arguments and Social Decision Schemes." *Journal of Personality and Social Psychology* 62.1 (1992): 50–61.

Index

307